ALEXANDER JACKSON
DAVIS

American Architect 1803–1892

ALEXANDER JACKSON

DAVIS

American Architect 1803–1892

Edited by Amelia Peck
Introduction by Jane B. Davies

THE METROPOLITAN MUSEUM OF ART

RIZZOLI
NEW YORK

First published in the United States of America in
1992 by Rizzoli International Publications, Inc.
300 Park Avenue South, New York, N.Y. 10010

This book has been published in conjunction with
the exhibition *Alexander Jackson Davis (1803–1892),
American Architect,* held at The Metropolitan
Museum of Art from October 20, 1992, to
January 24, 1993.

The exhibition is made possible by
The J. M. Kaplan Fund.

Color photography for the book was funded by the
William Cullen Bryant Fellows of the American
Wing, The Metropolitan Museum of Art.

Library of Congress Cataloging-in-Publication Data
Alexander Jackson Davis. American architect,
1803–1892 / edited by Amelia Peck; introduction
by Jane B. Davies.
p. cm.
Includes index.
ISBN 0-8478-1484-X
ISBN 0-8478-1485-8 (pbk.)
1. Davis, Alexander Jackson. 1803–1892—
Criticism and interpretation. 2. Architecture, 19th
century—United States. I. Peck, Amelia. II. Title:
American architect, 1803–1892.
NA737.D34A84   1992   92-8479
720'.92—dc20   CIP

Design by Abigail Sturges
Rizzoli Editor: Kate Norment
Printed and bound in Japan

Front cover: Ericstan for John J. Herrick,
Tarrytown, New York, 1855–59. Rear elevation.
Watercolor, ink, and graphite on paper, 25 5/16 x 30
in. The Metropolitan Museum of Art, Harris
Brisbane Dick Fund, 1924 (24.66.10).

Back cover: Study for a stained-glass window, ca.
1840. Elevation. Watercolor and ink on paper,
14½ x 10⅜ in. The Metropolitan Museum of Art,
Harris Brisbane Dick Fund, 1924 (24.66.1042).

Title page: Mary Freeman Goldbeck, Sketch of
A.J. Davis, ca. 1845. Graphite on paper, 14 x 10
in. Drawings & Archives, Avery Architectural and
Fine Arts Library, Columbia University
(1940.00.00740).

Contents

Acknowledgments

In this year, the one hundredth anniversary of Alexander Jackson Davis's death, the Metropolitan Museum of Art is happy to present the exhibition and catalogue *Alexander Jackson Davis: American Architect 1803–1892*. It is particularly fitting that this exhibition is held at the Metropolitan; since 1924, the Museum's collections have included more than five thousand drawings and watercolors in Davis's own hand. Our Davis collection was purchased from Davis's son; other parts of his extensive archives are housed at the New-York Historical Society, Avery Library at Columbia University, and the New York Public Library. Although Davis was one of nineteenth-century America's most widely acclaimed architects, the styles of architecture he popularized slipped out of fashion after the Civil War, and his work was generally forgotten by the twentieth century. This catalogue is the first book to be published on this seminal figure, and the exhibition is the first to consider the full spectrum of Davis's career.

Neither the exhibition nor the book would have existed without Jane B. Davies, Consultant Curator for the project. Alexander J. Davis has been the subject of Mrs. Davies's life work, and her superb research has brought this important figure to the forefront of American architectural history. Throughout the project, Mrs. Davies has been extremely generous with her knowledge and her time. All of the participants in the Davis project want to thank her first and foremost.

The William Cullen Bryant Fellows of the American Wing funded the shooting and processing of much of the color photography in the catalogue. We are greatly indebted for their support. In the American Wing, Assistant Curator Amelia Peck was in charge of all aspects of the book and exhibition. John K. Howat, the Lawrence A. Fleischman Chairman of the Departments of American Art, Morrison H. Heckscher, Alice Cooney Frelinghuysen, Peter Kenny, Paul Staiti, Ellin Rosenzweig, Seraphine Wu, and Emely Bramson were all most helpful to the authors. Neither the book nor the exhibition would have existed without the untiring help of Elizabeth De Rosa, Research Assistant for the project.

Many other members of the Museum staff contributed to the effort required in publishing the catalogue and mounting the exhibition. For their many hours of help, Colta Ives, Curator in Charge, David Kiehl, Janet Byrne, Tom Rassieur, and Elizabeth Wycoff of the Print Department deserve many thanks. Carol Ehler and Nina McN. Diefenbach of the Development Office made funding the exhibition a reality, and Barbara Burn of the Editorial Department believed in the importance of the catalogue and worked hard to find it a wonderful co-publisher. In Paper Conservation, Marjorie Shelley patiently contributed to the sparkling appearance of the Museum's drawings; Barbara Bridgers and Oi-Cheong Lee of the Photo Studio were a pleasure to work with; Kent Lydecker, Deputy Director for Education, and Stella Paul contributed many good ideas for creative public programs.

Several institutions kindly lent us works for the exhibition and helped supply images of their drawings for the catalogue. We are particularly indebted to the Avery Library at Columbia University, not only for the generous loans, but for the assistance provided to the authors by Janet Parks, Curator of Drawings and Archives, and Vicki Weiner, Assistant to the Curator. Our thanks also go to many on the staff of the New-York Historical Society: to Holly Hotchner, Director of the Museum of the New-York Historical Society, for her interest in and support of the exhibition; to Mary Beth Betts, Curator of Architecture, who was unstinting with both her time and her good humor; to Wendy Shadwell, Curator of Prints; and to the staff of the Society's library for research assistance.

We are grateful to several other institutions and individuals for their loans to the exhibition and in many cases for their research assistance as well: Rodney Armstrong, Director and Librarian of the Boston Athenaeum; John Dobkin, President of Historic Hudson Valley; Dr. Timothy Healy, President of the New York Public Library, and the staff of the Manuscript Division; Susanne Brendel-Pandich and Henry Duffy of Lyndhurst, a Property of the National Trust for Historic Preservation, as well as Frank Sanchis, Vice-President for Properties of the National Trust for Historic Preservation; Mr. and Mrs. Lyn Davies; Mr. and Mrs. Stuart Feld; Mr. Ralph Franklin, Director of the Beinecke Rare Book and Manuscript Library, Yale University; and Col. James Gaines, Director of Preston Library, Virginia Military Institute.

Mrs. Davies especially wishes to thank Elizabeth Mills Brown, Sarah B. Landau, and Alma deC. McArdle for their research assistance.

The catalogue would not have been realized without the superb editorial team from Rizzoli: David Morton, Senior Editor, Kate Norment, Editor, and Abigail Sturges, Designer.

The exhibition was made possible by a grant from the J.M. Kaplan Fund. We are most grateful to Joan K. Davidson for her vision and generosity.

Philippe de Montebello, Director
The Metropolitan Museum of Art

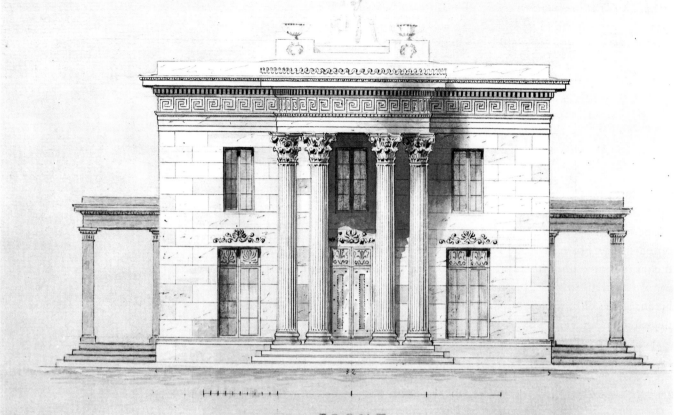

FRONT.

HENRY WHITNEY, N. HAVEN.   DAVIS. ARC. 1835.

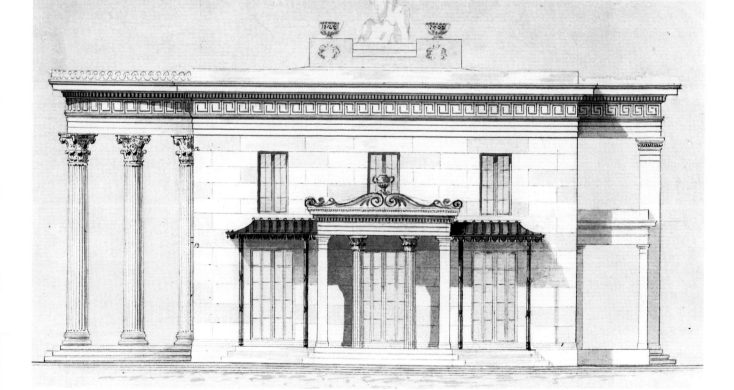

Alexander J. Davis, Creative American Architect

JANE B. DAVIES

Imaginative, innovative, and influential, Alexander J. Davis[1] was an extraordinary figure in American architecture in the rapidly changing and confusing period between Charles Bulfinch and Henry Hobson Richardson. He introduced and developed new ideas and new forms while producing some of the finest buildings of his time. In his designs he freely interpreted the classical heritage in new ways, explored many unfamiliar styles, and adapted for American houses the revolutionary ideas of the Picturesque aesthetic, relating houses to their landscape settings and opening up the traditional boxlike shape with irregularities, bold contrasts, and variety in textures and details. He was the outstanding American designer of villas and cottages in the Gothic and Italianate styles, and he invented the American bracketed style.

An "amazingly creative architect," as Talbot Hamlin described him, Davis had an "exuberant imagination"[2] that impelled him to devise new architecture for Americans. "A great innovator,"[3] he ventured beyond the accepted norms into styles that had scarcely reached these shores and into original conceptions that anticipated such developments of the modern age as strip windows and window walls. Many of his designs were in sharp contrast to those of other architects of his time; on the other hand, some became so much imitated that they started trends and even passed into the vernacular.

Davis entered architecture with active experience in art, and he considered architecture the highest and most inventive of the arts (see chapter 1). This was a different background and viewpoint from that of most American architects of his day, who usually began as builders. The imagination, temperament, eye, and skill of an artist gave Davis's work a special quality. With his visual approach to architecture he became a brilliant designer, experimenting constantly and developing exceptional skill in composition; he had a masterly control of proportion and scale and a scenic sense for the harmony of buildings with their settings and for the drama of bold features, deep shadows, and strong contrasts. His expansive imagination enabled him to envision buildings and schemes that were large for his day and sometimes even beyond the probability of construction. Some of his drawings had an element of fantasy, like his design for a church in the Egyptian style (fig. 2; colorplate 1). He was fascinated by geometric forms and by problems of light; he devised overhead lighting and used many skylights, large windows, and spacious bay windows. Many of his floor plans were unusual for his time; they frequently had rooms radiating from, or around, a central point and often exhibited an exceptional concern for space flow.

Davis designed in many styles—Greek, Roman, Tuscan, Egyptian, Oriental, Gothic, Romanesque, Elizabethan, Italianate, bracketed, Swiss. For him the diversi-

1. House for Henry Whitney, New Haven, Connecticut, ca. 1836. Front and side elevations. Watercolor, ink, and graphite on paper, 16¾ x 11¾ in. The Metropolitan Museum of Art, Harris Brisbane Dick Fund, 1924 (24.66.1416 [33], vol. XVII, leaf 38).

2. Study for a church in the Egyptian style, ca. 1834. Front and side elevations. Watercolor and ink on paper, 26¾ x 18¾ in. The Metropolitan Museum of Art, Harris Brisbane Dick Fund, 1924 (24.66.443).

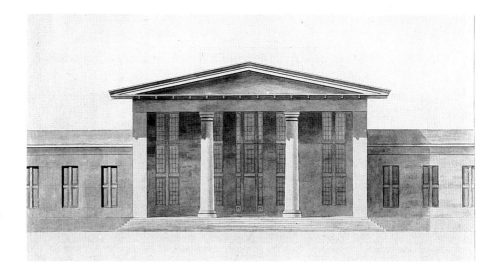

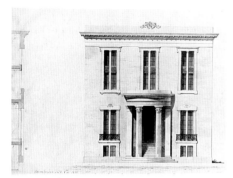

3. Study for the Pauper Lunatic Asylum, Blackwell's Island, New York City, ca. 1834. West elevation. Watercolor, ink, and graphite on paper, 18⅛ x 23¾ in. The Metropolitan Museum of Art, Harris Brisbane Dick Fund, 1924 (24.66.411).

4. House for William C. Rhinelander, New York City, 1836 (project). Front elevation and partial section. Watercolor, ink, and graphite on paper, 17½ x 25¹¹⁄₁₆ in. The Metropolitan Museum of Art, Arnold Bequest, 1954 (54.90.134).

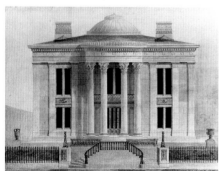

5. House for John Cox Stevens, New York City, 1845. Front elevation. Watercolor, ink, and graphite on paper, 15½ x 20½ in. Drawings Collection, The New-York Historical Society, Gift of Daniel Parish, Jr., 1908 (1908.27).

ty did not represent conflict, or a "Battle of Styles," but opportunity, an invitation to explore and experience new visual pleasures, to experiment with varied effects, and to invent for the American scene. Classicism and the Picturesque were but different aspects of romanticism, suitable for different situations and purposes—classical styles for monumental civic, institutional, and urban buildings, Picturesque styles for rural residences in hilly landscapes.

American classicism in Davis's period was predominantly Greek Revival, a style in which he and his early partner Ithiel Town designed outstanding buildings, but Davis reached beyond its bounds to Roman and Tuscan styles, to the dramatic force of tall Roman arches and massive Tuscan porticoes and deeply projecting eaves (fig. 3).[4] Working with great freedom, he did not hesitate to use features from other classical styles on buildings of basically Greek style to add drama, effectiveness, grace (as in the curved porticoes of the Whitney, Rhinelander, and Stevens houses, figs. 1, 4, 5; colorplates 2, 3), or symbolism (as in the domes used to denote government buildings).

The important modification of the Greek anta form into a bold, deeply projecting pilaster or pier may have developed in the Town & Davis office. They used it in forceful pilastrades, as in the Indiana and North Carolina capitols, the New York Custom House, and their distyle-in-antis church pattern (fig. 6). It became a widely copied feature of the American Greek Revival and later designs.[5] Town and Davis also created strong effects with freestanding anta-type piers in lieu of columns.

A remarkable original creation by Davis was the window he called Davisean. Multistoried, recessed in one plane with a panel at floor level and usually with mullions running its height, it gave unity and verticality to a facade. It anticipated the modern vertical strip window. Davis used it from around 1831, first in Greek Revival designs, then carrying it over into other styles—Tuscan, Egyptian (colorplate 32), and Gothic (fig. 7). It became such an integral part of his architecture that it was almost a signature. Occasionally imitated by other architects, it was too far ahead of its time to be adopted generally.

When framed by antae, Davisean windows gave the effect of intercolumnar voids. If extended the full width of the intervening spaces, they formed a virtual window wall, and the antae became piers of a masonry skeleton, as in several designs that foreshadowed the future: his third design for a Patent Office (1834), for an Astor Library (1843) (colorplate 33), and for a Commercial Exchange (1862) (fig. 8).

6. South Congregational Church, Middletown, Connecticut, 1829. Town & Davis. Front elevation. Watercolor, ink, and graphite on paper, 7 x 6¼ in. Drawings & Archives, Avery Architectural and Fine Arts Library, Columbia University (1940.001.00364A).

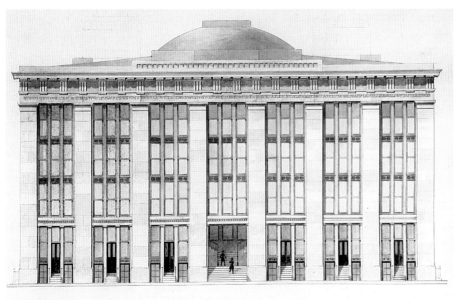

7. Hotel on Constitution Island, Hudson River opposite West Point, New York, 1837 (project). South elevation. Watercolor, ink wash, ink, and graphite on paper, 14⅝ x 20⁹⁄₁₆ in. A. J. Davis Collection, The New-York Historical Society (36).

8. Commercial Exchange, New York City, 1862 (project). Front elevation. Watercolor, ink, and graphite on paper, 18¾ x 26¾ in. A. J. Davis Collection, The New-York Historical Society (307a).

9. Study for a Greek Revival doorway, ca. 1831. Elevation. Watercolor, ink, and graphite on paper, 19 13/16 x 14 3/8 in. The Metropolitan Museum of Art, Harris Brisbane Dick Fund, 1924 (24.66.756).

10. Study for two residential rows facing across a court, New York City, ca. 1831. Perspective. Watercolor and ink on paper, 9 3/4 x 26 1/2 in. The Metropolitan Museum of Art, Harris Brisbane Dick Fund, 1924 (24.66.1291).

11. George W. Hatch, "Row of Dwelling Houses" (House of Mansions), New York City, ca. 1859. Perspective. Lithograph, 14 7/8 x 21 7/8 in. The Metropolitan Museum of Art, Bequest of Susan Dwight Bliss, 1967 (67.630.73).

Town and Davis had a strong impact on residential New York City, for they were the first to introduce Greek Revival doorways flanked by Doric or Ionic columns or pilasters and crowned by entablatures (fig. 9; colorplate 5).[6] These were quickly copied and became standard patterns, singly and in rows.

Davis made a number of unusual designs for rows and terraces, most of which were not executed. An inventive experimental design, probably from 1831 (fig. 10; colorplate 4), presented a new concept, siting two long rows crosswise through the block, facing each other over an open central court and crowned with pleasure walkways on their roofs. In early February 1845 he worked "Day and Night upon a Block of City Dwellings 800 ft. by 40 for Wm. Torrey";[7] his design was apparently the basis for London Terrace, a long block of houses with antae and Davisean windows, built that year by Torrey on Twenty-third Street between Ninth and Tenth avenues. Davis's most impressive row was not Greek Revival but Gothic. His unique House of Mansions (1858–59) covered the Fifth Avenue block between Forty-first and Forty-second streets (fig. 11), a striking contrast to the "desperate uniformity of style"[8] of Fifth Avenue's rows of high-stooped brownstones: eleven dwellings were designed as a unified edifice, a revolutionary predecessor to the development of the apartment-house concept.

In 1847, on West Twelfth Street just off Fifth Avenue, Davis designed two of the earliest Italianate town houses in the city (fig. 12). They were imitated, especially in a long row still standing on West Tenth Street, but their low stoops and restrained detailing were in contrast to the high stoops and ornate palazzo detailing that soon became the prevailing Italianate pattern.

New York's two most outstanding houses of the forties were both by Davis: downtown, at College Place, John Cox Stevens's elegant "palace" with its dome, tall Corinthian columns, and Davisean windows (1845) (see fig. 5); and the towered and turreted Gothic villa of W. C. H. Waddell on suburban Murray Hill at Fifth Avenue and Thirty-eighth Street (1844) (colorplate 52).

Davis brought the city other lively touches from his country-house designing. In 1843 he designed an extraordinary double house that stood at the corner of Fifth Avenue and Eighteenth Street (fig. 13), which was unusual not in size or basic shape

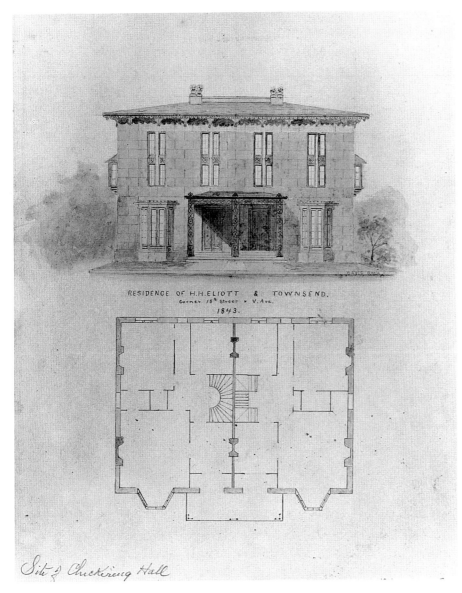

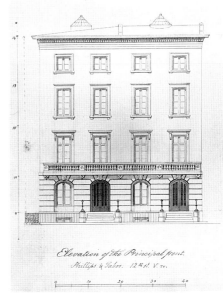

12. Town houses for James W. Phillips and Charles C. Taber, New York City, 1847. Front elevation. Ink and graphite on paper, 12¼ x 8½ in. Drawings & Archives, Avery Architectural and Fine Arts Library, Columbia University (1955.001.00317R).

13. Double town house for H. H. Elliott and R. C. Townsend, New York City, 1843. Front elevation and plan. Watercolor, ink, and graphite on paper, 11³⁄₁₆ x 8⁷⁄₁₆ in. Drawings & Archives, Avery Architectural and Fine Arts Library, Columbia University (1940.001.00128).

14. Study for a double town house, ca. 1843. Front elevation. Watercolor and ink on paper, 14½ x 20⁵⁄₁₆ in. The Metropolitan Museum of Art, Harris Brisbane Dick Fund, 1924 (24.66.55).

but in detailing. It had a low stoop, a small ornamental porch with honeysuckle supports, bracketed eaves, Davisean windows, and—most surprising of all—two bay windows, probably the first in New York City. Another bracketed design (fig. 14; colorplate 6) may have been a study for these houses. A few blocks away, on Gramercy Park's west side, are two houses with graceful cast-iron verandas (1843); these verandas too were probably designed by Davis,[9] and their lacy ironwork had widespread influence.

In 1838 Davis issued his only book, *Rural Residences,* a slender volume of designs full of new ideas for country houses. In a brief preface, he decried the "bald and uninteresting aspect of our [rural] houses . . . not only in the style of the house but in the want of connexion with its site—in the absence of . . . well disposed trees, shrubbery, and vines . . ."[10] To counter this American dullness, he turned to "the picturesque Cottages and Villas of England" and to the English aesthetic theory of the Picturesque, which had evolved and been expounded in reference to landscape gardening and the architecture of country houses in late-eighteenth-century England.

In contrast to the calm serenity of classical ideals, the followers of the Picturesque movement admired the wilder state of nature—its qualities of irregularity, movement, variety, rough texture, and bold contrasts. They urged that rural architecture be designed to harmonize with its setting and to contain these visual qualities, found especially in the Gothic, Italianate, and Swiss styles. The Picturesque theory had a crucial effect on house design, for along with its emphasis on irregularity came freedom and flexibility. It brought a release from the rigidity and limitations of the traditional box shape, which was opened in all directions, both upward and outward, and it liberated the composition of masses in plan and silhouette.

Davis and some of his clients, influenced by the Picturesque theory and inspired by the untamed nature in the Hudson River Valley, began to build country houses there that were in harmony with their surroundings. This brought about the exploration and development of the Gothic, Italianate, and bracketed styles and freer, more irregular shapes for houses in America. In English books Davis found ideas and details for his romantic villas and cottages, but his designs were his own. English designs were "not suited to the taste and wants of the American people," he wrote, as "the English plans are on a scale far more extended and expensive than we can accomplish with our limited means or . . . too inconsiderable and humble for the

15. Walnut Wood for Henry K. Harral, Bridgeport, Connecticut, 1846–50. Perspective. Watercolor and ink on paper, 14⁵⁄₁₆ x 20 in. Drawings & Archives, Avery Architectural and Fine Arts Library, Columbia University (1940.001.00038).

16. House for John B. James, Rhinebeck, New York, 1841 (project). Front elevation. Watercolor, ink, and graphite on paper, 13 ¼ x 19 ⅜ in. Drawings & Archives, Avery Architectural and Fine Arts Library, Columbia University (1940.001.00042).

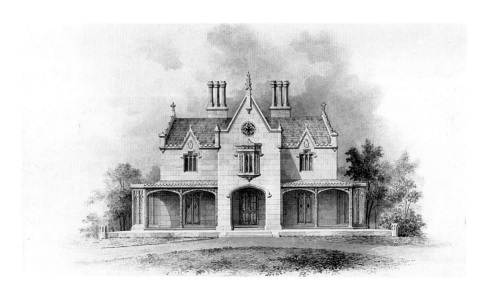

proper pride of republicans."[11] To convey impressions of Picturesque styles while working within this country's limitations, Davis used his sources freely, selecting a few forms and details, adapting and arranging them imaginatively with careful attention to scale. Towers, turrets, pinnacles, finials, high gables, and chimney pots broke the skylines of the Gothic villas, while projections, ample bay windows, and sweeping verandas reached out into the surrounding landscape (fig. 15; colorplate 7). Verandas (especially wraparounds), used as outdoor living spaces, became an important feature of American country houses and summer life.

Freely designed, most of Davis's villas were asymmetrical. Over the years, as the size of houses grew with the country's developing affluence, the asymmetry and complexity of the compositions increased until they reached a climax at Lyndhurst (colorplate 56). In the 1850s three castlelike villas, on very hilly sites, were built of rough-hewn, random-laid stone quarried on the grounds or nearby (colorplate 49). A few smaller villas were symmetrical (fig. 16; colorplate 8),[12] in order to maintain balance within their limited size.

The prototype for the American Gothic cottage was Davis's gatehouse for Robert Donaldson (1836) (colorplate 46). For a rustic, rough-textured effect, Davis sheathed the house in board and batten, a type of siding that was first introduced for domestic use here and became popular after being publicized by Andrew Jackson Downing. Davis's Gothic cottages were usually symmetrical, but they presented a lively appearance with their dramatically high gables ornamented by intricately carved vergeboards, their lofty chimney pots, decorative verandas, and large bay windows. Another of Davis's cottage designs was Kirri Cottage (fig. 17; colorplate 9), the house he had built for his mother in Newark, New Jersey, and which he described as Tudor. One of the gatehouses he designed was in a Norman Romanesque style, complete with portcullis (fig. 18; colorplate 10); in the drawing, the proposed Norman villa is sketched on the hilltop, although it was never built.

Probably the earliest Italianate villa begun in America was the house Davis designed for James Smillie at Rondout on the Hudson (1836) (fig. 19; colorplate 11 is an idealized version). Construction was soon abandoned as too expensive. An elaborated view was published in Downing's *Landscape Gardening* (1841) as "Mr. Smillie's Villa"; later editions called it simply "A Villa in the Italian Style." Also appearing there from the second edition (1844) on was Davis's first executed Italianate villa, Blandwood, for John M. Morehead, the progressive governor of North Carolina. Although the overall symmetrical layout was Palladian, with arcades linking the dependencies to the house, it had a central front tower, an influential idea much followed even into the Second Empire period. In the late 1840s and the 1850s, as the Italianate style became increasingly popular, Davis designed more than two dozen villas in the style. To distinguish them from their Anglo-Italianate inspiration, he frequently called them Americanized Italian. They were skillful asymmetrical compositions of geometric masses, often of extended length and with juxtaposed towers of different height, size, and shape; like the Gothic villas, they had extensive verandas and large bay windows, and their detailing was restrained (colorplate 55).

For some country houses of basically regular shape—such as an 1835 design for David Codwise—Davis devised ornamentation to disguise their rigidity, projecting the eaves and adding bay windows and ornamental verandas to give some irregularity to their appearance (colorplate 38). In 1836 he remodeled a Federal-style block for Robert Donaldson at Blithewood in Annandale-on-Hudson. Apparently working with Donaldson, he wrapped the house in a decorative veranda (fig. 20; color-

17. Detail of Kirri Cottage for Julia Davis, Newark, New Jersey, 1847–49 (later additions 1854, 1859). Front elevation. Watercolor, ink, and graphite on paper, 10 x 6 ¹⁵⁄₁₆ in. The Metropolitan Museum of Art, Harris Brisbane Dick Fund, 1924 (24.66.789).

18. Gate lodge for Amos G. Hull, Newburgh, New York, 1849. Front elevation. Watercolor, ink, and graphite on paper, 14⅜ x 19¹³⁄₁₆ in. The Metropolitan Museum of Art, Harris Brisbane Dick Fund, 1924 (24.66.71).

19. Detail of study for a villa for James Smillie, Rondout, New York, 1836. Front elevation. Watercolor, ink, and graphite on paper, 14½ x 10⅜ in. The Metropolitan Museum of Art, Harris Brisbane Dick Fund, 1924 (24.66.1416 [49], vol. XVII, leaf 56).

20. "View N. W. at Blithewood," Annandale-on-Hudson, New York, ca. 1841. Watercolor, ink, and graphite on paper, 7⅞ x 9¹⁵⁄₁₆ in. Drawings & Archives, Avery Architectural and Fine Arts Library, Columbia University (1955.001.00059).

21. Second gatehouse at Blithewood for Robert Donaldson, Annandale-on-Hudson, New York, 1841. Side elevation and plan. Watercolor and ink on paper, 9⅞ x 6⅛ in. Drawings & Archives, Avery Architectural and Fine Arts Library, Columbia University (1955.001.00057).

plate 12) and extended the roof to a broad gable with ornamental eave brackets; simplified from the Anglo-Swiss style, these were the origin of the American bracketed style, which Davis also used for a second gatehouse here (fig. 21). Blithewood's broad-gabled side elevation may have inspired the front elevations of two bracketed, board-and-batten designs of 1842 (figs. 22, 23; colorplates 13, 14). The more elaborate one is enlivened by the sparkle of carved brackets and the grace of vine-clad iron trellis supports on the encircling veranda; its simpler companion, with rafter brackets and plain bracketed veranda posts, was published twice by Downing.[13]

For appropriate situations and clients, Davis produced designs in a classical style, as in the graceful additions to Montgomery Place at Annandale-on-Hudson. He designed a small classical villa for Lewis B. Brown in Rahway, New Jersey (fig. 24), which he called his "American House" because of its popularity. Twice published by Downing, it was adapted by Davis at the request of several clients, and builders made copies directly from the published wood engravings. Classicism had been the language of Davis's early career, and it was a pervasive influence throughout his work. Together with his artist's eye it gave him a strong sensitivity to balance in composition and restraint in the handling of details.

Davis was born in New York City on July 24, 1803. His father, Cornelius Davis (1760–1831), was a bookseller and publisher of theological tracts, and an editor of theological periodicals. Benign but impractical, he made little money from his efforts, and the family often lived in near poverty. Studious though self-educated, like many Americans of his time, he stimulated in his son a love of books and reading, but in subjects very different from his own interests. His ancestors had been in America since the early seventeenth century, and he imparted to his children a strong sense of American identity through stories of his youth during the Revolutionary War—how he had fled with his family from the ravages of Burgoyne's army and the Indians on the Saratoga frontier and how he later had fought skirmishes in New Jersey.[14]

Alexander was the oldest child of Cornelius Davis and his second wife, Julia Jackson Davis (1772–1862), who came from Florida, New York, a pleasant village in the rolling countryside of Orange County, where Alexander occasionally visited relatives. He was named for his maternal grandfather, Alexander Jackson, who had migrated from northern Ireland in 1746 and had married an American wife of ancestry traced back to Annetje Jans Bogardus of New Amsterdam.

Although Davis was born in New York City and lived there during almost all of his mature life and career, his boyhood and youth were not spent there. Sometime between 1805 and 1808 his family seems to have moved to Newark, New Jersey, and again, probably in 1813, to central New York State, first to Utica for about four years, then farther west to Auburn for another year. Both villages were growing rapidly and were lively with construction. Utica, crossroads and gateway to the west and north, already had a fine Gothic church by Philip Hooker and impressive buildings by Hooker's father, while in Auburn a large prison was being erected in Gothic style. All the fervor and excitement of the building activity must have impressed young Alexander, for later he wrote that his "Mind [was] formed for Architecture at Utica and Auburn, while at school; and at Alexandria, and Washington, D.C. . . ."[15]

Davis's school days were over when he was not quite fifteen. In May 1818, he was sent to Alexandria (then in the District of Columbia) to learn the printing trade at the *Alexandria Gazette*, where his half-brother Samuel was editor. Typesetting taught him precision and manual dexterity, but other things were even more important in his development: the experiences offered by the sophisticated southern city,

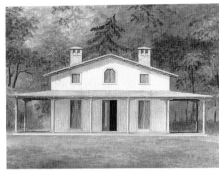

22. Study for a simple bracketed cottage, 1842. Front elevation. Watercolor, ink, and graphite on paper, 14⅛ x 20⅝ in. A. J. Davis Collection, The New-York Historical Society (564).

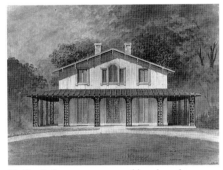

23. Study for an ornamented bracketed cottage, 1842. Front elevation. Watercolor, ink, and graphite on paper, 14⁵⁄₁₆ x 19¹⁵⁄₁₆ in. A. J. Davis Collection, The New-York Historical Society (565).

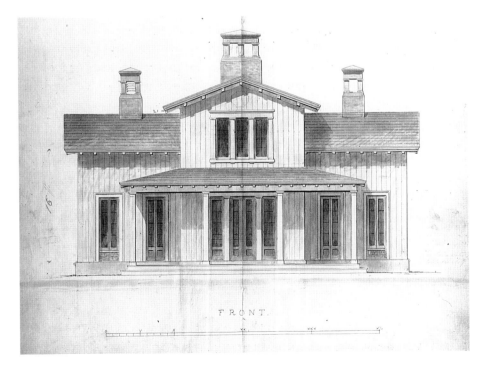

FRONT.

24. House for Lewis B. Brown, Rahway, New Jersey, 1848. Front elevation. Watercolor, ink, and graphite on paper, 13⅞ x 16⅞ in. The Metropolitan Museum of Art, Harris Brisbane Dick Fund, 1924 (24.66.1413, vol. XIV, leaf 14, recto).

25. Preliminary design for Kenwood for Joel Rathbone, south of Albany, New York, 1842. Rear elevation. Watercolor and ink on paper, 13¾ x 19¹¹⁄₁₆ in. The Metropolitan Museum of Art, Harris Brisbane Dick Fund, 1924 (24.66.22).

26. Library bay at Whitby for William P. Chapman, Rye, New York, 1853. Elevation and section. Watercolor and ink on paper, 17⅛ x 12½ in. The Metropolitan Museum of Art, Harris Brisbane Dick Fund, 1924 (24.66.16).

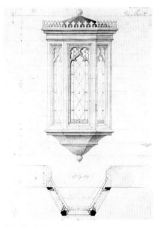

27. Oriel window in the Great Tower at Lyndhurst for George Merritt, Tarrytown, New York, 1865. Elevation and plan. Watercolor, ink, and graphite on paper, 21¾ x 14 in. The Metropolitan Museum of Art, Harris Brisbane Dick Fund, 1924 (24.66.15).

the sights of nearby Washington (which was being rebuilt after the destruction caused by the War of 1812), his exploration of literature, his sketching, and his fascination with acting in amateur dramatic performances. Drama became a longtime interest and a future asset to his work; his love of dramatic qualities in literature would translate into a sensitivity to visual dramatic effects in architecture.

Returning to New York in 1823, at age twenty, Davis supported himself for a few years by typesetting while he studied art. He began to draw buildings and city views for proprietors, publishers, and architects, and his interest turned increasingly to architecture. For a short time he did drafting in the office of Josiah R. Brady, and he studied in Ithiel Town's library, which was generously opened to interested persons. Town even loaned him Stuart and Revett's *The Antiquities of Athens* (1762), of which he recorded: "1828 March 15 First study of Stuarts Athens, from which I date Professional Practice."[16] In 1827 and 1828, on two trips of several months to Boston (to draw lithographs for William Pendleton), he studied in the Boston Athenaeum. By 1828 he was creating original architectural designs; that year he exhibited a design for a state house at the National Academy.

Davis drew expertly and was able to convey his ideas vividly and directly without hiring a draftsman as intermediary. He did almost all of his own drafting, from finished renderings (fig. 25; colorplate 15) to working drawings (figs. 26, 27; colorplate 16). William H. Pierson, Jr., has characterized Davis's drawing style as "versatile, expressive, and hauntingly beautiful."

> Davis produced the finest architectural renderings of his generation . . . Conceived in varying degrees of light and shade, and executed in water color with fluid ease, these drawings reveal with sureness and clarity the full-bodied substance of his designs. Through delicate precise lines they delineate the smallest elements of architectural detail; at the same time, they are richly luminous and vibrant, brought alive by an extraordinary control of tone.[17]

Davis's architectural career began auspiciously in 1829. In mid-January he received his first commission, for the design of a country house for the poet James A. Hillhouse at the head of Hillhouse Avenue on the outskirts of New Haven. In late December (1828) and early January Davis had acted as the draftsman of Hillhouse's own design for the house, made after attempts by outstanding architects and amateurs had left him dissatisfied. Now the "original design" of the young Davis pleased him where others had failed (colorplate 37).[18] An unusual, impressive design and an important commission, it brought Davis immediate recognition and led to friendship with Hillhouse and, eventually, to a succession of other New Haven houses.

Almost immediately, on February 1, 1829, Davis "entered into an association, (relating to Architectural Practice, for building) with Ithiel Town, Esq."[19] This was an extraordinary opportunity for a young, inexperienced beginner. Town (1784–1844), nearly twenty years Davis's senior, was a prominent architect and bridge engineer, an energetic leader in the new Greek Revival, and the inventor of the lucrative lattice truss for covered bridges. He owned by far the finest architectural library in America, thousands of volumes from incunabula to the latest English pattern books. Davis had already sampled it and now could explore it in depth. Since Davis never traveled abroad, books were his source of inspiration and of details throughout his career.

The Town & Davis firm lasted for six years, until May 1, 1835 (with the addition of James H. Dakin for a year and a half), and was revived briefly in 1842–43.

Some of the finest American buildings of the period came from their office: the capitols of Indiana and North Carolina, the New York Custom House, a courthouse and town hall, a hospital, an insane asylum, institutions, banks, stores, warehouses, churches (such as the Église du Saint Esprit of 1831–34, figs. 28, 29; colorplates 17, 18), and city and country houses, as well as advanced designs for unexecuted projects like the Astor Hotel of 1830–32 (fig. 30; colorplate 21). Most of the designs were free interpretations of the Greek Revival style, usually distinguished by bold antae, but there were also pioneering ventures into the Gothic, Egyptian, and Tuscan styles.

As he gained experience, Davis assumed an increasing role in the designs, especially during Town's frequent long absences while supervising construction of the two state capitols, developing his bridge-building enterprises, and traveling for eleven months in England and on the continent. Davis studied assiduously, made experimental designs in many styles (including Egyptian and Oriental), and started to compile an illustrated volume on the classical architecture of antiquity, a venture that evolved into an ambitious proposal, made jointly with Town, that was to be called "The American Architect" but was never completed.

After his association with Town was discontinued in 1835 and Town went off to New Haven, Davis "joined interests" briefly with Russell Warren for part of 1835–36. Then for four more decades (except for the year with Town in 1842–43), until 1878, he kept an office alone: he did his own drafting, with occasional help in very busy periods, and did not even have a clerk to keep his accounts. Burned out of the Merchants' Exchange in the Great Fire of December 1835, he moved to the new New York University building, at that time partly a studio building, where a number of artists rented rooms. He lived as well as worked in his rooms, a mode of life he continued when he moved back to the Merchants' Exchange from 1842 until 1862 (and then returned to the University until 1878).

The second half of the 1830s started as a period of buoyant optimism but then brought frustration and a new direction to his career. The Panic of 1837 and its aftermath doomed numerous ambitious projects that had been engendered by America's expansionist mood, including the Brooklyn City Hall, for which Davis submitted ten designs; a Gothic hotel on the Hudson River opposite West Point; and a large residential development scheme, Ravenswood, across the East River from Manhattan, for which he drew ten classical and Gothic villas and a church in 1836. His designs for the capitols of Illinois and Ohio and for the University of Michigan (colorplate 28) were not realized. The new American Institution of Architects, of which he and Thomas U. Walter were leaders when it was founded in December 1836, languished after 1837 and disappeared.

Through the 1830s Davis's residential designing strengthened. At New Haven a dozen suburban classical villas, including Henry Whitney's country house, Belmont (see fig. 1), demonstrated his imaginative skill in devising a variety of effects without duplication.

Davis began his designs for villas and cottages in Picturesque styles along the Hudson River in the 1830s. Although his Gothic villa designs for Robert Donaldson at Fishkill Landing (1834) (colorplate 43) were not executed and his Italianate villa for James Smillie at Rondout (1836) was not completed, in 1836 he introduced the bracketed mode in a cottage orné for Robert Donaldson at Blithewood and created the first American Gothic cottage as his gatehouse. In 1838 *Rural Residences* was issued, and William and Philip Paulding's amazing Knoll and Henry Sheldon's charm-

28. Detail of Église du Saint Esprit, New York City, 1831–34. Town & Davis. Front elevation. Watercolor and ink on paper, 11¼ x 8¹⁵⁄₁₆ in. The Metropolitan Museum of Art, Harris Brisbane Dick Fund, 1924 (24.66.82).

29. Detail of Église du Saint Esprit, New York City, 1831–34. Town & Davis. Section. Watercolor and ink on paper, 21⅞ x 14⅜ in. The Metropolitan Museum of Art, Harris Brisbane Dick Fund, 1924 (24.66.84).

30. Astor Hotel, New York City, ca. 1830 (project). Perspective. Watercolor, ink, and graphite on paper, 20⁵⁄₁₆ x 31½ in. The Metropolitan Museum of Art, Harris Brisbane Dick Fund, 1924 (24.66.30).

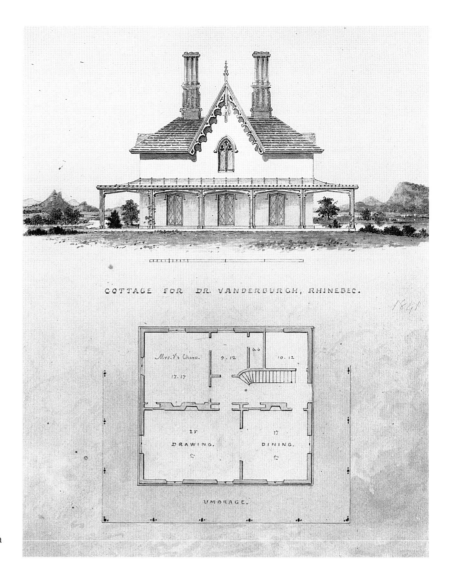

COTTAGE FOR DR. VANDERBURGH, RHINEBEC.

31. Cottage for Dr. Federal Vanderburgh, Rhinebeck, New York, 1841. Front elevation and plan. Watercolor, ink, and graphite on paper, 10 x 7 in. Drawings & Archives, Avery Architectural and Fine Arts Library, Columbia University (1955.001.00303).

ing Millbrook were designed. They were soon followed by other Gothic country houses, including Linwood Hill, Dr. Federal Vanderburgh's cottage at Rhinebeck (1841) (fig. 31), and Joel Rathbone's Kenwood near Albany (1842) (colorplate 45). In these early villas and cottages Davis created many of the patterns and details basic to his later designs.

For more than a decade, from 1839 to 1850, Davis collaborated with Andrew Jackson Downing (1815–52), drawing most of the architectural illustrations for the young landscape gardener's books and monthly magazine *The Horticulturist*.[20] Davis's work had a strong influence on Downing and his books. In the first book, *Landscape Gardening* (1841), many of the views were of Davis's recent Picturesque houses. In the subsequent pattern books some of the designs were Davis's, a few were Downing's, many were the joint work of Davis and Downing (though often dependent on prior work by Davis, especially those in Gothic and bracketed styles), and the remainder were by other architects. Davis's charming perspectives added much to the effectiveness of Downing's persuasive prose.

The books popularized the ideas of the Picturesque in America; their designs and details were copied and adapted widely. Davis's reputation spread, and by the 1840s and 1850s he had become the leading American designer of romantic country houses. His work extended not only along the Hudson and through central New

York State, but from Maine to Virginia and North Carolina and westward to Kentucky, Michigan, and Ohio. In the 1850s he made many designs for the romantic suburb Llewellyn Park (which he had probably helped to envisage) in West Orange, New Jersey, and for the development of New Rochelle, New York.

The 1840s and 1850s were the busiest years of Davis's career. His work included urban residences, a Gothic armory, the Wadsworth Atheneum (with Town, based on a plan by Henry Austin), Yale's Alumni Hall, a Tuscan Town Hall for Bridgeport, Connecticut, several small churches and academies, and important work in the South, both residential and institutional. At the University of North Carolina, he enlarged the Old East and Old West buildings, giving each distinctive bracketed eaves and a dominant central Davisean window, while his new Smith Hall had corn-and-wheat capitals. He designed a huge visionary Tuscan campus quadrangle for Davidson College and the impressive insane asylum in Raleigh. For the Virginia Military Institute he created a new Gothic campus: barracks, mess hall, three villas, and an octagonal porter's lodge. Further work in the South was being planned when the Civil War began.

The war interrupted Davis's career and ended his work in the South. His practice never fully recovered, although he did splendid work in the 1860s (including Montgomery Place and Lyndhurst) and continued to envision large schemes into the 1870s. Architectural fashions had begun to change even before the war, and he disliked both High Victorian Gothic and French Empire, the predominating styles. He dropped out of the American Institute of Architects, of which he had been an original trustee, but in the 1880s he became reconciled. Montgomery Schuyler wrote that Davis was "affectionately remembered by architects of the next generation following his own as 'Papa Davis.'"[21]

Until 1878, when Davis was seventy-five, he kept an office, where for many years he had lived as well as worked. In 1853 he had married Margaret Beale, by whom he had two children, Flora and Joseph, but for much of the time he lived apart from his family, completely absorbed in his architecture. In his retirement he joined his family and spent his declining years reliving his architecture—revising, "improving," copying, and arranging his drawings and papers. In 1856–57, on a cliff of Orange Mountain overlooking Llewellyn Park, he had built a small summer lodge, Wildmont, surrounded by partially wooded acres, where he indulged his love of nature. Enlarged in the 1860s, Wildmont was much expanded in 1878, intended to become eventually a year-round dwelling (colorplate 51), but it burned to the ground in 1884. Near the site his son built a simple frame house, to which the family moved in 1890, and there the architect died on January 14, 1892.

Davis had been an outstanding architect and had left his imprint on America. One of the most inventive interpreters of the Greek Revival and a daring explorer of many new styles, he had created great buildings of this country's mid-nineteenth century—the New York Custom House and North Carolina Capitol (with Ithiel Town), the Virginia Military Institute, the House of Mansions, the Stevens House, Montgomery Place, Walnut Wood, Lyndhurst, and Grace Hill, to name a few. His villas and cottages were the most evocative architectural expression of romanticism in America. He had influenced the evolution of American houses, initiated patterns, envisioned big schemes and prophetic forms, brought greater freedom to American architecture, and enriched the American scene with the achievements of his imaginative designs. His work, based in early classicism and blossoming with the unfolding of romantic styles, was an integral and formative force in the changing architecture of America in the nineteenth century.

1.1. Rustic landscape, ca. 1815–18. Graphite
on paper, 9 11/16 x 12 1/8 in. Drawings & Archives,
Avery Architectural and Fine Arts Library,
Columbia University (1940.001.00578).

CHAPTER 1

Alexander Jackson Davis and the Arts of Design

CARRIE REBORA

*If precedence is to be given to that branch of art, requiring the greatest amount
of acquired knowledge combined with force of imagination and strong judgment,
then Architecture must, unquestionably take the lead.* —A. J. Davis, 1834[1]

Alexander Jackson Davis might be called an historian's dream. The primary documentation on Davis is voluminous because, from the time he was a teenager, he saved everything: the diaries, journals, and notebooks he kept simultaneously; drawings and sketchbooks; papers from organizations he belonged to; clippings from newspapers and journals; and quotes he jotted down in volumes for future reference. Then he spent his old age organizing, alphabetizing, indexing, and annotating the papers for posterity. Even though some of this work confused matters, as when he altered drawings or rewrote old correspondence, Davis primarily facilitated historians' investigations of him. He wanted to make sure that his life and work would be understood by those who would take an interest in him years after his death. In his mind, there was no question that he would become an important historical figure. At one point in the 1870s, as he whiled away his time cutting and pasting, numbering sheets, titling drawings, rethinking his designs, and drafting autobiographical sketches, he wrote that he had attained "a prominence and influence not possessed by any architect before or since."[2] He meant in America, although he was undoubtedly certain of his high rank in the international, historical scheme of things. Davis had definite ideas about his legacy. So it seems ironic that for all his painstaking preparations for an afterlife defined not only by his buildings but also by his more general contribution to American culture, Davis's historical reputation is circumscribed by his built work and published drawings.

Davis's recorded actions and scribbled ideas, especially those that date from the time before he designed buildings, reveal the disposition behind his designs. One of the crucial, little-acclaimed facts of Davis's life is that he considered himself first and foremost an artist, with stature equal to that of any contemporary painter. In fact, he deemed architecture the highest form of artistic expression. He believed that painters and sculptors "seldom . . . rise to an unprejudiced and liberal contemplation of true beauty" and seconded his colleague George Wightwick's charge that "no body of men is more destitute of true architectural feeling than the gentlemen of the brush."[3] Davis did not dislike painters; he counted Thomas Cole, Asher B. Durand, Samuel F. B. Morse, Rembrandt Peale, and other gentlemen of the brush among his friends. His assailing comment against their profession betrays more strategy than true feeling. He demeaned painters, a relatively numerous and highly acclaimed group, in order to elevate architects, who he said were skilled in all aspects of design. Architecture, Davis wrote, paraphrasing Samuel Taylor Coleridge, "involves all the power of invention [and] design, and is sculpture and painting inclusively. It shews the greatness of man, and should at the same time teach him

1.2. Landscape, illustration for *Pilgrim's Progress*, 1818. Watercolor and ink on paper, 3⅞ x 6¹⁄₁₆ in. Drawings & Archives, Avery Architectural and Fine Arts Library, Columbia University (1955.001.00285).

humility."[4] Yet, architecture did not make Davis humble; in fact, its relation to the other arts made him angry. He protested against the perceived superiority of painting especially, waging a lifelong campaign for the preeminence of architecture.

Davis felt superior to his painter and sculptor colleagues because he had studied their craft early in his life and then surpassed them by acquiring the skills necessary for architectural design. In 1834, he wrote that "a knowledge not of the principles only, but even of *execution* in painting and sculpture are indispensable to the architect" and that "masters" of architecture must have "from their early youth, gradually climbed up to the summit" by acquiring proficiency in numerous fields.[5] As a boy, he probably did not conceive of learning to draw from the antique as a prerequisite for his future career as an architect, but in hindsight he considered his artistic training as predestination.

Davis's son gives the perhaps apocryphal account that his father, when just a young boy, traded his toys for a set of paints, probably watercolors.[6] Extant early drawings, such as the rustic landscape (fig. 1.1) that Davis drew probably during his early teens, reveal his young talent and suggest that he may have studied drawing manuals, prints, or book illustrations for help with composition and subject matter. When he was a little older, he experimented with a camera obscura, "in an attempt," he wrote, "to trace the beautiful reflections of natural objects."[7] One of his earliest dated landscapes, from 1818, of a man standing on a cliff looking at the town below (fig. 1.2), was likely to have been inspired by his work with a camera obscura, which was often used by landscape artists to capture proper perspective in rendering distant, wide-angle views. His inscription identifying this particular drawing as an illustration for "Bunion's Pilgrim's Prog." suggests that nature was not his only source; Davis was an avid reader, and nature and fiction probably mingled to inspire his artistic vision. His elaborate composition dated 1820 and entitled "View of the Village of Florida, Orange Co. N.Y. From the North-West" (fig. 1.3; colorplate 19) may have also been executed with the aid of a camera obscura and again reveals that Davis was not taking his view from nature alone. His detailed, if crudely executed, view from a distance, framed by trees, with gesticulating figures added for scale and a spark of narrative, shows that he might have been aware of views painted by Francis Guy, William Groombridge, or William Russell Birch; Davis even painted a faux

1.3. "View of the Village of Florida, Orange Co. N.Y. from the North-West," ca. 1820–22. Watercolor and ink on paper, 16⅛ x 20¼ in. The Metropolitan Museum of Art, Harris Brisbane Dick Fund, 1924 (24.66.749).

1.4. View of an imaginary city built on canals, 1820. Watercolor and ink on paper, 15 x 20⁹/₁₆ in. The Metropolitan Museum of Art, Harris Brisbane Dick Fund, 1924 (24.66.752).

frame around his composition to make it look like a finished work of art, ready for exhibition.[8]

Davis recalled that while drawing with a camera obscura "in an obscure country village . . . [he] conceived of the idea of becoming a professional artist." The village, actually a city, was probably Alexandria, Virginia, where Davis worked as a compositor in his brother's printing office beginning in about 1820. Apparently monotonous days spent setting type drove Davis further into books and his imagination. He spent his free time "designing streets in Venice, conjecturing the fashions of gondolas and planning interiors for churches, palaces, and prisons"[9] (fig. 1.4). Venice, a city Davis knew only from books, obviously struck him as a fantastic city, with monumental, colonnaded buildings stacked six stories high along the canals where leisured men and women floated along in embellished, canopied gondolas. His fixation with romance and drama also inspired various painted illustrations for Shakespearean tragedies, such as *Othello* (fig. 1.5), which allowed him to explore the dark and sublime subject matter that appealed to his inquisitive mind.

The way Davis tells his story, by the time he was ready to leave his brother's shop in about 1823, he was intoxicated with artistic inspiration and there was no changing his course; "he [had] imbibed a portion of that high imaginative spirit so necessary to constitute an artist destined to practise in the field of invention."[10] Davis moved to New York at the age of twenty and, by his own account, soon decided to study perspective, "the grammar of his art," and "devote himself to architecture."[11] In fact, he did not choose a career so quickly, but spent a few years attempting to broaden his artistic experience. At the time, New York offered scant opportunity for artists to sell or exhibit their work and even less opportunity for study. The painter Samuel F. B. Morse, who arrived in New York at about the same time as Davis, was discouraged after only a month; in late 1823, he wrote to his wife that the artists "all agree that little is doing in the city of New York. It seems wholly given to commerce."[12] For Davis, though, New York must have seemed an exciting and welcome contrast to Alexandria. Evenings at the theater supplemented his study of dramatic literature, and he probably browsed in artists' supply shops and bookstores and met other aspiring young artists around town.

Davis also must have visited the gallery at the American Academy of the Fine

1.5. "Bed Scene in *Othello*," ca. 1820–22. Ink and wash on paper, 2¼ x 3⅜ in. The Metropolitan Museum of Art, Gift of Richard H. Pratt, 1946 (46.114.8).

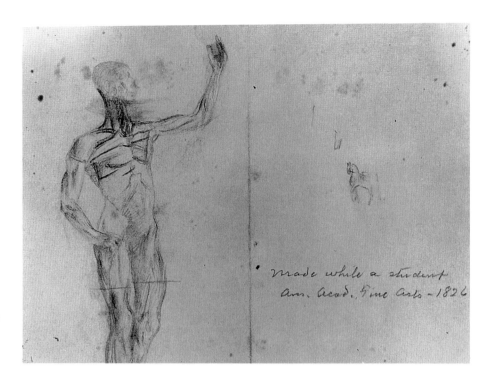

made while a student
Am. Acad. Fine Arts - 1826

1.6. Sketch from the antique, ca. 1824. Graphite on paper, 6⅛ x 7¹³⁄₁₆ in. Drawings & Archives, Avery Architectural and Fine Arts Library, Columbia University (1940.001.00404).

Arts, and possibly studied there in the fall of 1824, when the board of directors offered a sketch class. The academy had been founded in 1802 by Edward and Robert R. Livingston, then mayor of New York and American Minister to France respectively, who called for subscriptions from merchants, doctors, lawyers, politicians, and other elite city residents to establish "the first American School for the fine Arts," complete with plaster casts from classical sculpture, copies of old masterpieces, architectural models and drawings, and a library.[13] The Livingstons succeeded in acquiring a sizable collection of casts from the Louvre and a respectable selection of paintings, books, and prints, but they failed to develop a program of exhibitions and artists' classes. After John Trumbull became president of the board in 1817, the academy held annual exhibitions but still did not fulfill its founders' plans for an art school.

In 1823, when Davis surely entered the gallery in the refurbished Alms House in City Hall Park, he would have seen paintings by Trumbull, Benjamin West, John Singleton Copley, Washington Allston, and John Wesley Jarvis, along with a number of European pictures of dubious attribution and many portraits. The academy allowed sketching in the gallery but did not offer supervised instruction. In the summer of 1824, in response to criticism from local artists, Archibald Robertson, the Scottish draftsman and author of *Elements of the Graphic Arts* (New York, 1802), set up a program of study in the academy. Students drew the large sculptures in the gallery during the morning and moved into a studio for additional study from small casts later in the day.[14] Robertson did not keep a record of attendance, so there is no way of knowing who studied with him, but Davis's sketch of an antique statue, perhaps Germanicus (fig. 1.6), offers some proof that he sketched at the academy.[15] The only artist who is postively known to have studied there is Ambrose Andrews, a painter two years older than Davis, and Andrews's account of what he learned at the academy might be construed as further proof that Davis studied there too. Andrews's words ring remarkably close to many of Davis's ideas about the arts:

The student . . . should not neglect the daily practice of drawing from some correct model of imitation— Excellence in drawing is the foundation of excellence in every department of art. . . . Few people are aware of the requisites to form any artist, or of the variety of studies necessary in historic or poetic composition—A knowledge of Anatomy and perspective, correctness of drawing, which can only be acquired by long practice . . . is necessary to combine Portraiture, Landscape, and Architecture, with beauty of form and appropriate expression.[16]

Andrews regretted that his study at the academy coincided with Trumbull's absence from the city. Davis, too, would have had very little contact with the academy president, who was in Washington, D.C., working on his commission for the rotunda of the Capitol during much of 1823 and 1824. Trumbull has traditionally been assigned a great deal of influence on Davis; decades later Davis acquired a scrapbook of Trumbull's drawings and wrote in it that he was Trumbull's "pupil and friend," but this is merely telling of his respect for Trumbull and should not be considered proof of their teacher-student relationship. In any case, during the mid-1820s, Davis probably received more attention from other artists. Andrews explained that the painter William Dunlap and the sculptor Hugh Reinagle lent him books and small statues and offered helpful advice. Davis probably knew these artists, and he undoubtedly knew Morse, who returned to New York in November 1824 and soon moved into a spacious home and studio on Canal Street, where he often hosted informal gatherings of artists. By the autumn of 1825, Morse's soirees had grown so popular that a group of painters and sculptors began looking for a bigger meeting room where they could also sketch. Dunlap, the painter Thomas Seir Cummings, and others contacted Trumbull about holding their meetings at the American Academy, but the group was too big for the gallery. Trumbull arranged to move a selection of statues into the New-York Historical Society and then, when the group attracted more artists, to the more commodious Literary and Philosophical Society.[17] The New York Association of Artists, as the group was formally named, convened at least once a week for talking and sketching. Davis was welcomed as a member on November 16, 1825, and was also recorded in attendance on November 21.[18] When the Association of Artists became the National Academy of Design in January 1826, the official roster of members and students listed Davis as a student in the Antique School.[19]

According to the National Academy's rules, students were admitted to the Antique School, which was open three evenings a week, "by presenting a drawing" to the committee on arrangements.[20] Through his membership in the Association of Artists, however, Davis may have been automatically enrolled in the National Academy. His drawings from 1825 and 1826 suggest that he probably would have been admitted in any case.

Davis's drawing titled "Apollo and the Muses," which was engraved by James Eddy and published as the 1827 volume frontispiece (fig. 1.7) for the New-York Mirror's first four volumes (1827–30), suggests that he was capable of depicting figures in motion. His 1825 design for a grand, eclectic proscenium (fig. 1.8), with Egyptian columns and Greek bas-relief sculpture surmounted by a figure of Zeus, also shows that his drafting skill was much improved. Clearly his fascination with theatrical invention persisted. The effect of his study of antique statuary can be seen in small portraits of actors in character, such as "Brutus in the Rostrum" (fig. 1.9), "Mme. Augusta in La Bayadere," and "Mr. Kemble as Roma" (fig. 1.10). With these dramatic likenesses, Davis contributed to the current vogue of theatrical portraiture, as

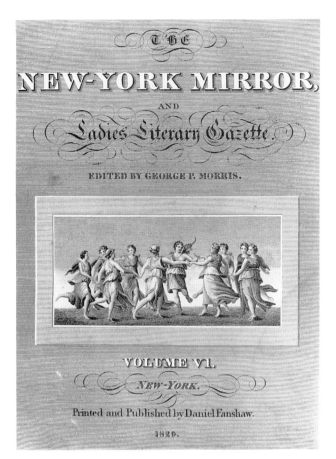

1.7. "Apollo and the Muses," ca. 1827. Engraved by James Eddy after original drawing by Davis for *The New-York Mirror and Ladies' Literary Gazette,* frontispiece to vols. 4–8, 1827–30. The New-York Historical Society Library.

DESIGN,   PROCENIUM,   DAVIS,

1.8. Study for a proscenium, 1825. Elevation. Watercolor, ink, and graphite on paper, 18⁹⁄₁₆ x 14¾ in. The Metropolitan Museum of Art, Harris Brisbane Dick Fund, 1924 (24.66.442).

BRUTUS IN THE ROSTRUM.

SHAKESPEARE.

*I mean that Brutus, who in open Senate
Stabb'd the first Cæsar that usurp'd the world.*

Mr. KEMBLE as ROLLA,——

Rolla— *My brave associates—partners of my toil.
my feelings and my fame:——*✳

popularized by Thomas Sully, John Wesley Jarvis, and Henry Inman. Yet, unlike these artists, whose goal was to produce vivid characterizations of actors, Davis seems to have been more interested in the theatrical trappings than the figures.

Davis showed no inclination toward portraiture, the art of choice at the time for any artist hoping to support himself by his art. In 1826, landscape painting was gaining acceptance as a salable, worthy form of art, in part due to the auspicious popularity of Thomas Cole, whose paintings of Catskill Falls thrilled local art patrons at the American Academy's 1825 exhibition.[21] Davis, however, did not pursue landscape painting either. Sometime in 1826, he received commissions for architectural renderings from A. T. Goodrich, a prominent bookseller and publisher of city guides, and Josiah R. Brady, a noted architect. For Goodrich, Davis drew graphite and wash renditions of important buildings throughout the city, and he helped Brady with plans for various architectural projects. Also, at about this time, Rembrandt Peale told Davis that "he appeared to be peculiarly well fitted" to be an architect.[22] In 1827, at the age of twenty-four, Davis claimed his profession: the city directory listed him as an "architectural composer" with an office or studio on Wall Street.

Davis's choice of title for himself suggests a compromise between professions. He was not an architect, he was not an artist; he composed views of existing buildings in embellished settings for use by engravers, a process that required a draftsman's skill and an artist's inventiveness. If the account of his boyhood is to be believed, then it seems he was inclined toward this sort of work ever since he bartered toys for paint. Later, he would explain that his temperament, or "intellectual thermometer," was governed by his parents, from whom he had genetically inherited "sound judgment, tempered . . . by poetic fervor, and . . . a brilliant imagination,

1.9. "Brutus in the Rostrum," ca. 1826. Ink wash on paper, 9 x 5 ½ in. Drawings & Archives, Avery Architectural and Fine Arts Library, Columbia University (1940.001.00572).

1.10. "Mr. Kemble as Roma," ca. 1826. Ink wash on paper, 5 ¾ x 3 ¾ in. Drawings & Archives, Avery Architectural and Fine Arts Library, Columbia University (1940.001.00571).

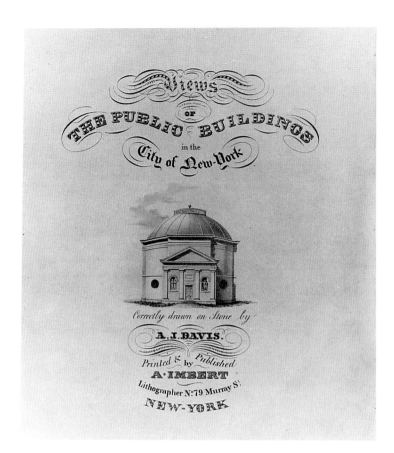

1.11. Title page for *Views of the Public Buildings in the City of New-York,* 1827, illustrating the Vanderlyn Rotunda. Lithograph issued by Anthony Imbert, 19 7/16 x 15 15/16 in. A. J. Davis Collection, The New-York Historical Society (25).

governed by reason that made him fit to be an architectural composer."[23] But there was another, more recent, influence that might have had an impact on his choice of career.

Gulian C. Verplanck's address on the fine arts, delivered May 11, 1824, to celebrate the tenth exhibition at the American Academy, was one of the most powerful events in the New York art world during the 1820s. His eloquent discourse on the national value of the arts was published, reprinted, excerpted, and praised in newspapers and journals, and arguably inspired the intense growth of the fine arts in New York in the following years.[24] If Davis did not hear the address himself, he certainly read it.

Verplanck, an author, a lawyer, and later a congressman, spoke at great length to convince his audience of artists, city officials, academy members, and others that "the arts of design have a direct and positive utility" on the lives of all Americans and the good of the nation. He discussed painting, sculpture, the development of taste, the relationship of the arts to freedom, and many other subjects, and made a particularly passionate argument for the special importance of architecture:

> There is no walk of the elegant arts in which our defects of science and taste are more palpable than in that of architecture. . . . There is, in fact, scarcely any single circumstance, which can contribute more powerfully towards elevating the reputation of a people, . . . than the grandeur or beauty of their public structures. . . . The taste, the rules, the character of architecture, as well as its materials, having not less the expression of durability than the reality of it, tend to lift the mind above the 'ignorant present,' to connect our thoughts with the past, and expand them into the future. Of all the achievements of human skill or industry, this noble art approaches most nearly to the sublimity and vastness of nature.[25]

Verplanck's emphatic speech might very well have convinced Davis to pursue a career in architecture. The speech almost certainly boosted business for Brady, who would have been reassured about the nobility of his profession, and for Goodrich, whose illustrated guidebooks, according to Verplanck, actually contributed to the good of the nation by publicizing the appearance of the city's finest edifices.

During 1826, Davis began producing renderings of New York's most celebrated buildings, including the New York Theatre, the Merchants' Exchange, and Trinity Church. New York's premier lithographer, Anthony Imbert, printed twelve of these views and issued them as a set in a wrapper embellished with Davis's drawing of the New York Rotunda (fig. 1.11).[26] This work was seminal for Imbert, who carried on a prolific lithography business through the 1830s, and for Davis, whose skills as a draftsman became known throughout the city.

At the same time, Davis began exhibiting his drawings in the National Academy's annual exhibitions. As an alternative to the American Academy, where Trumbull and his board mounted exhibitions juxtaposing contemporary and historical American paintings and sculptures with European art from all ages, Morse and other National Academy officers admitted works exclusively by living artists in the four branches of the arts of design—painting, sculpture, architecture, and engraving.[27] Davis did not submit work to the first exhibition in 1826, but in 1827 he was represented by four entries: three drawings from his series of views of buildings in New York and another drawing titled "Architectural Design."[28]

According to the reviewer for *The United States Review and Literary Gazette*, Davis's view of the New York Theatre was "in bad perspective," as were his views of Trinity Church and St. Thomas Church, Broadway (fig. 1.12; colorplate 20), "although the defects [in the latter two] are not so obvious."[29] The critic had kinder words for Davis's fourth entry: "A design of some merit, from a young artist; the Doric portico is good; the rusticated corners are in bad taste, and give the whole building a heavy appearance. It is neatly colored." In general, the reviewer preferred "Original Plans and Elevations of Buildings" to "Views of Buildings" because, he wrote, "that work of art should rank the highest which requires the greatest exercise of mind, or, in other words, that *mental is superior to manual labor*."[30] In his review, which is considered by historians to be a seminal document in the history of American art criticism, the writer attempted to impose "a just scale" for judging paintings, sculptures, engravings, and architectural drawings. He rated "Architectural Painting," or interior views, fifth in the field of painting (the only example of this category in the 1827 National Academy exhibition was Morse's *The Old House of Representatives* [1822, Corcoran Gallery of Art]). He separated this category from the specific field of architecture to make the point that architecture was a professional skill, not to be confused with painting or any other art:

1.12. View of St. Thomas Church (Josiah R. Brady, architect), ca. 1827. Black ink, gray and brown wash on paper, 8 x 10 in. Drawings Collection, The New-York Historical Society, Foster Jarvis Fund, 1953 (1953.201).

> Much has been said of late, and with great justice, of the want of taste in architecture in the City of New York. The remedy for the evil is very plain,—*Employ every man in his own department*. . . . We do not go to our physician for advice in a lawsuit, nor to our lawyer for prescription in a fever; why should we go to either for a design in architecture, while the architect is ready with his professional skill to aid us. . . . A building, particularly a public building, should be under the sole direction of the professed, educated architect; limit him, if you please, in his expenditure, give him a catalogue of the conveniences you desire; but leave him unshackled in his design. Throw on *him* the responsibility of taste.[31]

Davis probably had a mixed reaction to this review. The criticism of his own entries aside, he surely must have realized that the critic had in mind the betterment of the architectural profession. On the other hand, the critic made his plea by separating architecture from painting; Davis was still working on combining the two. He had just begun drawing scenic, architectural views for the *New-York Mirror*.[32] In his "View of St. John's Chapel, From the Park" (fig. 1.13), for example, the landscape setting was as important as the featured building. Likewise, Davis's "view through a monumental Greek portico" (fig. 1.14; colorplate 22), in which massive columns frame the romantic vista beyond, successfully employs architectural elements as a foil for the natural landscape.

Davis ignored the critic's artistic hierarchy in 1828 and sent the National Academy ten views of buildings, including some from his recent trip to Boston, and three original designs.[33] At the same time, he invited editors from two of New York's leading newspapers to see more of his work. To M. M. Noah, editor of the *National Advocate,* he wrote that his architectural drawings, "the highest branch of fine Art," were quite accomplished.[34] To the editor of the *Commercial Advertiser,* he explained that

> I aim at a higher department, within the hole [sic] of the fine arts than mere *picture making*—at excellence in *Architectural* Design]. . . . I occupy room 42 Merchants Exchange, where I am proud of receiving visits from amateurs of Art and if there [sic] criticism is severe, my improvement is more rapid.[35]

Perhaps neither editor paid a call to Davis's room; nothing about his work appeared in the papers. Reviewers of the National Academy exhibition saved their remarks for paintings. Yet the academy's board acknowledged Davis's talent by making him an associate member.[36] This election not only honored Davis but also signified the academy's progress in encouraging architecture. Although architecture was recognized as one of the four arts of design, the board had done very little to indicate that the academy intended to support it. Plans to hire an instructor of architecture were not pursued; the 1827 *United States Review* critic had pleaded with the board to appoint such a professor, to "spread correct principles on this subject, and form for us

1.13. "View of St. John's Chapel, From the Park." Engraved by W. D. Smith after original drawing by Davis for *The New-York Mirror,* 6 (April 11, 1829), opp. p. 313. The New-York Historical Society Library.

well educated architects."[37] After Davis's election, he nominated himself for the position:

> To relieve the lecturing Professor of Perspective of a portion of his labor, I proffer my services in draughting such illustrations of the *practical* part of the science (being myself an imperfect theorist) as he may be unprovided with. This I also do that I may not be held an [sic] useless member of the Academy.[38]

The academy's board voted favorably on Davis's offer but apparently did not follow through to hire him.[39]

Davis was, at that time, one of three architect-members of the National Academy. The others were founding members Martin E. Thompson and Ithiel Town, who asked Davis to become his partner in February 1829. In some ways, the partnership marked an important intellectual transition for Davis, from architectural composition to pure architecture. This was not a change in his working method or technique; his drawings continued to be characterized by his facility for rendering settings and context. The change concerned Davis's resolution of his compromised position between architecture and art, between being an architect and being an artist. An important signal of his newly confirmed sense of his professional identity is written on his copy of the National Academy's 1829 list of members, published with the constitution and bylaws. Davis crossed out his name under the roster of associate members and wrote it in at the very bottom of the page, as if the academy had no category to accommodate him: "Davis, A. J., Architect." Then he altered the title National Academy of Design to read "N. Y. Academy of Painters."[40]

Davis exhibited eight drawings in the 1829 exhibition—four views and four designs—but it was the last time he wholeheartedly participated in the academy's affairs.[41] One of his entries, a "Design for an Academy of Arts," which may be the extant watercolor rendering with the same title (fig. 1.15), shows an ideal academy, where spacious galleries are devoted to each branch of the arts. The National Academy, unfortunately, had no permanent exhibition galleries at all, and Davis's designs may have appeared grandiose, but they illustrated his point.

In May 1830, perhaps in recognition of his persistent view of architecture as art, the academy's board invited Davis to deliver a lecture on architecture. By that time, however, he had given up on the academy:

> Indeed, enthusiastically devoted as I am, to my art, and heretofore in voluntary seclusion from society, I suspect my *power* to please a mixed audience, who, for the most part, listen with attention to subjects of a *light* and *general* nature, and would, infallibly find the dry techniques of Architectural detail in which my soul is bound, *peculiar and tedious.*[42]

Davis's seemingly polite, self-deprecatory tone has been misinterpreted as showing fear "that his ideas were not fully crystallized."[43] On the contrary, Davis mocked the academy, suggesting that they would not have been able to comprehend his serious thoughts on architecture. His apology that he could not give a lecture "of a *light* and *general* nature" was an indictment of painters—the academy's usual audience—and painting—the academy's usual subject.

Davis's withdrawal from the National Academy did not necessarily mean that he had divorced himself from New York's art community. The American Academy, while it was not the exhibition gallery of choice for most contemporary artists and had never instituted an active educational program, remained a vital institution through the mid-1830s. The primary reason most artists gave for preferring the Na-

1.14. View through a monumental Greek portico, ca. 1828–30. Watercolor, ink, and graphite on paper, 17⅞ x 21¼ in. A. J. Davis Collection, The New-York Historical Society (575).

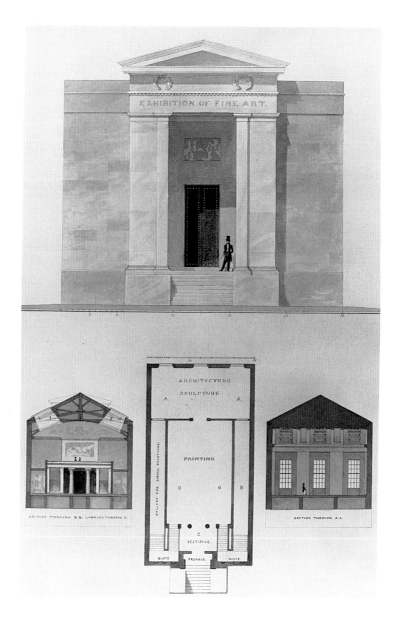

1.15. Design for an Academy of Arts, ca. 1828–29. Front elevation, plan, and two sections. Watercolor and ink on paper, 20 x 14½ in. A. J. Davis Collection, The New-York Historical Society (10).

tional Academy was that it was run by and for artists. The American Academy, by contrast, was run by and for art patrons. Attempts to unite the two academies during the late 1820s had come to naught, since neither group was willing to compromise its views on whose taste—artists' or patrons'—should prevail when it came to exhibition juries, building the permanent collection, and other activities.[44] For all Davis's aspirations to be taken seriously as an artist, it might be suspected that he would, in principle, side with the painters and sculptors. In fact, he sided with the patrons, as demonstrated by a toast he delivered at a dinner attended by artists and art patrons at the New York Hotel on May 4, 1830:

> To the spirit that animated the soul of Pericles, patron of Phidias and Polygnotos, to the House of Medici, patrons of Art:—O, rise some other such! Gentlemen will repeat the last clause: 'O, rise some other such!'[45]

Davis was attracted to the American Academy for other reasons as well. He shared with other members a fondness for European art and had begun collecting prints and copies of paintings in about 1829.[46] Perhaps the greatest attraction the American Academy held for Davis, though, was Trumbull, who presided over the

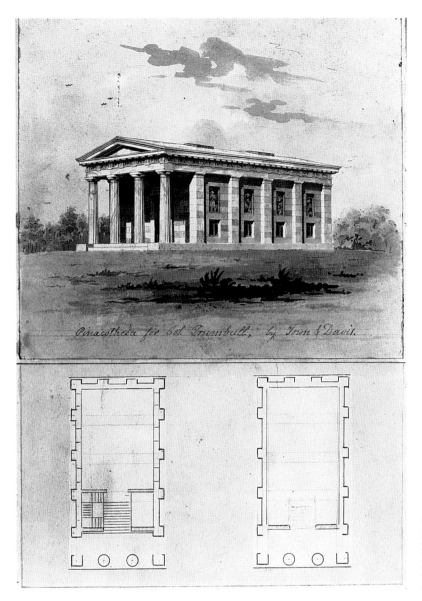

1.16. "Pinacotheca for Col. Trumbull, by Town & Davis," 1831 (project). Perspective and two plans. Watercolor and ink on paper, 10 3/16 x 7 1/8 in. I. N. Phelps Stokes Collection, Miriam and Ira D. Wallach Division of Art, Prints and Photographs, The New York Public Library, Astor, Lenox and Tilden Foundations.

board until 1836. Davis's earliest documented contact with Trumbull, a gentleman-architect as well as a celebrated painter, was in about 1830 when Town and Davis designed a Pinacotheca for his paintings (fig. 1.16). Trumbull eventually designed his own gallery for Yale College, where he bequeathed his life's work, but the firm's ideas impressed him and influenced his own design. Trumbull thought highly enough of Davis to propose him for membership in the American Academy in October 1832.[47]

That year, Davis began exhibiting his work at the American Academy; he submitted a "Design from the Antique" and a watercolor "View from the Park Gate, Broadway, N.Y. with St. Pauls' Trinity, and Grace Churches."[48] The American Academy, like the National Academy, put no particular emphasis on architecture, and art critics did not review architectural entries at either academy. The difference for Davis seems to have been a matter of pretense and false advertising. By taking the word "design" for its title, the National Academy had a responsibility to represent the arts of design with equitable wall space in their gallery. The American Academy, by virtue of its more general title, had no such obligation. The fact that the board showed architecture at all was proof that architecture was art.

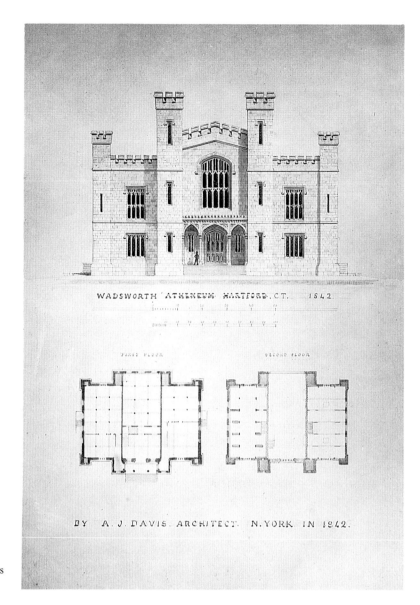

WADSWORTH ATHENEUM. HARTFORD. CT. 1842.

FIRST FLOOR   SECOND FLOOR

BY A. J. DAVIS. ARCHITECT. N. YORK. IN 1842.

1.17. The Wadsworth Atheneum, Hartford, Connecticut, 1842. Town & Davis and Henry Austin. Front elevation and two plans. Watercolor, ink, and graphite on paper, 14⅜ x 10 in. The Metropolitan Museum of Art, Harris Brisbane Dick Fund, 1924 (24.66.866).

Davis was elected to the American Academy's board of directors in 1834, the same year he drafted an essay on the arts for a proposed journal on the fine arts.[49] In his essay, Davis argued for a reordering of the traditional prioritization of the arts—painting, sculpture, architecture, and engraving—because architecture, he wrote, "must, unquestionably take the lead."[50] He paraphrased an unnamed professor of architecture at the Royal Academy in London:

> Architecture, the Queen of the fine arts, assisted by her handmaids, Paintings and Sculpture, combines and displays all the mighty powers of music and poetry. . . . Hence arises that proud pre-eminence which architecture by prescriptive right seems to hold over the fine arts.

It is not known how far Davis got in the planning for this publication, but it is likely that his co-editors, Asher B. Durand for painting and John W. Casilear for engraving, objected to this essay for the first issue. The idea for the journal was probably born on a trip to the Catskills that Davis took with Durand and Casilear in July 1834, but it never got any further than Davis's first draft.[51] Still, he maintained his friendship with the painters, apparently by separating his professional grudges from his personal enjoyments. He took a great risk in 1836 when he proposed an attempted unification of the two academies.

Davis, then secretary of the American Academy, was not alone in this venturous business; Town, who had joined the American Academy in 1833 and was elected vice-president in 1836, was with him to represent the older academy. By this time, Trumbull had retired to New Haven and Rembrandt Peale was president. Town and Davis, who were no longer architectural partners, Peale, the art dealer and collector Pierre Flandin, and the artist James Herring formed a committee to solidify the New York art world. If successful, they would save the American Academy, which faced its demise from lack of support, and, perhaps more important, reestablish their original interest in the National Academy.

For Town, the proposed union was a plan of recourse rather than choice. The year before, he published his *Outlines of a Plan for Establishing in New-York, an Academy and Institution of the Fine Arts* (New York, 1835). In this pamphlet, which described a two-branch institution with a school operated by artists and a collection and library administered by non-artist stockholders, Town explained that he had come up with this idea since uniting the two existing academies had been proven a futile exercise.[52] Yet his United States Academy, as he called it, did not attract support.

Neither did the 1836 negotiations between academies. The National Academy's conference committee—Dunlap, Durand, Morse, John Ludlow Morton, and Thomas Seir Cummings—could not be convinced that the union was to their advantage. In fact, the union favored the American Academy, which declined very quickly after 1836. Davis, Town, and others tried to maintain the institution for as long as possible, partly in rebellion against the National Academy, as Davis wrote to Trumbull in February 1839:

> It is with the greatest pleasure I have to inform you that our Academy is still 'alive and kicking.' . . . We were tossing for sometime in the frying-pan—but fell not into the fire. Some thirty new Stockholders are to pay into the treasury and get up an exhibition and they threaten that the N. A.s [National Academicians] shall find a 'swarm of bees in the carcase of the dead lion'—(if they poke it). The present board, however, will furnish no jawbones, even to slay Philistines, but wish 'brethren to dwell together in unity and peace.' What hero was that who peopled his country by throwing stones over his shoulder?—There are many legitimate ways of strengthening the right—we have only to conceive them![53]

The academy barely lasted through that year. But all was not lost for Town and Davis. On the eve of reconstituting their architectural partnership in 1842, they orchestrated the sale of the academy's paintings to a group of art patrons led by Trumbull's nephew-in-law, Daniel Wadsworth, who had commissioned the architects for a new gallery in Hartford, Connecticut (fig. 1.17). To their credit, they designed and helped fill the Wadsworth Atheneum. In addition, Town & Davis's office in the Merchants' Exchange took over part of the gallery function of the American Academy. With drawings, paintings, prints, and books on display, they entertained "the most celebrated savans of the city."[54]

Davis's efforts on behalf of the American Academy did not ruin his friendship with National Academicians. His expulsion from the National Academy in 1836 was merely for lack of interest; he had not exhibited there for two consecutive years and effectively annulled his membership.[55] Davis still remained friendly with Morse, the

1.18. Samuel F. B. Morse, "Landscape," 1836.
Oil on panel, 4 3/16 x 6 7/8 x 3/8 in. Drawings &
Archives, Avery Architectural and Fine Arts
Library, Columbia University (1940.001.0016).

academy's president, who painted the landscape for the frontispiece of Davis's *Rural Residences* (figs. 1.18, 1.19), and Davis later helped him design a home in Poughkeepsie. Davis, Morse, and other artists joined to form an "artists' agency" following the Panic of 1837 to help artists sell their work, or, in Davis's words, "to execute order in every department of the Arts, with their best ability, at prices appropriate to the depressed state of the times."[56]

Still, Davis never forgave the National Academy for shirking its responsibility to architecture. Even after the founding of the American Institute of Architects in 1857, when Davis knew architecture had an institution of its own, he still harped on the National Academy:

> I do not accuse the painters, it is the Academy I accuse for defrauding architecture of its just rights to which they are bound to attend, and to see supported, as those of painting. How happens it that architecture is so inadequately represented in the academy as to be looked upon as a mere cypher? Is it because, although a partner in the firm with painting and sculpture, architecture has only a very small share indeed in the concern, perhaps not more than one fiftieth part of the whole? . . . Is there anything in the Academy charter to such effect? Is it expressly stipulated that the painters are to have the lion's share, and the architects be content with being admitted to the honor of participating by looking on? . . . Whether in other respects the Academy be more than a mere club of artists, I leave to the consideration of others, and only add that whatever may have been the case formerly, there is, now that the Institute has been established, not the slightest reason wherefore architecture should continue to submit to the contumelious treatment it receives at the heads of the Academy.[57]

When he addressed the Apollo Association in March 1841, Davis respected the painters in his audience by refraining from overt criticism of the National Academy. Instead, he devoted his remarks to aggrandizing the old American Academy:

> The cultivation of the arts, and the refinement of national taste, depend not on artists alone; but on the general education of society, and the stimulus given by the patronage and munificence of opulent and educated men, without which, artists become useless, and their talents sink into obscurity.[58]

Even years later, Davis maintained his opinion of the National Academy. He thought its 1863 building, designed by P. B. Wight in imitation of the Doge's Palace in Venice, was an outrage, perhaps more so because he had not been invited to submit a design to the competition.[59] He interpreted the building as telling evidence of the academy's ignorance of architectural design. In an address before the New-York Historical Society in 1874, he said that it was "merely an Academy of Painters, and under the government of painters only, as their new building would seem clearly to evince. 'By their works shall ye know them'."[60]

Davis's critical remarks that night in 1874 were pertinent to his subject that evening, which was his gift of the American Academy's papers to the Historical Society. As the academy's last secretary, he had taken the liberty of preserving all of the minutes, correspondence, and other documents, and in his presentation address, he made it clear that he was giving the papers to the Historical Society because the National Academy was not worthy of receiving them. He told the same to the painter T. Addison Richards, secretary of the National Academy, who wrote him in 1881 to ask for autograph letters for the academy's collection. Davis told Richards that he had given numerous letters from distinguished artists to the New-York Historical Society:

> The papers might with propriety have gone to the [National Academy], . . . but the painters, ignoring the pretensions of the older arts awarded small room for their display, and thus became merely an Academy of Paintings. . . . Thus the higher departments of invention, composition, grandeur of form with simplicity and force of expression, without the meretricious or irrelevant, as taught by architecture and sculpture, is too much left to a vagrant conception of the pupils own inorganized [sic] mind, or the inspiration of untutered [sic] genius governed by no wholsome [sic] geometric laws, or approved precedent.[61]

As if to spite the National Academicians, Davis listed, at length, the famous autographs contained in his voluminous papers: artists, writers, merchants, foreign dignitaries, and American politicians. But he was not so embittered that he shunned the academy entirely. He enclosed an original letter written by Benjamin West, a letter from a gentleman of the brush to other gentlemen of the brush, as the symbolic gift from an architect who hoped that artists, architects, and others would one day recognize that his campaign for the art of architecture had not been in vain.

1.19. Title vignette of *Rural Residences,* 1836, published 1838. Wood engraving by J. A. Adams after original painting by Samuel F. B. Morse. Sheet: 14 x 9 $^{15}/_{16}$ in., image: 3⅝ x 6⅛ in. The Metropolitan Museum of Art, Harris Brisbane Dick Fund, 1924 (24.66.1888).

DESIGN FOR A STATE HOUSE.

AT INDIANAPOLIS, INDIANA

TOWN, and DAVIS, ARCH.?

2.1. Indiana State Capitol, Indianapolis,
1831–35. Town & Davis. Perspective.
Watercolor, ink, and graphite on paper, 14 ¼ x
19 ¾ in. The Metropolitan Museum of Art,
Harris Brisbane Dick Fund, 1924 (24.66.391).

CHAPTER 2

Simplicity and Dignity: The Public and Institutional Buildings of Alexander Jackson Davis

FRANCIS R. KOWSKY

The most endearing memory we have of Alexander Jackson Davis is the remark he penned about himself recalling his days as a youthful assistant in his brother's printing office in Alexandria, Virginia. "Being a quick compositor, he would soon complete the task assigned him," wrote Davis, adopting the third person, "and fly to his books, works of imagination, poetry, and the drama, whence he imbibed a portion of that high imaginative spirit so necessary to constitute an artist destined to practise in the field of invention."[1] Here is the essence of Davis's thoroughly romantic view of architecture as an art of creation that springs from cultivated imagination. And the fact that he entered the profession following experience with painting and the theater further reinforced his pictorial and emotional bias. Even at its most rationalist moments, Davis's public architecture is informed by sentiments of greatness, earnestness, history, and feeling.

Davis expressed his architectural ideas most eloquently through the medium of drawing. His watercolors of public buildings reveal how he conceived each project as an heroic statement. Depicted in noble centrality, boldly lit from the side in a bright middle distance, his handsome buildings stand before the viewer as if a curtain had been pulled aside to reveal them. Nature or the surrounding cityscapes seem to shrink modestly into the background, reverently deferring to the commanding presence of the building in their midst. Such imagery is familiar to us now, but how impressive it must have been to viewers in the 1830s and 1840s who were accustomed to seeing architecture represented in flat line drawings. No wonder Ithiel Town and later Andrew Jackson Downing engaged Davis to transform their conceptions into architectural images they knew would have wide appeal. In the Age of Jackson, Davis, more than any other person, "popularized" the image of architecture—especially the civic building—as a symbol of American aspirations. Drawing on the elevated mood and artistic devices of the early Hudson River School painters, especially his friend Thomas Cole, Davis achieved a remarkable synthesis of fact and feeling.

But together with his romantic fascination with buildings as evocative symbols, Davis possessed a sensible, "scientific" mind. "He that embarks on the voyage of life," wrote Davis, "will always wish to advance rather by the impulse of the wind than [by] the strokes of the oar."[2] Although Davis lacked the advantage of European training and he entered the field before schools of architecture existed in this country, he worked hard to obtain, largely through his association with Josiah Brady and Town, adequate understanding of structure and scholarly knowledge of architectural tradition. Thomas Cole wrote of Davis that he readily talked of "violations of first principles in erudite phraseology."[3] Not only did Davis study and draw out-

2.2. Custom House, New York City, 1833. Town & Davis. Perspective. Watercolor, ink, and graphite on paper, 24 3/16 x 30 1/4 in. M. & M. Karolik Collection of American Watercolors and Drawings, 1800–1875, Courtesy Museum of Fine Arts, Boston (50.3851).

standing American buildings, but he also planned to publish a book on the architecture of ancient Greece. To that end, he made many painstakingly accurate drawings of Greek temples, an undertaking based on long hours of careful book study, for Davis never saw the originals. His drawings aspire to the kind of authority communicated in the work of Stuart and Revett, one of his cherished sources,[4] and testify to the depth and breadth of his self-acquired knowledge of classical architecture. Perhaps his more fanciful appreciation of Gothic design mirrors, conversely, the limited number of scholarly books on this subject available in the United States before the 1850s.

As a designer of public and institutional buildings, Davis applied his historical knowledge to plans for a wide range of specialized structures. Few American architects before him had had to meet the challenge of devising plans for so many large and distinctly different building types. Courthouses, state capitols, town halls, asylums, college and educational buildings, museums, libraries, and art galleries all occupied Davis's attention and reflected the new demands that expanding American social needs placed on the architectural profession from the 1830s forward. Davis's response to the claims of the new age was threefold: as an eclectic he chose to work chiefly in the Greek, Gothic, Egyptian, and Tuscan styles; as a rationalist he showed reluctance to use ornament, stressed simple compositions, and developed efficient ground plans; and, as a visionary, especially in the later part of his career, he devised highly imaginative, even eccentric, schemes for both large and small buildings.

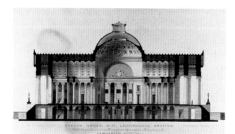

2.3. Custom House, New York City, 1833. Town & Davis. Longitudinal section. Watercolor and ink on paper, 13 7/8 x 19 1/2 in. Drawings & Archives, Avery Architectural and Fine Arts Library, Columbia University (1940.001.00132).

Davis had his best opportunity to put his love for ancient Greek architecture to effective use when he dealt with civic buildings. The United States Custom House (present Federal Hall Memorial) in New York City (figs. 2.2, 2.3; colorplate 23), which Davis designed in 1833 in conjunction with Town, displayed many of the elements that were characteristic of Davis's civic architecture.[5] The temple form based on the Parthenon, the central dome, and the Doric piers alternating with windows along the building's sides constituted an effectively simple composition that provided a dignified setting for the business of government in an era of ardent democracy. And in the manner of Davis's great rural villas, the Custom House took full advantage of its conspicuous site on Wall Street at the head of Broad Street.

Unfortunately, Town & Davis's design for the Custom House, which won first place in a competition sponsored by the Treasury Department, suffered at the hands of Samuel Thomson, who wrested supervision of its construction away from the original architects. Modifications to the exterior robbed the building of much of the sense of monumentality that so proudly informs Davis's watercolor drawing. (The interior scheme was also altered without the participation of Town & Davis.) The changes, apparently dictated to Thomson by Treasury Department officials,[6] resulted in the elimination of the dome (which was reminiscent of Bulfinch's dome for the United States Capitol) and the deletion of the inner row of columns from the porticoes. A writer in *The American Monthly Magazine*[7] had leveled harsh criticism at the use of the protruding dome as the external expression of the rotunda. The article may have turned the commissioners in charge of the project against the dome, despite the fact that domes had become closely associated in the American consciousness with the architecture of democratic government. The result of these alterations was particularly upsetting to Davis. To his painterly eye, the reduction of the scale of the porticoes was as disastrous as the absence of the dome, for it all but eliminated the area of shadow behind the front columns. Sadly, despite the fact that by winning the Custom House competition Davis moved to the front ranks of the architectural profession in New York, he took no pride in the building once it was constructed. "The U. S. Treasury building would have been a masterpiece of its Architects," lamented Davis, "had its portico been executed with a proper depth for shelter and shade and its external dome been preserved to give an expression of purpose. These features were changed by the commissioners, without the sanction of the Architects, and the result is a caricature of the Grecian temple."[8]

Davis's beautiful perspective drawing forcefully conveys his intentions for the Custom House. (The original drawings for the building were lost in a fire in March 1833; Davis created a second set later that year.) He demonstrates not only his advanced knowledge of Greek Doric architecture (although the dome and podium base are, of course, foreign to that order) but also his "composer's" understanding of proportion and its effect on the viewer. As portrayed in the drawing, the strong cornice line, the range of lateral piers, and the band of podium windows (a feature perhaps derived from the United States Capitol) diminishing down the side of the building are calculated to produce an emphatic sense of horizontality. This characteristic of the classical style made it especially appropriate as a choice for public buildings. Echoing Palladio, Davis wrote that if "width predominates over height in an edifice, we are struck with the idea of majesty and strength."[9] And perhaps the role of the dome, aside from its symbolic function, was significant in Davis's mind because it acted as a counterpoint to the building's lowness, for he cautioned that "an excess of width degenerates into heaviness . . . perfect proportion, then, consists in a medium between these two extremes."[10] Davis may also have calculated that the dome would have made the building seem more imposing to people coming up from the harbor along Broad Street.

The New Haven Statehouse, begun by Town in 1827 and worked on in its final stages by Davis,[11] and the Indiana State Capitol (fig. 2.1), for which Davis recorded a $150 premium in October 1831,[12] initiated ideas that would inform Town & Davis's other temple-form public buildings. At Indianapolis, Town & Davis experimented for the first time with the temple and dome combination, as well as with the use of massive Doric piers along the sides.[13] The dome of the Indianapolis building, which Henry-Russell Hitchcock and William Seale suggest may have been

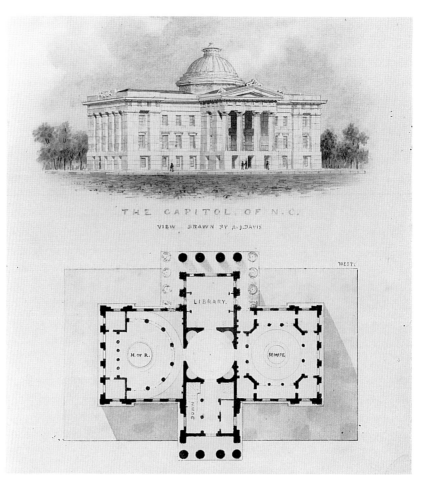

2.4. North Carolina State Capitol, Raleigh, 1833. Town & Davis. Perspective and plan. Watercolor and ink on paper, 9 3/16 x 6 9/16 in. The Metropolitan Museum of Art, Harris Brisbane Dick Fund, 1924 (24.66.1401 [23], vol. II, leaf 29).

2.5. The Patent Office, Washington, D.C., designed 1832, drawn 1834 (first project). Town & Davis. Perspective. Watercolor, ink, and graphite on paper, 19 1/2 x 27 3/4 in. The Metropolitan Museum of Art, Harris Brisbane Dick Fund, 1924 (24.66.423).

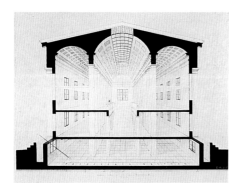

2.6. Detail of the Patent Office, Washington, D.C., 1834 (first project). Town & Davis. Transverse section. Watercolor and ink on paper, 25 3/4 x 17 5/8 in. The Metropolitan Museum of Art, Harris Brisbane Dick Fund, 1924 (24.66.448).

added by Town at the suggestion of local legislators,[14] rested on a cylindrical drum and was capped by a cupola. Much taller than the Custom House dome, it tended, at least in Davis's drawing, to look somewhat spindly. Its awkwardness may have been the reason why two years later the architects experimented with the shallower and heavier saucer form for the dome of the New York City building. The cruciform-plan capitol at Raleigh, North Carolina (fig. 2.4), built according to Town & Davis's designs between 1833 and 1840, shared elements with these buildings, notably Doric porticoes and a central dome. On his own, Davis designed temple-form buildings for local governments, notably the Town Hall and Courthouse at Bridgeport, Connecticut, the plans for which he made in 1853, and the County Courthouse at Powhatan, Virginia, for which Davis asked $30 for elevations and plans in May 1843.[15] (The Virginia building did not have a dome.)

Town & Davis's design for the Patent Office in Washington started out as a pristine Doric temple building based on the Theseum (figs. 2.5, 2.6; colorplates 24, 25) but with only one portico. Davis's involvement with this major Washington project was complicated and entailed the making of several designs.[16] The second version (fig. 2.7) consisted of a three-story rectangular building with a shallow portico in the center of one of the long sides. The elevations were unified by anta piers, the solid spaces between which were greatly reduced by tall slender windows. This openness was carried much further in the final design of 1834 (fig. 2.8), a long U-shaped structure with a portico and saucer dome in the center and Doric pavilions at each end. The entire long building rested on a high stone base pierced with windows between the intercolumniations of anta piers above. Between these giant piers,

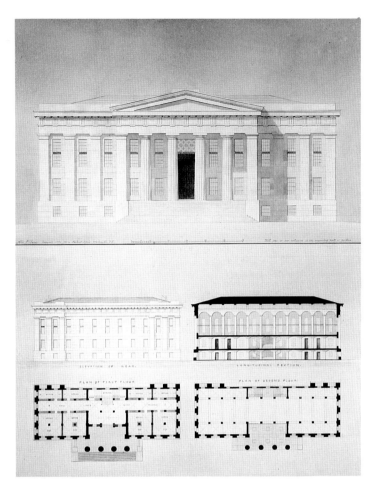

2.7. The Patent Office, Washington, D.C., 1834 (second project). Town & Davis. Front and rear elevations, first and second floor plans, and longitudinal section. Watercolor, ink, and graphite on paper, 27 ¼ x 19 ¹⁵/₁₆ in. The Metropolitan Museum of Art, Harris Brisbane Dick Fund, 1924 (24.66.470).

2.8. The Patent Office, Washington, D.C., 1834 (third project). Town & Davis. Front elevation and plan. Watercolor, ink, and graphite on paper, 18 ⅛ x 23 ¹³/₁₆ in. The Metropolitan Museum of Art, Harris Brisbane Dick Fund, 1924 (24.66.451).

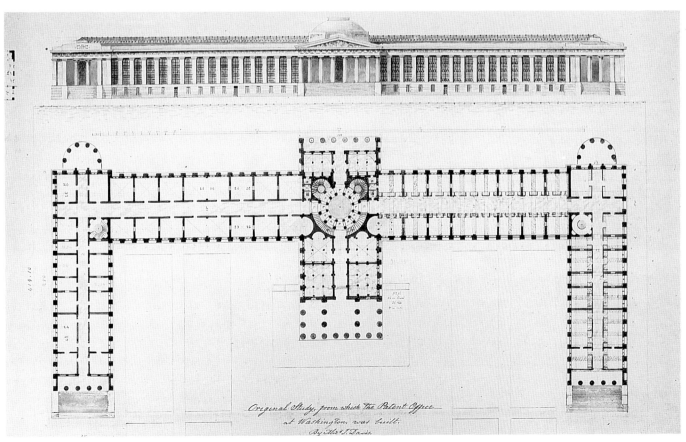

2.9. Study of the Temple of Erment, ca. 1830. Elevation and plan. Watercolor, ink, and graphite on paper, 18¾ x 26¾ in. The Metropolitan Museum of Art, Harris Brisbane Dick Fund, 1924 (24.66.445).

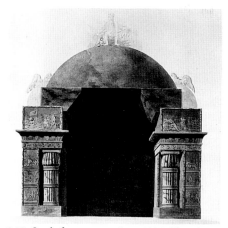

2.10. Study for a proscenium, 1825. Elevation. Watercolor, ink, and graphite on paper, 18⁹⁄₁₆ x 14¼ in. The Metropolitan Museum of Art, Harris Brisbane Dick Fund, 1924 (24.66.442).

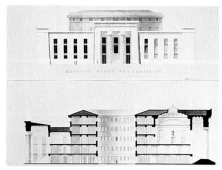

2.11. Competition drawing for the Halls of Justice, New York City, 1835. Centre Street elevation and longitudinal section. Watercolor, ink, and graphite on paper, 25½ x 31⅛ in. The Metropolitan Museum of Art, Harris Brisbane Dick Fund, 1924 (24.66.437).

all vestiges of solid walls disappeared; the intercolumniations consisted of "curtain walls" of glass that lighted three floors of offices within.

This latter design, which Jane Davies calls "no paltry scheme for limited minds,"[17] points to the influence on Davis's thought of the French seventeenth-century architect Claude Perrault. Davis's elevation drawing clearly recalls the east front of the Louvre, which Perrault designed in 1667. Davis read (probably in translation) at least parts of Perrault's *Ordonnance des cinq espèces de colonnes* and was especially intrigued by the problem the Frenchman had encountered when designing the colonnade of paired columns on the Louvre. "All half pilasters, and the coupling of columns is condemned by Perrault," wrote Davis, "who defends himself against the practice in the Louvre on the score of convenience."[18] And Davis writes further that "coupling columns...is degrading to their dignity, and subservient to ostentation."[19] In his third Patent Office design, Davis rejected Perrault's use of coupled Corinthian columns and relied instead on his favored Doric piers, spaced equidistantly. These multistory piers march in quiet procession across the front of his building, their structural role made more obvious by the totally empty spaces between them. Davis transformed Perrault's elegant Baroque model into a severe statement of republican simplicity and ingenuity.

Although Davis held that "Greece brought architecture to its extreme perfection," he regarded Egypt as the true birthplace of the building arts.[20] Davis drew elevations of Egyptian temples (fig. 2.9; colorplate 26) with the same care and devotion he lavished on Greek temples, and as a stage designer he turned this knowledge of Egypt to clever use (fig. 2.10). Davis's grandest architectural scheme in the Egyptian mode was his unsuccessful competition entry of 1835 for the New York City Halls of Justice, known popularly as "the Tombs" (fig. 2.11; colorplate 27). The building was to fill the block between Elm and Centre streets in Manhattan, requiring two major facade designs. The recessed entrance Davis drew for Centre Street featured a monumental pylon gateway supported by two papyrus columns in antis. Three-story-tall windows pierced the flanking walls, and battered towers terminated each end of the facade. Behind the low front loomed the great round cell block. On the opposite side of the building, on Elm Street, Davis drew a tall Doric portico, the height of which masked the interior cells. Through this portico one entered the domed courtroom. Davis's dual Greek and Egyptian facades neatly demonstrated how the architect could think of style in terms of its appropriateness to the purpose of a building. His design effectively conveyed the message to the visitor that Centre Street was the penal entrance and Elm Street was the judicial entrance.

From the early decades of the nineteenth century, public care of the mentally ill had become a greater and greater burden on city and state governments. Prior to the reform movement of the 1830s and 1840s, most disturbed individuals of limited means were incarcerated in poor houses or county jails. For a time, the Bloomingdale Asylum in Manhattan was the only place in the state where insanity was treated as a disease. In the mid-1830s, New York City, which formerly paid the Bloomingdale Asylum for the care of indigent patients, erected its own Island Retreat or Pauper Lunatic Asylum on Blackwell's Island in the East River (fig. 2.12). Davis received $300 in 1834 for drawing the plans,[21] which the Board of Aldermen approved in January 1835. The large, two story U-shaped structure (which was only partially constructed) faced Manhattan, affording many residents views of lawn and water. The administration of the hospital was to occupy a three-story hipped-roof structure

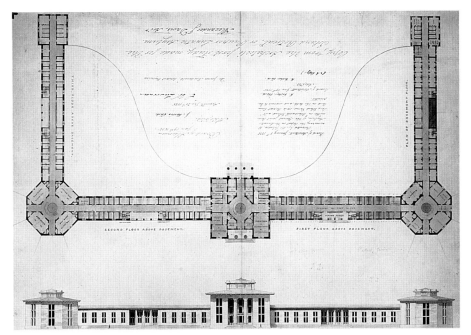

2.12. Preliminary design for the Pauper Lunatic Asylum, Blackwell's Island, New York City, 1834–35. East elevation and overall plan showing basement, first, second, and third floors. Watercolor, ink, and graphite on paper, 27⅞ x 37⁷⁄₁₆ in. The Metropolitan Museum of Art, Harris Brisbane Dick Fund, 1924 (24.66.452).

in the center of the complex. Through this building one would gain access to the long corridors of the patient wings, which were lined on either side with rooms for inmates. Each ward was to have opened in the center (on the side away from the interior court) to a columnar porch where patients could enjoy fresh air. At the angles, Davis designed octagonal pavilions (one of which survives and is under consideration for adaptive reuse) that held dayrooms, baths, storerooms, and dining halls. Davis's plan, which was influenced by the recent Middlesex County Asylum at Hanwell, near London,[22] was a model of efficient management of people and services. Its long wide corridors provided both access and control, for entry to them was through the central administration building. The octagonal corner pavilions, features inspired by the Hanwell asylum, compactly accommodated staircases and service facilities, as well as betraying Davis's interest in the use of centralized plans, a theme he would develop in later domestic and public architecture.

The exterior design of the Blackwell's Island asylum shared the rationalist spirit of its well-ordered plan. The elevations, in the economical Tuscan style (only the two north wings and the central octagon were erected), were devoid of ornament and historical references, except for the Tuscan Doric columns, in antis, at the entrance to the central building and on the porches. Otherwise, Davis expressed the geometry of the design in pure shapes, relying only on the repeated rhythms of the tall windows—a type he called "Davisean"—the texture of the stone, and the shadows of the bracketed eaves to create a mood of quiet dignity. Davis was always sparing with ornament, but it was in his design for the Blackwell's Island asylum that he best illustrated the statement that appeared on his business handbill: "Admit nothing that can be called meretricious, but let the character, the proportion, expression, and ornament, be that of acknowledged beauty and truth."[23]

Although the Blackwell's Island asylum was a significant commission for Davis, it was generally regarded as less than successful as a reform mental institution. Its most damning critic was Charles Dickens, who on his trip to America in 1842 visited the institution. "I cannot say," he wrote, "that I derived much comfort from the inspection of this charity. . . . I saw nothing of the salutary system which had im-

47

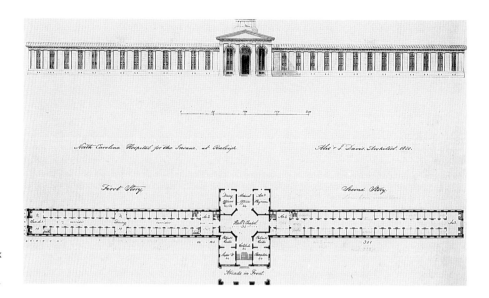

2.13. North Carolina Hospital for the Insane, Raleigh, 1850–52. Front elevation and overall plan showing both first and second floors. Watercolor, ink, and graphite on paper, 17⅛ x 27⅞ in. The Metropolitan Museum of Art, Harris Brisbane Dick Fund, 1924 (24.66.431).

pressed me so favorably elsewhere; and everything had a lounging, listless, madhouse air which was very painful."[24]

Dickens's observations notwithstanding, Davis wrote that because of his association with the Blackwell's Island hospital the state of North Carolina chose him to design its new asylum at Dix Hill, near Raleigh (fig. 2.13).[25] This commission came to his office in 1850. By the time he went to Raleigh in May of that year, Davis had already consulted the directors of the well-respected state institutions at Trenton, Staunton (Virginia), and Philadelphia on matters of heating, ventilation, and planning.[26] At the Pennsylvania Hospital in Philadelphia, Davis had met Dr. Thomas Story Kirkbride, the leading thinker on the architecture of asylums. Inspired by English practices, Kirkbride had developed a humane system of asylum design and management that stressed the need to classify patients according to the nature and degree of their disorders. Davis spent the month of November 1850 in Raleigh preparing his plans, which he finished back in New York the following month.[27]

The Raleigh hospital, which had been undertaken at the urging of Dorothea Dix, showed the influence on Davis of Kirkbride's ideas. The plan consisted of a central administration building comprising offices, storerooms, chapel, and quarters for the superintendent, and two flanking wings, approximately 150 feet long, for separately housing male and female patients. As in the Blackwell's Island asylum, which was built at the time when Kirkbride was first formulating his recommendations, the wards were reached through the superintendent's building and held patients' rooms along either side of a central ten-foot-wide corridor. Residents dined together in the middle of each floor and enjoyed amusements and arts and crafts on the third floor of the main building; the "moral" treatment that Kirkbride prescribed stressed the therapeutic value of socializing and manual labor.

The exterior of the Raleigh building, which was surrounded by ample grounds and enjoyed fine views from its hilltop site, was less severe in appearance than Davis's New York City asylum. Wayne Andrews called it "Davis' most imposing Italian design."[28] Above a low base, the walls of the patient wings bore Doric pilasters between which blank wall space alternated with full-length windows. The administration building (demolished) acquired dignity from a three-story Tuscan Doric portico and a large cupola that crowned its roof, announcing the presence of the chapel hall beneath. The Raleigh hospital was one of Davis's last large commissions, for

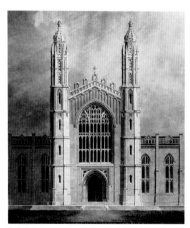

2.14. Library and Chapel, University of Michigan, Ann Arbor, 1838–39 (project). Front elevation. Watercolor, ink, and graphite on paper, 31⅛ x 26⅛ in. The Metropolitan Museum of Art, Harris Brisbane Dick Fund, 1924 (24.66.41).

during the 1850s he became more and more exclusively devoted to domestic architecture. Nonetheless, with the Raleigh and Blackwell's Island asylums, Davis made important contributions to what historian Albert Deutsch has called "the forces of progress in humanitarian reform."[29]

As a designer of institutional buildings, Davis did his most prolific work for educational clients.[30] In fact, he might be called the "education architect" of the antebellum period. From his office came plans for over a dozen schools, including the University of Michigan (fig. 2.14; colorplate 28) at Ann Arbor, the University of North Carolina at Chapel Hill, Davidson College (fig. 2.15) at Davidson, North Carolina, the Virginia Military Institute in Lexington (fig. 2.16), and New York University (fig. 2.17; colorplate 30).

For New York University, Davis conceived a monumental classical edifice, but one that never got beyond the exquisite watercolor drawing he made for it. The design and the rendering were masterpieces of Davis's work as designer and artist. Restrained in massing and detailing, the marble building had walls articulated by Doric engaged piers that deferred in the center to majestic columns which screened the recessed entrance. A slight pediment and a tower recalling the Tower of the Winds in Athens accentuated the entry. Light entered the interior through aedicula-framed

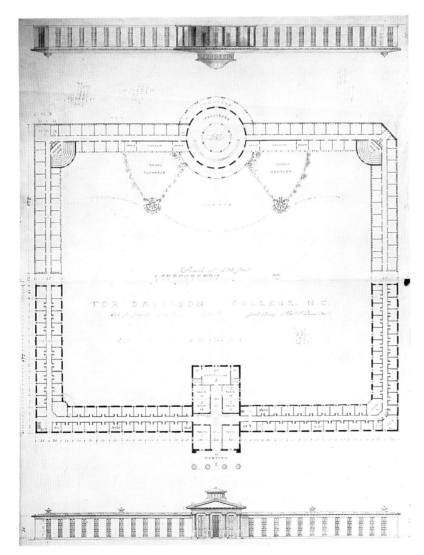

2.15. Davidson College, Davidson, North Carolina, 1856. Front and rear elevations and overall plan. Watercolor, ink, and graphite on paper, 27⅜ x 19⁹⁄₁₆ in. The Metropolitan Museum of Art, Harris Brisbane Dick Fund, 1924 (24.66.435).

2.16. Casimir Bohn, "View of Virginia Military Institute," 1857. Campus designed by Davis, 1848, 1850–61. Lithograph, 13 ¼ x 21 ¾ in. Preston Library, Virginia Military Institute Archives.

2.17. New York University in the classical style, 1832 (project). Perspective. Watercolor, ink, and graphite on paper, 14 ⅝ x 20 ⅝ in. A. J. Davis Collection, The New-York Historical Society (16).

2.18. Design for the interior of New York University Chapel, 1835. Perspective. Watercolor, ink, and graphite on paper, 25 ¹⁵/₁₆ x 19 ¼ in. A. J. Davis Collection, The New-York Historical Society (15).

windows at the base of the tower, through acroterion-capped skylights, and through tall narrow facade windows. The building also had sculptural embellishment, for all of the metopes were to have been carved, although the subjects Davis had in mind are unknown. At once monumental and delicate, the building marked a more inventive approach to classical tradition than Davis's temple-form public buildings.

The university rejected Davis's scheme in favor of a Gothic design prepared by his partners, James Dakin and Ithiel Town.[31] Davis's drawing, however, may have played a role in the formation of the proposal that Thomas Cole submitted to the competition for the Ohio State Capitol in 1838. The Columbus statehouse, on which Davis consulted after the state had accepted Cole's design, was a large squarish structure with a simple cylindrical dome. In the manner of the front of Davis's New York University building, each facade held a recessed entrance screened by Doric columns and flanked by walls articulated with thick Doric pilasters.

Although Davis yielded supremacy to Dakin on the New York University commission, he did have some participation in the work. In 1835, drawings attributed to Davis were prepared for the interior of the school's new chapel, a towering Gothic space the end wall of which was given over to a huge paneled window (fig. 2.18; colorplate 31). The inspiration for the chapel came from English Perpendicular examples, chiefly King's College Chapel, Cambridge, the Chapel of Henry VII at Westminster Abbey, and the choir of Oxford Cathedral, historic landmarks that would have been familiar to Davis and Dakin from books and prints.[32] For the ceiling of the chapel (fig. 2.19) Davis used plaster to imitate English pendent vaulting. Its elaborate pattern of ribs was lit by clerestory windows running above the roofline of adjoining wings that housed the library and classrooms. The chapel, which faced Washington Square, significantly advanced the growing importance in this country of Gothic as the style most appropriate for Christian architecture. In terms of scale and detail, it must have been a splendidly evocative medieval interior, one of New York City's first monuments of the Gothic Revival.

Three years after he had designed the New York University chapel, Davis, who Paul Turner speculates was the first architect to use the term "Collegiate Gothic,"[33] planned a similar chapel and library building for the University of Michigan (see fig.

2.14). (Davis also prepared an alternative design in the classical style, together with a forty-acre campus plan.) His drawing for the Michigan chapel, which was never constructed, relies on slanting rays of light emanating from the heavens to reinforce the romantic identification of the Gothic with the realm of the spirit. One can only wonder if Davis had seen Cole's recent "Voyage of Life" series, where similar effects of light were employed. Choosing the Perpendicular style, the favorite phase of Gothic for early revivalists, Davis drew the twin-towered facade of the Ann Arbor building in emulation of King's College Chapel, Cambridge, turning to the example of that famous collegiate building in the same way that he had looked to the Parthenon for many of his public buildings. Davis simplified his sources and prepared a very "chaste" Gothic design.

In addition to concerning himself with the architecture of higher education, Davis took an interest in schools for primary instruction. The "Village School-House" (figs. 2.20a, 2.20b) that appeared in his book *Rural Residences* (1838),[34] was, Davis stated, "adopted by the American Common School Society and offered to the public as a model of fitness and economy." The design is one of the most rationalist of all Davis's creations. Children entering the board-and-batten building (the architect recommended that the wood be merely oiled) were admonished by an inscription above the door to "Get Wisdom And With All Thy Getting Get Understanding." (A globe, missing in Davis's first design, atop the forty-foot tower recalled a similar emblem of knowledge crowning his New York University building.) Inside, the school held one large polygonal, windowless room. Davis justified the unaccustomed absence of fenestration on the grounds that windows produced unhealthy drafts and created unnecessary distractions for the young scholars. Ventilation and light, he said, could be better provided by openings in the roof.

Like his Blackwell's Island asylum, Davis's model village schoolhouse was well thought out in terms of function. "The form should be semicircular or polygonal, with the master's seat at the center, and each scholar facing it," Davis insisted, "so that at times lessons may be given to the whole school at once, and the attention of the pupils gained, with less effort, to themselves and the teacher." The architect even provided dimensions for pupils' desks, allowing them "a space of 18 inches, side to

2.19. Design for the ceiling of New York University Chapel, 1835. Watercolor on paper, 12¾ x 19⅞ in. The Metropolitan Museum of Art, Arnold Bequest, 1954 (54.90.907).

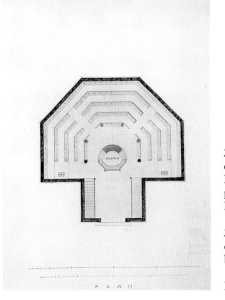

2.20a. Village Chapel and School, Annandale-on-Hudson, New York, 1837. Front elevation. Brown ink, brown ink wash, and graphite on paper, 20 x 14¼ in. A. J. Davis Collection, The New-York Historical Society (214a).

2.20b. Village Chapel and School, Annandale-on-Hudson, New York, 1837. Plan. Brown ink, brown ink wash, and graphite on paper, 20 x 14¼ in. A. J. Davis Collection, The New-York Historical Society (214b).

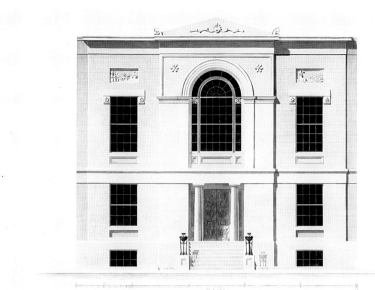

2.21. First Mercantile Library, New York City, 1828 (project). Front elevation. Watercolor, ink wash, ink, and graphite on paper, 16⅝ x 20½ in. A. J. Davis Collection, The New-York Historical Society (348).

2.22. Lyceum of Natural History, New York City, 1835. Town & Davis. Front elevation. Watercolor, ink, and graphite on paper, 20⅝ x 14⁷⁄₁₆ in. The Metropolitan Museum of Art, Harris Brisbane Dick Fund, 1924 (24.66.614).

side," and included a small window in the master's room from which he could survey the class.[35]

Obviously intrigued by the problems of designing an efficient small school, Davis had come up with a highly imaginative design. Freed from imitating historical style by the demands of economy, Davis reduced eclecticism to abstraction. In the batter of the walls we sense the legacy of Egypt, while the scale and centrality of the bell tower echo early Gothic Revival church architecture. These elements, together with the natural color of the wood, constitute Davis's most simple and original formulation of the picturesque tradition. And at least one community is known to have been swayed by the logic of Davis's design. Unfortunately, two drawings by Davis are all that survive of the chapel and school erected after his exemplar by Isabella Donaldson, wife of Robert Donaldson of Blithewood, at Annandale-on-Hudson, New York.[36]

Along with statehouses, asylums, colleges, and schools, Davis sought commissions to design libraries and art galleries. Projects for cultural institutions recur throughout his career, beginning with a drawing for the First Mercantile Library in Nassau Street in New York City (fig. 2.21), dated 1828. This extremely severe double-story building is unlike any of his later library projects, and in its linearity, planarity, and mood of timelessness it recalls the works of the French Romantic Classicists. The only indications of Davis's Greek Revival ideals are the small Doric columns flanking the entrance and the diminutive pediment above the central round arched window. The decidedly residential appearance of the First Mercantile Library gives way in Davis's later libraries and lyceums to a more monumental and "public" architectural vocabulary. In his mature work, Davis almost exclusively alternated between classical and Gothic designs for cultural institutions. The Wadsworth Atheneum (see fig. 1.17) of 1842, still standing in Hartford,[37] is a simple castellated building, while the unbuilt Pinacotheca for his one-time mentor John Trumbull (see fig. 1.16) took the form of a temple ringed by Doric piers, a program familiar from his civic buildings.

On several occasions, Davis had to accommodate his client's needs to city lots. The Lyceum of Natural History (fig. 2.22), which Town & Davis designed in 1835 for a New York City site (the building stood at 561-63 Broadway), interprets the temple facade in giant pilasters standing above a street-level base.[38] The lower level held shops on either side of the central entrance. (According to Davis, Town devised for these stores the first metal shopfronts in New York City.) The Lyceum design, which is related to Davis's Egyptian Revival design for an American Institute (fig. 2.23; colorplate 32), clearly expressed the importance of the exhibition and library rooms on the second floor and also indicated Davis's desire to include large areas of glass in his buildings. The beautiful watercolor drawing he made in 1838 for a "Bibliotheca" in the Gothic style (fig. 2.24; colorplate 29) takes the issue of streetfront lighting a step further. An oversize oriel bay window reaches out daringly to gather brightness for the interior, while at the same time sheltering visitors entering the triple portal beneath it.

Davis's 1843 study for the Astor Library in New York City (fig. 2.25; colorplate 33), which he said he made at the request of Washington Irving,[39] advanced the evolution toward openness to its fullest development. Here Davis dispensed with the base floor and used three-story Corinthian piers, filling the intercolumniations entirely with windows. (In this respect, the Astor Library study is related to the third Patent Office design of nine years earlier.) The big plate-glass windows lighted a

2.23. American Institute, New York City, ca. 1834–35 (project). Town? & Davis. Front elevation. Watercolor, ink, and graphite on paper, 31 x 25⅛ in. The Metropolitan Museum of Art, Harris Brisbane Dick Fund, 1924 (24.66.438).

2.24. Study for a library, 1838. Front elevation. Watercolor, ink, and graphite on paper, 25⁹⁄₁₆ x 17¾ in. The Metropolitan Museum of Art, The Elisha Whittelsey Collection, The Elisha Whittelsey Fund, 1949 (49.102.9).

2.25. Study for the Astor Library, 1843. Front elevation. Watercolor and ink on paper, 20¾ x 14½ in. The Metropolitan Museum of Art, Harris Brisbane Dick Fund, 1924 (24.66.419).

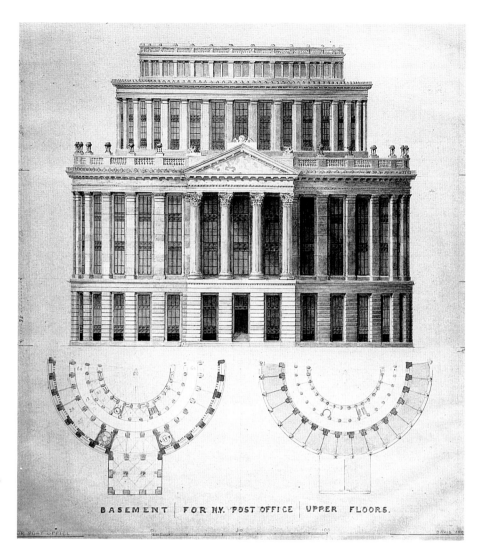

2.26. Competition drawing for the New York City Post Office, 1867. Front elevation and two plans. Watercolor, ink, and graphite on paper, 23 $\frac{5}{16}$ x 18 in. The Metropolitan Museum of Art, Harris Brisbane Dick Fund, 1924 (24.66.386).

BASEMENT | FOR N.Y. POST OFFICE | UPPER FLOORS.

large rotunda, the shadowy presence of which can be glimpsed behind the portico. Although Davis condemned the Romans for having "disfigured [architecture] by gaudy and tasteless decorations, and [the] ruinous spoliation of its purity and beauty of outline," perhaps he thought Jefferson's decision to adapt the Pantheon form for the University of Virginia library sanctioned his own reference to that monument in this instance. He may also have had in view James Gibbs's Radcliffe Library at Oxford, a print of which was in Davis's possession. Davis generally subscribed to the practice of seeking guidance from history; on his business advertisement he admonished, "study your plans carefully and compare them with approved examples sometime before beginning to build."[40]

But if the plan was Roman, there was also much here to please the Greek taste. Davis emulated the north porch of the Erectheum in Athens in the design of the portico and quoted more precisely from that same building in the central doorway, which reproduces, with the addition of a bust (presumably of the donor), the temple's famous north door. Because of its beautiful embodiment of the Ionic order, the Erectheum frequently inspired nineteenth-century buildings housing cultural institutions; Davis himself had made drawings of the temple, which he extolled as "most elegant, and valuable, as a model for imitation."[41] And in this would-be costly piece of work, the striving for ornamental refinement led Davis to embrace sculpture. A copy of Phidias' Athena Promachus, symbol of wisdom and enlightenment, crowned the gable, and a row of books, somewhat haphazardly arranged on either side of a medallion (possibly representing Apollo), filled the pediment. If the iconographic program for this ancestor of the New York Public Library seems to us too self-consciously directed toward educated taste, it nonetheless is a forceful document of the Jacksonian faith in the power of democracy and knowledge to affect human progress.

Davis's career as a leading architect of public buildings failed to survive the Civil War. Indeed, by the end of the 1850s, he was devoting himself almost exclusively to the design of houses. His last attempt to garner an important public commission, to make a comeback, was his decision in 1867 to enter the competition for the new Manhattan post office. Davis had little chance of success; the premium went to Alfred Mullett, who produced an extravagant Second Empire-style structure (now demolished). Davis's proposal (fig. 2.26) took him beyond the eclecticism and rationalism that had guided most of his earlier work and into the realm of personal vision. Davis based his three-tiered stone and glass structure on the circle, which he felt had both mystical and practical properties. "The circle, in which neither end nor beginning can be found, [is] uniform in all its parts . . . ," he wrote, quoting Malton. "The circle is therefore the most proper figure to show the unity, infinite essence, the uniformity and justice of God."[42] In his Journal, especially in the later years of his life, Davis returned repeatedly to the circle, picturing to himself all sorts of structures based upon it. Undoubtedly, the shape did hold metaphysical meaning for him—he designed at least one church, Holy Apostles, with a centralized ground plan (figs. 2.27, 2.28; colorplate 35) and imagined an artist's villa in the form of a circular tower.[43]

The circle also possessed special aesthetic and pragmatic properties for Davis that the rectangle lacked. Once again letting Malton be his spokesman, Davis wrote: "The circular form would present a front, and invite approach at every point, would be most strong and durable, would have neither angle or corner, most convenient and capacious."[44] As early as 1835, Davis had demonstrated these characteristics of the centralized plan for a major public building in his hexagonal plan for the Brooklyn City Hall (figs. 2.29, 2.30; colorplate 34), truly one of the most distinguished and original designs of his long career. Eight years later, he drew in his Journal a plan for a public library in the form of a circle within a square.[45] Many years after that, in a carefully penned statement that he must have intended for publication, Davis, again writing in the third person, elaborated on the special appropriateness of the circular plan he had proposed for the New York post office:

Mr. Davis made a design for the N.Y. Post Office, but it was not considered or examined by the Commission, in-as-much as he did not comply with the printed instructions for covering the whole ground, preferring to exercise his own judgment in regard to the form and size of the building, and only observing the specification of requisites. His plan was round, and differed essentially from all others. It furnished more room within a diameter of 150 ft. than was required, yet the commission . . . had their minds wholly filled with the idea that the entire area of ground must be covered, without regard to acute or obtuse angles, therefore, his plan was the first rejected, without examination. The ground is triangular in form, 320 ft on the park north; and 375 ft on Broadway, and same on Park Row. Mr. Davis contended that as covering any part of the park by building upon it was an outrage on the people, the least area which would

2.27. Church of the Holy Apostles, New York City, 1845 (project). Front elevation. Watercolor, ink, and graphite on paper, 19⅞ x 14⅝ in. The Metropolitan Museum of Art, Harris Brisbane Dick Fund, 1924 (24.66.88).

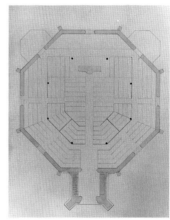

2.28. Church of the Holy Apostles, New York City, 1845 (project). Plan. Brown ink, brown ink wash, and graphite on paper, 17⅝ x 12⅛ in. A. J. Davis Collection, The New-York Historical Society (197b).

2.29. Competition drawing for the Brooklyn City Hall, 1835. Front elevation. Watercolor, ink, and graphite on paper, 25 x 30⅛ in. The Metropolitan Museum of Art, Harris Brisbane Dick Fund, 1924 (24.66.472).

fully serve postal and court uses, in the building, ought to be preferred, and that as 150 or 200 ft would suffice to do this, and also, as a round form, the only one suited to a triangle, would appear like a monument in the park, as does the Radcliffe Library at Oxford; and leave open space for fountains, trees, and statues on the angles, this form would be chosen by the Commission, and serve to gratify those of artistic feeling and confer honor upon all citizens.[46]

Closely related in spirit to the Brooklyn City Hall and post office designs was the plan for a Museum of Geography, History, Art, Science and Literature (fig. 2.31) that Davis put on paper in the early 1870s. This grandiose construction, which may have been undertaken purely for the architect's delectation or to crystallize his thoughts about the new Metropolitan Museum of Art (for which Davis volunteered plans and advice), consisted of four rotundas connected to each other by "verandas" crossing open light courts. The entire structure, which held libraries dedicated to Asia, Africa, America, and Europe, was inscribed within a square. A huge central rotunda containing a raised platform reached by monumental flights of steps focused both interior space and exterior composition. Vaguely reminiscent of the United States Capitol, of which Davis was making scale drawings as late as 1876,[47] and perhaps influenced by Davis's imperfect knowledge of the École des Beaux-Arts brand of classicism, the museum was a dream that he probably knew could never be realized.

Isolated in his later years from the New York architectural scene by reason of the radical changes in practice and taste that had come about after the Civil War, Davis turned from being a designer of public buildings to being a vitriolic critic of the architecture of his time. Most of his remarks were made in private, in his Journal, or recorded in his unfinished manuscript "Abuses in Architecture." In 1878, however, his feelings boiled over, and citing himself as New York's "oldest architect and the designer of more buildings than seem to have fallen to the lot of any other architect in America," he addressed a letter "to the Mayor of New York and the Pub-

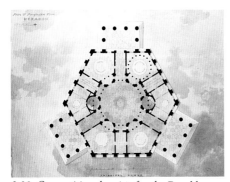

2.30. Competition drawing for the Brooklyn City Hall, 1835. Plan. Watercolor, ink, and graphite on paper, 25½ x 31½ in. The Metropolitan Museum of Art, Harris Brisbane Dick Fund, 1924 (24.66.471).

lic through the Press" that appeared in the October 28 issue of the *Sun*.[48] Davis enumerated many examples of "hideous deformity" in public architecture, condemning High Victorian Gothic and Second Empire buildings with equal vigor. Calvert Vaux's Belvedere in Central Park,[49] Frederick Withers's Jefferson Market Courthouse, Kellum and Eidlitz's New York County Courthouse, and Richard Morris Hunt's Lenox Library came in for special opprobrium, as did Mullett's post office, which Davis termed "a broken pile of costly vulgarity." In this, perhaps his last public pronouncement, Davis wanted the metropolis he so loved but that no longer desired his services to know that "at least one of its native citizens has no part in the abuses of the time, perpetuated in the later public buildings of the city and its vicinity."

By the time of Davis's death in 1892, American architects had all but forgotten the contributions he had made to their profession and to the legacy of American public architecture. Late-twentieth-century audiences, however, find much to respect in such buildings as the Manhattan Custom House, which despite its vastly altered surroundings still manages to impress the viewer with its pleasing proportions and fine detailing. It and other governmental buildings by Town & Davis helped establish classicism as the preferred architectural idiom of American democracy. In the field of collegiate architecture, we recognize that Davis's work influenced the layout and expression that many universities espoused well into the present century. And his Gothic Revival Wadsworth Atheneum still stands to remind us that Davis was one of the first American architects to tackle the problem of creating buildings for art and culture. It is to be regretted that so many edifices of all types that he designed are now demolished. Fortunately, his striking drawings remain to illuminate our understanding of the simple and dignified architecture he conceived to serve the institutions of a young, optimistic nation.

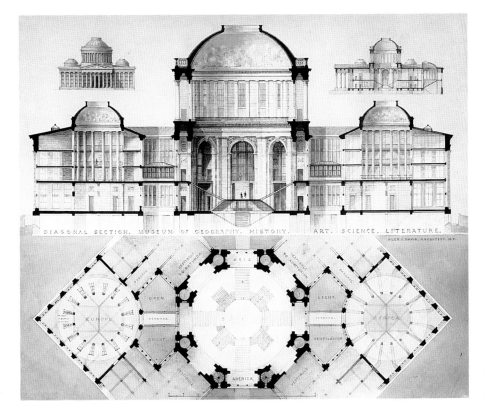

2.31. Study for a "Museum of Geography. History. Art. Science. Literature.," ca. 1872. Diagonal section, partial plan, elevation, and longitudinal section. Watercolor, ink, and graphite on paper, 25 ½ x 31 ¼ in. The Metropolitan Museum of Art, Harris Brisbane Dick Fund, 1924 (24.66.458).

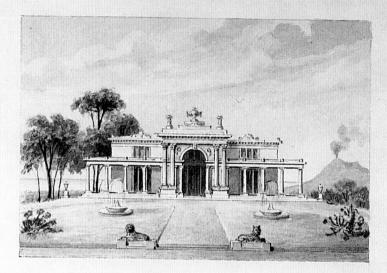

ROMAN VILLA.

GREEK VILLA.

CHAPTER 3

From Cottages to Castles: The Country House Designs of Alexander Jackson Davis

SUSANNE BRENDEL-PANDICH

During the course of Alexander Jackson Davis's long and productive architectural career, he designed almost every type of building, ranging from hotels and warehouses to universities, capitols, and churches. The majority of his commissions, however, were private residences, designed in every major historical style. The creative qualities of his architecture were found not in his eclectic virtuosity but rather in his talent for manipulating geometric massing, light, siting, technology, and archaeological detail.

His mature compositions broke from the Late Georgian tradition of houses with balanced facades and central hall plans featuring flanking double parlors. Palladio's principles of proportion and reverence for classical orders had served as strict guidelines for the previous generation of designers, but Davis searched through diverse sources for inspiration. The proliferation of English prescriptive literature in the late eighteenth and early nineteenth century provided rich material for the young architect. Davis also studied the French rationalists and particularly admired the writings of Jean Nicolas Louis Durand (1760–1834), who advocated a system of floor-plan design based on geometric forms.[1] Davis's fascination with compositions of unusual geometric relationships left him dissatisfied with the confining formulas of Palladio. Even some of his early classical floor plans had semicircular side wings and unusual room arrangements. The later Gothic and Italianate villas, such as Ericstan and Grace Hill, broke open the box completely with round and octagonal rooms, towers, and wings.

In his earliest work in the Greek Revival style, Davis devised his own order, in which strong antae separated by continuous window strips or planar piers gave his facades a simple, bold appearance. Multiple window units rose vertically through two or three stories between the piers. The interior floor levels were indicated by shallow wooden panels made flush with the glass. He referred to this facade treatment as the "Davisean Order."[2] These designs, which provided great expanses of glass on the building's exterior, were the precursors of the window wall.

With an early background in theater design and drawing, Davis showed an ability for using light to create drama both on the interior and exterior of his buildings. He designed projecting bay windows to gain more interior light, and consistently specified French doors leading to terraces or verandas. These verandas cast shadows on the facade; the rooms behind them received only filtered light. Colored light flowed through the stained-glass windows of his Gothic, castellated, and Italianate villas. Davis also skillfully incorporated skylights in the residences he designed, especially in picture galleries, stairwells, or other major second-floor rooms.

On the first floor, "plant cabinets," glassed-in portions of the veranda, were

3.1. Studies of Roman and Greek villas, ca. 1829. Front elevations. Watercolor and ink on paper, $9\,^{15}/_{16}$ x $7\,^{1}/_{8}$ in. The Metropolitan Museum of Art, Harris Brisbane Dick Fund, 1924 (24.66.1401 [98], vol. II, leaf 113).

standard features of his villas. These glass rooms were included even when the estate had a major greenhouse, as in his design of Lyndhurst for George Merritt. A clear reminder of the period's fascination with horticulture, plant cabinets were meant to bring nature indoors, and Davis often noted on his drawings that they should be furnished with shrubs as well as flowers.

For Davis, the view from a window was as important as the light admitted. Contemporary literature paid particular attention to the siting of a house. An 1843 article entitled "The Architects and Architecture of New York" that appeared in the New York weekly magazine *Brother Jonathan* set forth one of the criteria for the selection of a country house's site.

> The view of scenery to be had from the house when finished should be considered; and this cannot be too bold or too grand. Large masses of foliage, cliffs, mountains, water and cultivated land should if possible be compassed by the vision and the fewer village houses to be seen the better.[3]

The article praised the residences of Philip R. Paulding and Henry Sheldon, both designed by Davis and both in Tarrytown, New York, as being "eminently well located, and they owe much of the beauty for which they are celebrated to the scenes in which they are embosomed."

It is clear that Davis considered his buildings part of a larger composition and their siting in the landscape essential to their artistic success. He had read the major English treatises on the philosophy of landscape gardening and felt that the picturesque villas and cottages of England were examples worthy of emulation for Americans. In his own published work, *Rural Residences* (1838), he wrote that American homes were defective "not only in the style of the house but in the want of connection with its site,—in the absence of . . . well disposed trees, shrubbery, and vines."[4] During the course of implementing his most important commissions, it is likely that his clients sought his advice on landscape design. There are a few significant references in his Day Books to landscaping; for example, he records on October 5, 1864, that he wrote a letter to George Merritt advising on gardening at Lyndhurst. Davis also prepared a list of more than 200 suggested books for Merritt, in which he recommended numerous works on landscape gardening.[5] A partial listing includes the collected works of Humphrey Repton, edited by John Claudius Loudon (1840), four additional titles by Loudon himself, including his *Encyclopaedia of Cottage, Farm, and Villa Architecture* (1833) and *Suburban Gardener and Villa Companion* (1838), as well as more theoretical works such as Richard Payne Knight's *The Landscape, A Didactic Poem* (1794) and Thomas Whately's *Observations on Modern Gardening* (1770), of which Davis said "this is *the classic* on modern gardening."[6]

Davis practiced much of the advice he found in the English source books, as seen in his preference for placing his large villas on architectural terraces with urns or garden sculpture at the corners. While terraces had a formalizing effect, they also provided a graceful transition into the landscape.

As carefully as Davis studied the relationship of his residences to their setting, he was also keenly sensitive to how his houses functioned for the families who lived in them. Technology and comfort were important components of his house designs. He designed ventilation systems to circulate fresh air through the interiors. Water closets and bathrooms were included in some of his earliest houses of the late 1830s, and he later added new amenities such as speaking tubes and dumbwaiters at houses such as Lyndhurst and Grace Hill. Andrew Jackson Downing, for whom

Davis delineated many of the illustrations published in his works, wrote about the "fitness" of such improvements for Americans.

> In a country like ours, where the population is comparatively sparse, civil rights equal, and wages high, good servants or domestics are comparatively rare, and not likely to retain their places a long time. The maximum of comfort, therefore, is found to consist in employing the smallest number of servants actually necessary. This may be greatly facilitated by having all the apartments conveniently arranged with reference to various uses, and still further by introducing certain kinds of domestic labor saving apparatus to lessen the amount of service required, or to render its performance easy. Among those which we would, from experience, especially recommend for cottages are the rising cupboard or dumb waiter, the speaking-tube, and the rotary pump.[7]

Compared with the country houses of England and Europe, Davis's residences were modest, but they were mansions by American standards. While the facades were often impressive, the interiors were more intimate expressions of the privacy of family and its relationship to the public world. In a diary entry of 1841, Philip Hone commented on these new interior arrangements in a backhanded way by describing Davis's house for the Pauldings as "an edifice of gigantic size, with no room in it."[8] This was a common reaction to the new ordering of space seen in Gothic interiors and other irregular floor plans, which differed substantially from the strictly ordered and cubic volumes in classical villas. The romantic spaces of a Gothic villa were filled with angles created by vaulted ceilings and room shapes broken up with projecting bays. These rooms were not arranged along a strict axis, but often placed in radial or cross plans that created provocative vistas within the house. Irregular corridor views of rooms partially visible provided both interest and surprise.

Seen with a sympathetic eye, these room arrangements were described as elegant and spacious by Andrew Jackson Downing in his *Treatise on the Theory and Practice of Landscape Gardening*, published the same year as Hone's entry. Downing deplored the "formal sameness" of classical designs and wrote that rooms should be of varying size and irregular placement, with openings and windows of different sizes. He also advocated separation between private family spaces, service areas, and entertaining areas as the best way to order a floor plan.[9] The irregular outline of this free planning allowed the house to be more closely integrated with the site, extending out into its surroundings with terraces and porches. This engagement with nature was the primary characteristic of picturesque design.

Davis made numerous other unseen improvements in his buildings. He included a system of floor deafening that made the various levels of the house impervious to the sound of activities above and below. By the 1840s, most of his masonry buildings were of a hollow brick wall construction. The bricks were then stuccoed or faced with stone to produce what he believed would be a drier and more fireproof building.[10]

By introducing innovative detailing that required complex building techniques, Davis often encountered problems with the builders who executed his designs. In response, he was one of the first architects to use written specifications for contractors. Throughout his Day Books and Journal, Davis expressed his frustration with or disappointment in buildings executed without his supervision. An 1847 letter from a potential client in Ohio articulated the problems of building in the new picturesque style: " . . . our builders know no other way than the old monotonous straight lines . . . I want only a *little wild sweet house*—with just room enough."[11]

Davis designed country houses in a wide range of styles. While classical designs predominated at the beginning of Davis's career and during his partnership with Ithiel Town (1829–35 and 1842–43), he worked in a variety of styles simultaneously. His first Gothic design was in 1832 for Joseph Moulton of Brooklyn, and his Tuscan designs, such as Ravenswood for Charles Roach, also date to the 1830s. While more picturesque styles make up the majority of his commissions after the 1830s, he continued to offer classical designs throughout his career, such as his work on Montgomery Place into the 1870s.

The Classical Designs

A discussion of Davis's first commissions must start with his classical designs. Davis noted in his Day Book that on March 15, 1828, he made his "First study of Stuarts Athens, from which I date Professional Practice . . . borrowed from Town."[12] Indeed, this volume had a profound effect on Davis and his contemporaries. The archaeological recordings made by James Stuart and Nicholas Revett and published in their masterpiece, *The Antiquities of Athens* (1762), were to provide the inspiration for the new Greek Revival style so enormously popular for the first half of the century. Davis's early designs reflected this new interest in the pure Greek Doric and Ionic orders, drawings of which, Stuart and Revett had pointed out, were lacking in Palladio. Stuart and Revett advocated the restoration of the orders from their Roman corruption. Davis embraced their philosophy but at the same time studied Palladio and other classical sources.[13] Several of his early study drawings show his recreation of Pliny's Villa at Laurentinum, Ostia, as well as historically inspired designs of Roman and Greek villas (fig. 3.1). These early explorations are illustrative of his interest in archaeological examples and their application to modern villas.

Davis used a Greek design in his first architectural commission, for James A. Hillhouse (1789–1841). Hillhouse was a sophisticated client; he had been educated at Yale and had traveled abroad. A prominent resident of New Haven, he was also a noted contemporary poet and a patron of the arts. He collected works by Davis's friend, the Hudson River School painter Thomas Cole, and knew Ithiel Town, another leading citizen of New Haven. Davis first met Hillhouse in the fall of 1828 while on a trip to Boston and New England, during the course of which he produced a commissioned series of architectural views. He must have made a favorable impression because he began work on the Hillhouse villa in December 1828. Several other more established architects had also proposed designs for Hillhouse, including William Strickland and Ithiel Town. Davis's design was chosen, and he began his first commission as an architect.

The house was located on the crest of a hill at the head of Hillhouse Avenue in New Haven. From the outset, Hillhouse had strong ideas about his house and had sketched floor plans of his own. He wanted Davis to provide him with elegant and well-proportioned facades. There are several versions of Davis's design which show interesting variations on the final house. The design is, in essence, a three-bay, two-story house with a pedimented portico consisting of two central Ionic columns flanked by two square piers. In an alternate design, Davis displayed a startling imagination by adding a one-story open colonnade on the rear of the house that extended on both sides. This loggia faced out to an architectural terrace with a garden pavilion or service building on one end. With the addition of this colonnaded porch, a simple design acquired dramatic proportions (fig. 3.2; colorplate 36). At some lat-

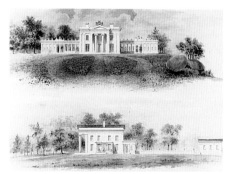

3.2. Detail of study for Highwood for James A. Hillhouse, New Haven, Connecticut, ca. 1830. Front and side elevations. Watercolor, ink, and graphite on paper, 15½ x 12⅛ in. The Metropolitan Museum of Art, Harris Brisbane Dick Fund, 1924 (24.66.1416 [22], vol. XVII, leaf 23).

er date, Davis made further additions to his drawings, expanding the house with corresponding one-story additions and pavilions on the ends of the colonnade. This Palladian scheme of flanking pavilions was not adopted, and the simpler plan prevailed. The final version of the design contained only the central core; however, the severity of the Doric order had been softened to the Ionic order (fig. 3.3; colorplate 37). Originally called Highwood, the house was renamed Sachem's Wood in honor of Hillhouse's deceased father and commemorated in a poem by the same name.[14]

In the next few years, other Greek villas were built on Hillhouse Avenue, including residences for Ithiel Town and for Aaron Skinner, the mayor of New Haven. Hillhouse owned the land on the avenue terminating at the hill where his villa stood (fig. 3.4). He encouraged his friends to use Town & Davis as architects and sold them the land on which to build their houses. Davis's commission for Hillhouse and the villas that followed on Hillhouse Avenue established a sophisticated version of the domestic Greek Revival style in New Haven.

Davis's relationship with James Hillhouse continued over the next ten years. Built from Davis's designs, an ice house, a children's playhouse, and a farmer's house were added to the estate. It is not surprising that Hillhouse was also instrumental in encouraging Davis's publication of his architectural pattern book, *Rural Residences*, in 1838. The dedication indicates that several gentlemen (James Hillhouse and Robert Donaldson) "with a View to the Improvement of American Country architecture" assisted in the publication. Donaldson had also commissioned early designs from Davis, and the design for Donaldson's "Residence in the English Collegiate Style" appeared in *Rural Residences*. It is uncertain what financial or other support Hillhouse may have given Davis, but he stands as one of his most important patrons. He helped to launch the young architect's career and to encourage the dissemination of Davis's ideas.

Only a few classical designs appeared in *Rural Residences*. Davis explained in his introduction, "The Greek Temple form, perfect in itself, and well adapted as it is to public edifices and even to town mansions is inappropriate for country residences."[15] When Davis used classical forms for his country houses, he transformed them with great creativity. The "American Cottage," a three-room log cabin with a temple front of bark-covered tree columns, served as an example appropriate for

3.3. Highwood for James A. Hillhouse, New Haven, Connecticut, 1829. Perspective. Watercolor, ink, and graphite on paper, 14 5/16 x 19 15/16 in. A. J. Davis Collection, The New-York Historical Society (289).

3.4. View of "Sachem's Wood. Newhaven Ct.," 1839. Ink and wash on paper, 9 7/8 x 14 in. Drawings & Archives, Avery Architectural and Fine Arts Library, Columbia University (1955.001.00523).

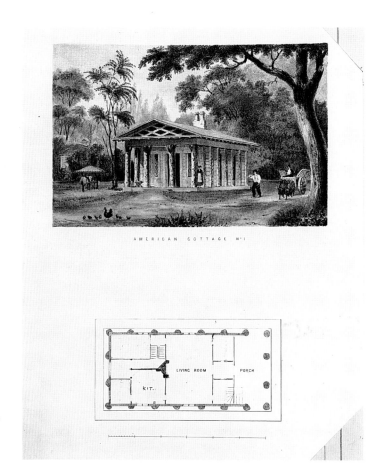

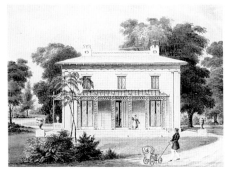

3.5. "American Cottage No. 1" from *Rural Residences,* 1836, published 1838. Perspective and plan. Lithograph with watercolor and ink, 13⅜ x 10¼ in. The Metropolitan Museum of Art, Harris Brisbane Dick Fund, 1924 (24.66.1406, vol. VII, leaf 31).

3.6. Detail of House for David Codwise, near New Rochelle, New York, 1835 (project). Front elevation. Watercolor, ink, and graphite on paper, 14⅜ x 9 in. The Metropolitan Museum of Art, Harris Brisbane Dick Fund, 1924 (24.66.790).

country living (fig. 3.5). The primitive temple hut finds its archaeological roots in sources such as Vitruvius's *Ten Books of Architecture*, which refers to the earliest Greek temples as being constructed of wood. Davis ingeniously crossed this temple with the native American log cabin to produce a tasteful home that could be constructed by hand on the frontier. His design rusticated the classical dwelling to blend into a wilderness setting.

As romanticism gained acceptance, Davis increasingly explored a more eclectic vocabulary for his country buildings. He also modified his use of the classical vocabulary in order to adapt his designs to a more picturesque style suitable for suburban living. In his *Rural Residences* design entitled "Cottage Orne . . . for David Codwise," Davis took a simple box with a central hall plan and gave it visual interest through creative detailing (fig. 3.6; colorplate 38). He raised the house on a terrace and added an exotic veranda on the front and a smaller porch to one side. Broad overhanging cantilevered eaves, diamond-paned windows, and French doors contributed to the informality of the house. Classical-style detailing appeared on the double pilasters at the corners, the frieze board running under the eaves, and the chimneys decorated with wreaths. Although this vocabulary was derived from classical forms, the effect was romantic. In his text, Davis describes the house as Oriental: "The design partakes of an oriental character, from its veranda-like porch of entrance, the light pilasters on the angles, for projecting cornice and cantilevers."[16] The concave roof of the porch with the upturned curve of the eaves was suggestive of the roofline of a pagoda. The green roof and the lightness of the supporting trellis also created the impression of an awning or a tent. Through this important detailing, the design took on an exotic character. While there is no evidence that Codwise built

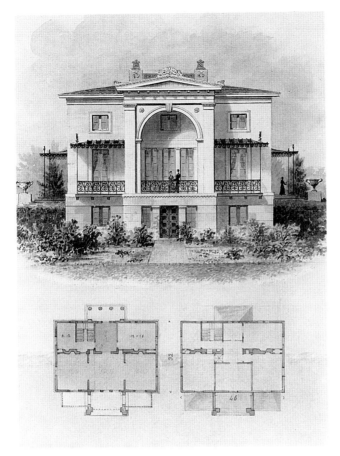

3.7. House for Henry W. T. Mali, Manhattanville, New York, 1839 (project). Front elevation and two plans. Watercolor, ink, and graphite on paper, 14⅛ x 10⅜ in. The Metropolitan Museum of Art, Harris Brisbane Dick Fund, 1924 (24.66.1416 [37], vol. XVII, leaf 44).

this house, the design was used by James Hillhouse and his father-in-law for a cottage on Trumbull Street in New Haven, located near Davis's Greek design of six years earlier.

Codwise's "Cottage Orne" of 1835 pointed the way to Davis's increased use of eclectic detailing for his villas. Davis designed fewer country villas in the classical style as the decade progressed, although he continued to employ it for city commissions. In the few instances in which he used a more formal classical style for the country, he often employed open pavilions, side wings, and porches that invited the landscape into the design. Two houses in the Roman style illustrated his stylistic adaptations for rural settings. A design for Nathaniel Jocelyn of New Haven in 1835 displayed a central block with two flanking arched pavilions. Another design, for Henry W. T. Mali of Manhattanville in 1839, contained a pedimented triumphal arch on the main facade with awning-style porches similar to the Cottage Orne (fig. 3.7). Neither of these Roman Revival houses was built, but his elegant design for an open-sided pavilion can still be seen at Montgomery Place (1843–44) near Red Hook, New York. He used the architecture of this unusual outdoor room to frame the landscape into a picture (fig. 3.8).

Davis's classical designs for the country exhibited symmetry and a harmonious relationship with nature, fulfilling the romantic precepts of the Beautiful as set forth in the publications of Downing and his English predecessors.[17] As Downing explained in his *Treatise on Landscape Gardening* (first edition, 1841), the Beautiful was characterized by a simplicity of form and outline together with ornament that was graceful and refined. The Picturesque, the contrasting ideal to the Beautiful, was based on asymmetry and an organic vitality stemming from irregular forms and a boldness of

3.8. "View From Montgomery Place," ca. 1847. Watercolor, ink, and graphite on paper, 8¼ x 7⅛ in. Drawings & Archives, Avery Architectural and Fine Arts Library, Columbia University (1955.001.00012).

3.9a. "Example of the Beautiful in Landscape Gardening," fig. 15 from Andrew Jackson Downing's *A Treatise on the Theory and Practice of Landscape Gardening*, 1841.

3.9b. "Example of the Picturesque in Landscape Gardening," fig. 16 from Andrew Jackson Downing's *A Treatise on the Theory and Practice of Landscape Gardening*, 1841.

composition. A house that was Picturesque was characterized by rooflines of varied profile, ornamented with such elements as chimney pots, towers, and dormers, and by verandas, loggias, and balustrades that broke up the main block of the house. Downing illustrated both the Beautiful and the Picturesque in his *Treatise on the Theory and Practice of Landscape Gardening* (figs. 3.9a, 3.9b). According to Downing, Italianate and Gothic styles embodied the characteristics of the Picturesque.

Some of Davis's buildings anticipated the writings of Downing. His ability to translate these concepts into architectural designs helped to turn the American house builder away from classicism and toward an architecture more closely attuned to the American landscape. This was made possible through Downing's publication and endorsement of Davis's work. While other notable architects such as Richard Upjohn and John Notman had designs published by Downing, it was Davis's work that had the most influence on him.[18]

The Italian Designs

Under the general heading of Italian, Davis designed houses in the Roman, the Tuscan, and the Italianate styles. Both the Roman and the early Tuscan works were classically derived designs, adapted from Roman and Tuscan orders. His first Journal entry for a Tuscan villa was in 1833, when he designed a house for E. H. Conway

3.10. Detail of House for Edmund H. Conway, proposed location unknown, 1833 (project). Perspective. Watercolor and ink on paper, 9⅜ x 6⅝ in. The Metropolitan Museum of Art, Harris Brisbane Dick Fund, 1924 (24.66.1166).

(fig. 3.10; colorplate 39). This first small transitional villa for Conway was strikingly simple in its form, and the drawing was titled "Greek Pilaster Villa" in pencil. Square Tuscan piers fronted the house; the flat roof terminated in wide overhanging eaves. Single-story semicircular side wings articulated with engaged pilasters flanked the central house. Three years later Davis designed Ravenswood, a more dramatic example of a Tuscan villa, for Charles H. Roach (fig. 3.11; colorplate 41). Roach was planning a residential development on Long Island for which Davis designed a number of villas in a variety of styles (fig. 3.13). Ravenswood was a boldly designed Tuscan villa with a square floor plan. The main block of the house was surrounded by a peristyle porch of square piers in a Tuscan order. The roof's wide cantilevered eaves extended past the piers of the porch, and a parapet at its crown contained a pair of balanced chimneys. The three-bay facade had a two-story entrance flanked by Davisean windows. Although the design was strictly symmetrical, picturesque details are evident in the sweeping eaves and the broad veranda/loggia. Davis included a small woodcut of this design as an illustration in *Rural Residences* (fig. 3.12). Although his planned community was never realized, Roach's villa was probably built.

The Italian styles provided a link between classicism and the romantic styles. Downing wrote:

> The Italian style is we think, decidedly the most beautiful mode for domestic purposes that has been the offspring of Grecian Art. It is the style which has evidently grown up under the eyes of painters of a more modern Italy.[19]

Downing was referring to the farmhouses of Tuscany and the Italianate country villas influenced by Renaissance design. Tuscan architecture, as Davis interpreted it in his later career, was irregular in plan and picturesque in its boldness of outline and sparsity of ornament. In a larger villa of 1851, Davis showed the Tuscan style with a more vernacular vocabulary of stuccoed walls, towers, and arcaded loggias. He composed a very elegant and austere residence for Richard O. Morris in Green Springs, Virginia (fig. 3.14; colorplate 40). The house, known as Hawkwood, had a cruciform plan with an arcaded porch around one end. A two-story entry projection was placed slightly off center on the facade to balance the higher three-story tower behind. The projecting gable of the entry and Palladian windows were the signature of Davis's later Tuscan designs. Light and shade played on the broken and plain surfaces of the facade, and the bracketed projecting eaves cast dark shadows. The

3.11. Detail of Ravenswood for Charles H. Roach, Long Island, New York, 1836. Front elevation. Watercolor, ink, and graphite on paper, 16½ x 12⅝ in. Drawings & Archives, Avery Architectural and Fine Arts Library, Columbia University (1940.001.00027R).

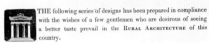

3.12. Advertisement from *Rural Residences,* 1836, published 1838. Wood engraving, 2 1/16 x 2½ in. The Metropolitan Museum of Art, Harris Brisbane Dick Fund, 1924 (24.66.1887).

3.13. Ravenswood Development for Charles H. Roach, Long Island, New York, 1836 (project). Lithograph by N. Currier, architecture drawn by A. J. Davis. 17⅛ x 52⅜ in. A. J. Davis Collection, Print Room, The New-York Historical Society.

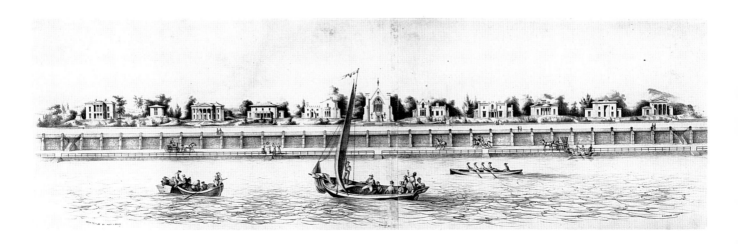

3.14. Hawkwood for Richard O. Morris, Green Springs, Virginia, 1851–54. Front elevation. Watercolor and ink on paper, 14⁵⁄₁₆ x 19¹⁵⁄₁₆ in. The Metropolitan Museum of Art, Harris Brisbane Dick Fund, 1924 (24.66.60).

roofline and chimneys all provided a dramatic outline against the sky. The windows were emphasized with heavy projecting architraves that were repeated over the arch of the entryway. While Davis produced other more ambitious Tuscan designs for clients C. B. Sedgewick (1852) and Samuel F. B. Morse (1851–52), this house for Morris was striking in its simplicity and almost sculptural qualities.

A more elaborate version of the Tuscan style was the Italianate. While the Tuscan was characterized by a single tower, pitched roofs, and restrained ornament, the Italianate utilized multiple towers with flat roofs topped with balustrades. Davis's most ambitious Italianate villa may have been the one he designed for Edwin Clark Litchfield (1815–85) in Brooklyn, named Grace Hill by the family because Mrs. Litchfield's maiden name was Grace Hill Hubbard. Litchfield was a lawyer by training but spent most of his career in railroad enterprises and in developing real estate in Brooklyn. In November 1853 he commissioned Davis to begin drawings for his house. By May of 1854, Davis produced two alternative studies for the house, a "Villa in Castleated Style of Gothic" (fig. 3.15a) and a "Villa in American Style of Italian" (fig. 3.15b). The two facades were identical in composition, varying only in the detailing; the towers terminated with battlements in the Gothic design and with balustrades in the Italian. Litchfield chose the Italian villa, a style that was gaining in popularity throughout the 1850s.

The Litchfield design contained a highly imaginative floor plan that radiated from the central hall or rotunda (see figs. 4.16a, 4.16b). None of the principal rooms were square or rectangular in shape; many of them were octagonal or round, and some contained large round or angled bays. In this design Davis was able to indulge his love of the play between geometric volumes. This is typical of the irregular floor plans seen in Davis's most complex picturesque villas. The rooms are of varying shapes and sizes and close off from one another, creating incomplete and intriguing vistas within the house. The house was placed on an architectural terrace and set into a hill; an exposed basement story on the rear elevation added height to this facade and dramatized the house's prominence in relation to the hill.

While more strictly classical houses are designed to emphasize only the front facade, Davis's picturesque houses incorporated complex elevations on all four sides. Grace Hill's front facade was unusual because the entrance tower did not project out in order to announce the portal. It gained prominence through height; it was the tallest tower on the front elevation. A broad octagonal tower, to the entrance tower's right, stepped out on the undulating facade and was ornamented with more ornate detailing. This broad tower had a semicircular bay window on the first floor and a balustraded balcony on the second floor. On the north end of the house, a smaller round tower with a conical roof relieved the central emphasis of the two large towers and provided balance to the composition.

On the rear or east elevation, an identical round tower ended the north corner and was connected by a terrace to the projecting octagonal block of the dining room. The dining room had a semicircular bay window on the first floor with a balcony above. An elaborate rotunda skylight topped the third floor of this element and rose above the main roofline. The towers of the front facade, behind the roofline, added interest to this rear elevation. On the south end, a columned loggia with a plant cabinet continued around the south facade and terminated at the corner of the front facade. This interlinking of elements such as towers and verandas on multiple facades provided four varied elevations that could almost be unfolded into one continuous design.[20]

Inside, a skylight added drama to the entry rotunda, which included a picture gallery on its second level. The second-story game room also had a skylight. The large porch on the south end was entered through French doors, and smaller verandas appeared on both the front and rear facades. Many of the windows incorporated stained-glass borders to give variation of color and light to the interiors.

Davis's specifications for Litchfield's villa called for "scientific bricklaying" and included sophisticated systems for comfort such as central heating, advanced ventilation and plumbing, an elevator, and a dumbwaiter. Davis oversaw the construction of the villa while the Litchfield family toured Europe from October 1855 to July 1857. The family moved into the house in October 1857. The construction cost was $60,000; Davis charged 3 percent of that total as his architectural fee. At the outset of his career, he charged by the drawing and by the number of supervisory trips, but by the 1850s he sometimes used the practice of a percentage charge for his larger projects.

The villa for Edwin Litchfield was the culmination of Davis's work in the Italianate style, designed at the height of his career. It displayed his virtuosity at geometric massing, lighting, siting, and building technology. During the course of the 1850s, he worked on at least eighteen other designs in the Italianate style for clients such as Alexander E. Outerbridge near Philadelphia and Llewellyn Haskell in Belleville, New Jersey. Davis developed his Italianate villas into complex compositions, but employed a more restrained style than seen in houses by some other architects, such as the Morse-Libby Mansion, designed by Henry Austin. His designs incorporated the essence of the picturesque in their balanced asymmetry and bold composition without relying on excessive or exaggerated ornament.

3.15a. "Villa in Castleated Style of Gothic," study for Grace Hill for Edwin C. Litchfield, Brooklyn, New York, ca. 1853–54. Front elevation. Watercolor and ink wash on paper, 8½ x 14 in. Drawings & Archives, Avery Architectural and Fine Arts Library, Columbia University (1940.001.00529).

3.15b. "Villa in American Style of Italian," study for Grace Hill for Edwin C. Litchfield, Brooklyn, New York, ca. 1853–54. Front elevation. Watercolor and ink wash on paper, 8½ x 14 in. Drawings & Archives, Avery Architectural and Fine Arts Library, Columbia University (1940.001.00530).

The Gothic Designs

Although Davis was a leading designer in the Italian styles, it was his work in the Gothic style that made him the principal proponent of picturesque architecture in America. More than any classically derived architecture, the Gothic style embodied romantic sensibilities. As Downing explained in the text of *Landscape Gardening*:

> The ideas connected in our minds with Gothic architecture are of highly romantic and poetical nature contrasted with the classical association which Greek and Roman styles suggest. . . . He who has extended his researches, *con amore*, into the history of domestic life and habits of those illustrious minds, will not . . . forget . . . the tasteful residence of Pope at Twickenham; or the turrets and battlements of the more picturesque Abbotsford [the home of Sir Walter Scott]; and numberless other buildings of England, once the abodes of renowned genius.[21]

Indeed, these two residences, along with Horace Walpole's Strawberry Hill and Richard Payne Knight's Downton Castle, promoted the picturesque garden and the Gothic style as symbolic of the intellectual and artistic home (fig. 3.16). American authors such as Washington Irving, James Fenimore Cooper, and Edgar Allan Poe returned from English tours to gothicize their own houses (fig. 3.17). Town & Davis's first major Gothic commission, for Robert Gilmor in 1832, was the direct result of Gilmor's English travels. He had stayed at Strawberry Hill for five days in 1830 as a guest of Horace Walpole's heirs, Earl and Lady Waldegrave, and had also traveled to his ancestral Scotland, where he visited Abbotsford and met Sir Walter Scott.[22]

Robert Gilmor was an enlightened client. Born to a wealthy merchant family, he became an attaché with the American Embassy in France after graduating from Harvard in 1828. He wrote poetry and aspired to be a gentleman farmer. Gilmor established his country seat, Glen Ellen, on a site overlooking the banks of the Gunpowder River about twelve miles from Baltimore. He contributed to the design provided by Town & Davis, and the main house had elements that were suggestive of both Strawberry Hill and Abbotsford (fig. 3.18; colorplate 42). The continuous line

3.16. Paul Sandby, "View of Strawberry Hill from the South East," ca. 1783. Watercolor on paper, 5⅜ x 7⁷⁄₁₆ in. Courtesy of The Lewis Walpole Library, Yale University.

3.17. "View of Sunnyside," ca. 1841. Wood engraving after a drawing by A. J. Davis. Detail, 3 15/16 x 2 9/16 in. Historic Hudson Valley, Tarrytown, New York (A85426).

of battlements along the eaves punctuated by pinnacles and towers, the pointed arch windows, and the prominent bay window of Glen Ellen were also features of Strawberry Hill. Glen Ellen's roofline was also interrupted by a dramatic four-story octagonal tower and a pinnacled roof screen above the octagonal bay. The facades were consciously asymmetrical, with historically correct detailing. In plan, the progression of the octagonal corner tower, the two-story bay window, and the small projecting square tower on the rear elevation echoed the outline of the main facade of Abbotsford.[23] Reduced from three stories in the first design to two, Glen Ellen's exterior presented none of the sophisticated massing of Davis's later designs and ventured cautiously outside the confines of the rectangular box. Its cruciform plan had a three-room entry axis with a large drawing room running parallel to it on the left and a perpendicular hallway on the right with flanking rooms and stairway. Davis used a similar spatial relationship in later villas such as Lyndhurst.

Glen Ellen was America's first Gothic Revival-style villa. Prior to its design, the Gothic Revival style had been primarily used for churches by architects such as Ithiel Town, Benjamin Latrobe, and Josiah Brady. Latrobe's 1799 Sedgeley, a residence for Philadelphia merchant William Crammond, has been cited as an earlier Gothic Revival example. Latrobe employed Gothic forms such as pointed arch windows with hood moldings, but the traditional hipped roof with dormers and the symmetry of both plan and elevations linked the house more strongly to classicism, resulting in a hybrid design.

After Town & Davis's partnership ended amicably in 1835, Davis continued to develop his designs for Gothic Revival residences over the next thirty years. During the 1830s and 1840s, Davis favored the English Collegiate Gothic, a facet of the Gothic Revival style that was influenced by the buildings of Oxford and Cambridge. He also used the terms Pointed Gothic and Tudor Gothic interchangeably. Davis had read Thomas Rickman's *An Attempt to Discriminate the Styles of Architecture in England from the Conquest to the Reformation* (1817), which was the first text to take an historical approach to the Gothic and divide it into stylistic periods: Norman, Early English, Decorated, and Perpendicular. Among other English sources, Davis relied on details from the archaeological recordings of Augustus Pugin's *Specimens of Gothic Architecture; selected from various Ancient Edifices in England* (1821–23) and

3.18. Glen Ellen for Robert Gilmor, Towson, Maryland, 1832–33. Perspective, elevation, and plan. Watercolor, ink, and graphite on paper, 21 3/4 x 15 5/8 in. The Metropolitan Museum of Art, Harris Brisbane Dick Fund, 1924 (24.66.17).

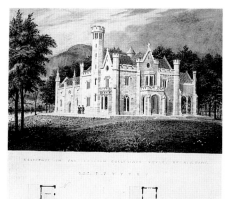

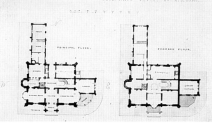

3.19. Villa for Robert Donaldson, Fishkill Landing, New York, 1834 (project). Perspective and two plans. Watercolor, ink, and graphite on paper, 12 15/16 x 10 in. The Metropolitan Museum of Art, Harris Brisbane Dick Fund, 1924 (24.66.865).

Examples of Gothic Architecture Selected from various Ancient Edifices in England (1831–38). He faithfully adopted many of the details illustrated in Pugin's works and the later works of his son A. W. N. Pugin, thus giving his buildings historical and intellectual validity.

Davis's first major design in the English Collegiate style was for Robert Donaldson in 1834 (fig. 3.19; colorplate 43). Although never built, it appeared as an illustration in Davis's *Rural Residences* in 1838. The villa design for Donaldson provided Davis with the opportunity to explore and develop the new Gothic style at a critical juncture in his career.

The design for Donaldson's villa had many outward similarities to the earlier Glen Ellen, but it was a more sophisticated design. Both houses included features such as a four-story octagonal tower, small corner towers, pointed arch windows with smaller squared windows above, and battlements. However, the two houses were quite different in plan. The Donaldson villa had an "L" floor plan with the service wing behind the main block, instead of the self-contained cruciform plan of Glen Ellen. This allowed the Donaldson design to flow more freely. On the front elevation, Davis lifted the house upward with a gabled bay that broke the roofline and projected the house outward with a single-story entry porch. A second-story oriel window also enriched the main facade. The side elevations were extremely varied; the library was topped by another gabled end roof and contained a plant cabinet. The opposite elevation was composed of a four-story tower, another gable with bay window below, and the service wing. The whole composition was placed on a terrace. Both a client and a friend, Donaldson continued to call on Davis to make designs for a series of Hudson River estates, including a gatehouse that also appeared in *Rural Residences*.[24] Together with client James Hillhouse, Donaldson supported the publication of *Rural Residences* and was an advocate for Davis's ideas throughout his career. He wrote to Davis in 1863:

> My recollection of the *initial* steps (taken in 1834 or 1835 by late *Mr. Hillhouse & Ourselves*) sometimes recurs to me—of the rural Architecture & Villa embellishments which have gone on to the great *improvement of country life* notwithstanding the overdone gingerbread work & begabled houses which abound. *Downing stole your thunder*, for a while—but I always, on suitable occasions, claimed for you the *seminal* ideas which have been so fruitful.[25]

In 1838, Davis designed and built his first important Gothic villa, for General William Paulding. Descended from a prominent old Dutch family, Paulding had been a two-term mayor of New York, a brigadier general in the War of 1812, and a congressman. The Paulding family resided in Tarrytown, twenty miles outside New York City. Washington Irving's brother had married William Paulding's sister, and James Kirke Paulding, a brother, collaborated with Irving on *Salmagundi; or, the Whim-Whams and Opinions of Launcelot Langstaff & Others* (1807–08). Within a year of Washington Irving's renovations to his picturesque Sunnyside, William Paulding decided to construct a house on an adjacent riverfront parcel. It may have been through introductions by Irving that Paulding came to choose Davis as his architect. However, soon after the project began in 1838, the elder Paulding seems to have handed over the planning to his son, Philip.

The house was situated on an open promontory overlooking the Tappan Zee section of the Hudson River, and was appropriately named Knoll (fig. 3.20; colorplate 44). In the 1841 edition of *Landscape Gardening*, Downing illustrated Knoll and stated that "both externally and internally, the most minute attention has been paid to a careful correspondence with the best examples of the Tudor era."[26] The house exhibited all the refined detailing of this picturesque style, with pointed gable ends, parapet walls, and a roof decorated with crockets, pinnacles, and clustered chimney pots. The windows were varied in size and shape; some had pointed arches, some had squared tops with dripstones, and there was an oriel. The elaborate twelve-by-ten-foot stained-glass library window was a prominent feature of the rear elevation. Most windows contained panels of colored glass. Davis designed a veranda encircling two sides of the house; this was an important picturesque element that had not been included in his earlier Donaldson design. On the front facade, a gabled entrance projection with a porte cochere and a smaller square stair tower on the right end were the principal foci. The river elevation had a corresponding central gabled projection; the veranda ran through the first story and extended to each side of the gable. A small octagonal tower completed the left corner of the river facade (see fig. 4.4).

The cruciform plan Davis chose showed a striking resemblance to the plan of Glen Ellen. It had a similar progression of a three-part entry axis with a large drawing room running parallel on the left and a perpendicular hallway with flanking rooms and stairs on the right. However, Davis changed the plan of Knoll to incorporate voids under the east-west transept. When viewed together with the verandas, this interpenetration of space broke up the massing of the building and brought a sense of lightness to the design. Quaint dormer windows with bargeboard trim (which Downing called "gablets") helped bring further domestic qualities to the Gothic Revival style of the house.

There is a set of drawings in the Metropolitan Museum's collection that contains three elevations and plans marked "Paulding #1 & #2" in pencil. They reveal another possible version of the house, in a more cottage Gothic treatment.[27] The floor plans proposed were of particular interest since they displayed a radiating plan around a central round hall. This type of plan was developed further in Davis's 1842 design of Kenwood for Joel Rathbone (fig. 3.21; colorplate 45), and brought to its fullest elaboration in houses of the 1850s, such as the Litchfield villa. Permutations on the cruciform, radial, and "L" plans formed the basis of Davis's floor planning for his picturesque villas of the 1830s and 1840s.

When completed in 1842, Knoll was a radical departure from the homes heretofore built in the American landscape. It drew comment in contemporary literature and signaled the arrival of the picturesque residence in this country. The versatility of Knoll's Gothic Revival design was tested almost thirty years later when Davis returned to expand the house for the new owner, George Merritt.[28] Few architects have the opportunity to design the same house twice, and it was fortunate that Davis was chosen to expand this seminal building of his early career (fig. 3.22). On the front, a large four-story tower was added to the northeast corner, which provided a counterpoint to the existing gabled transept. A new dining room and service wing were also added on the north end, which were stepped down in two sections, following the downslope of the site. The existing entryway was glassed in and a new one-story porte cochere was added. On the riverfront the dining room wing incorporated an impressive three-story oriel window and was topped with a roof cupola. The addition flowed seamlessly into the existing house; the new facade, although asymmetrical, remained balanced. Lyndhurst, as it was renamed, proved the adaptability of the new picturesque concept of freedom in planning.

3.20. Knoll for William and Philip R. Paulding, Tarrytown, New York, 1838. South and east (front) elevations. Watercolor and ink on paper, 14¼ x 10⁵⁄₁₆ in. The Metropolitan Museum of Art, Harris Brisbane Dick Fund, 1924 (24.66.70).

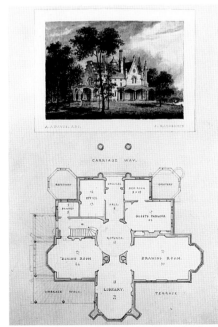

3.21. Kenwood for Joel Rathbone, south of Albany, New York, 1842. Perspective and plan. Watercolor, ink, and graphite on paper, 10⁵⁄₁₆ x 7¼ in. Drawings & Archives, Avery Architectural and Fine Arts Library, Columbia University (1955.001.00133).

3.22. Lyndhurst for George Merritt, Tarrytown, New York, 1865. West (rear) elevation and plan. Watercolor, ink, and graphite on paper, 18⅞ x 26⅝ in. The Metropolitan Museum of Art, Harris Brisbane Dick Fund, 1924 (24.66.14).

3.23. Millbrook for Henry Sheldon, Tarrytown, New York, 1838–40. Fig. 60 from Andrew Jackson Downing's *A Treatise on the Theory and Practice of Landscape Gardening,* 1841.

3.24. Detail of Gatehouse at Blithewood for Robert Donaldson, Annandale-on-Hudson, New York, 1836. Perspective. Lithograph, watercolored by George Harvey, 13½ x 9⅝ in. Drawings & Archives, Avery Architectural and Fine Arts Library, Columbia University (1940.001.00093R).

English Gothic villas and cottage villas were in great demand through the 1840s. Davis's major villa commissions included Joel Rathbone's Kenwood (1842) near Albany, New York, Henry Kent's villa (1846) on Gowanus Bay in Brooklyn, and Philip St. George Cocke's Belmead (1845) in Powhatan County, Virginia. Davis also designed a large group of "cottage villas." These were more modest houses, often built primarily of wood. In the same year that Knoll was built, Davis provided Henry Sheldon with a cottage design for a site to the north of Knoll (fig. 3.23). The house was a somewhat larger version of the gate lodge design Davis made for Robert Donaldson at Blithewood (fig. 3.24; colorplate 46). The prominent vergeboard-trimmed central gable with a finial at its apex became characteristic of Gothic cottage architecture in America. The design for Sheldon included features symbolic of domestic comfort, such as verandas overlooking the river and clustered chimney pots topping the steep roof. In addition to the residence, Davis designed a greenhouse and decoratively renovated a grist mill which gave the property its name, Millbrook (fig. 3.26).

Davis's cottage villas were straightforward structures, usually symmetrical in plan but irregular in outline. Their picturesque character was derived from the bold pitch of the gabled roofs bordered with vergeboards, the overhanging eaves, and the light verandas. Many of these designs were carried out in board-and-batten wood siding. Cottage designs were simple enough to be readily copied by local carpenter/builders and were soon seen throughout the United States. This type of vernacular cottage architecture is often called Carpenter Gothic.

While cottage villas lent themselves to economical construction in wood, Downing always promoted the superiority of those made of masonry construction. Davis designed many fine examples in both materials. Henry Delamater's house (1844) in Rhinebeck, New York, was of wooden board-and-batten construction, while a cottage for William J. Rotch (1845) in New Bedford, Massachusetts, was made of wood painted to look like stone (fig. 3.25; colorplate 47). The house for S. E. Lyon (1842) in White Plains, New York, was a handsome stone example.

The cottage villa form was further simplified with the evolution of the bracketed cottage. A typical bracketed cottage was a simple board-and-batten house with bracketed eaves and a porch. This style could be gracefully applied to a larger villa, and was derived from more elaborate Swiss designs. With broad gabled eaves, it was well adapted for simple farmhouses and homes for the working man. Downing advocated the bracketed mode of cottage building, particularly in his last two books, *Cottage Residences* (1842) and *The Architecture of Country Houses* (1850). Many of the bracketed cottages in these publications were collaborative designs by Davis and Downing.[29] Davis had included a design for a bracketed farmhouse in his *Rural Residences* (fig. 3.27).

Davis continued to design in the Gothic Revival style into the 1850s, but during this decade the Castellated Gothic was favored over the Pointed or Tudor Gothic. While the earlier style had English roots, the fortified architecture of the castellated style was strongly influenced by medieval Italian castles. English author John Claudius Loudon was referring to the castellated style and not the more Renaissance-inspired Italianate when he wrote:

> The Beau Ideal of the Italian Style of Villa Architecture, it is justly observed by Meason, it to be found in the landscapes of the great Italian painters, and more especially in the backgrounds of their pictures.[30]

Early in his career, Davis rendered this type of medieval castle in the background of his design for a "Villa in the Oriental Style" in *Rural Residences*. During the 1850s, these castle designs were brought into the foreground as viable houses for his clients.

Andrew J. Downing was less enthusiastic about the castellated mode of building because it suggested baronial castles that were too ambitious and expensive for a republic. It was a style that was difficult to portray on a small scale because the medieval fortified characteristics were conveyed through large massive parts. Com-

3.25. House for William J. Rotch, New Bedford, Massachusetts, 1845. Front elevation. Watercolor, ink, and graphite on paper, 16⅝₆ x 25¼ in. The Metropolitan Museum of Art, Harris Brisbane Dick Fund, 1924 (24.66.20).

3.26. Old mill remodeled as a billiard room at Millbrook for Henry Sheldon, Tarrytown, New York, ca. 1840. Elevation. Watercolor, ink, and graphite on paper, 14⅜ x 10 in. The Metropolitan Museum of Art, Harris Brisbane Dick Fund, 1924 (24.66.115).

3.27. "Farmer's Cottage" from *Rural Residences,* 1836, published 1838. Front elevation and two plans. Lithograph, with watercolor, ink, and graphite, 17 x 12 in. The Metropolitan Museum of Art, Harris Brisbane Dick Fund, 1924 (24.66.1416 [6], vol. XVII, leaf 5).

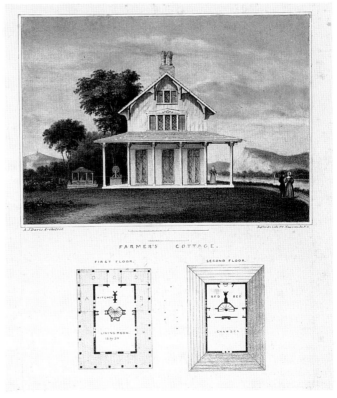

3.28. Ericstan for John J. Herrick, Tarrytown, New York, 1855–59. Rear elevation. Watercolor, ink, and graphite on paper, 25 ⁵/₁₆ x 30 in. The Metropolitan Museum of Art, Harris Brisbane Dick Fund, 1924 (24.66.10).

pared to the English Tudor style, the castellated villa had little ornament beyond the battlements and heavy, rough-hewn stone work. The design depended on the relationship of various towers in plan and in height to provide interest. Davis's alternative designs for the Litchfield villa demonstrated a similar spatial relationship between his designs in Italianate and castellated styles. However, the castellated house was usually more ponderous, requiring careful siting for the design to be successful. It was best sited in wild and romantic scenery, such as the rocky cliffs portrayed in the Italian paintings.

Davis created his most elaborate castellated design for John Herrick in 1855. A wealthy flour merchant, Herrick chose a site high above the Hudson River in Tarrytown, New York. The design was dominated by a massive round tower that rose three stories on the west, overlooking the river. A two-story rectangular block extended eastward from the tower and terminated in a square tower. The service wing continued on the east end but was stepped back with a lower roofline. A veranda ran from the square tower westward, encircling the parlor and terminating at a smaller round tower on the rear elevation (fig. 3.28; colorplate 49). The use of interlinking facades described in the design for Litchfield's villa was characteristic of many of Davis's later works.

The first plans for Herrick's "castlette" were fairly modest and showed only a round parlor, a hall, a library, a dining room, and a kitchen on the main floor. As later designs progressed, more rooms were added along an east-west hall perpendicular to the entrance hall, and the service wing was also expanded. The final plan was

3.29. Ericstan for John J. Herrick, Tarrytown, New York, 1855–59. Rear elevation and plan. Watercolor and ink on paper, 13 ³/₈ x 8 ³/₈ in. Drawings & Archives, Avery Architectural and Fine Arts Library, Columbia University (1955.001.00125).

3.30. Interior of the parlor at Ericstan, ca. 1933. Drawings & Archives, Avery Architectural and Fine Arts Library, Columbia University (Natalie Morris Collection).

basically cruciform, but the balance of the design had shifted from Davis's previous house types. The emphasis was on the geometry of the circular tower (fig. 3.29).[31]

The round parlor in the tower was one of Davis's most elaborate domestic interiors. The intricate vaulting of the ceiling sprang from a central cluster of delicate Gothic columns and radiated to a series of single columns along the circular wall of the room. Elaborate bosses decorated the junctions of the ribs, and the capitals of the columns were gilded. This room provided a fitting centerpiece for the imposing house (fig. 3.30).

Davis also provided Herrick with designs for a round coach house as well as furniture for the mansion. Construction took four years, and was completed in 1859 at a cost of $60,000. The Herrick family occupied Ericstan for only a few years. Financial setbacks, together with the enormous costs of construction, forced Herrick to sell the property to Dr. Edward Maynard in 1865 for $150,000.

Concurrent with the building of Ericstan, Davis was designing other castellated villas. Two notable examples were the residence for Augustus C. Richards (1855–58) in Fort Washington, New York, and Castlewood (1857–59) for Joseph Howard in Llewellyn Park, New Jersey. The Richards villa had a conservative floor plan with all the major rooms accessible from the entry hall. The front elevation displayed a round tower next to a square tower containing the entry porch. In somewhat similar fashion, a pair of earlier Gothic villas, Whitby (1852–55) for William Chapman in Rye, and Ingleside (1853–54) for Edwin B. Strange in Dobbs Ferry, had high towers nestled next to the front projection. These houses still employed Tudor Gothic forms, but the simplified detailing and battlements created a heavier, more fortified appearance. Castlewood related more closely to Ericstan since it had a round central tower that dominated the design (fig. 3.31; colorplate 48).

3.31. Castlewood for Joseph Howard, Llewellyn Park, West Orange, New Jersey, 1857–59. Rear elevation. Watercolor, ink, and graphite on paper, 8 ½ x 14 in. Drawings & Archives, Avery Architectural and Fine Arts Library, Columbia University (1955.001.00088).

This fascination with circular forms was repeated in various projects designed for Llewellyn Park, a five-hundred-acre planned romantic suburb in West Orange, New Jersey. The park was the vision of Llewellyn Haskell, a pharmaceutical entrepreneur from New York City who espoused progressive philosophies about the interrelationship of man, nature, and community.[32] Davis was in sympathy with these ideas, and worked with Haskell and Eugene Baumann, a landscape gardener, in designing and laying out the community. Davis's designs included several residences and follies in the park, as well as houses for both Haskell and himself on the cliffs above it (fig. 3.32). A contemporary account credited Davis as the creative force behind Llewellyn Park.

> A ramble through the grounds is a Poet's dream . . . We thank Mr. Davis—the Architect—the Michael Angelo of his time, for what he has done for us. No other man could have combined nature and art, and have produced such a wilderness of loveliness.[33]

Haskell's home, Eyrie, was situated on Eagle Rock, with magnificent panoramic views encompassing more than a hundred miles (fig. 3.33). It was an exotic, asymmetrical design consisting of two round towers connected by a square central block. The larger tower, containing the parlor, was constructed of local rock, while the smaller library tower was built of vertical wood siding. This siding was milled to preserve the bark and any fragile lichen or moss, and a porch off the parlor was constructed with rough tree trunk supports. The conical roofs of the towers were covered with decorative slate and terminated in umbrella-like finials. Davis's gate lodge for the park echoed the design of Eyrie with its pointed conical roof, rough-cut stone, and round design. Both buildings had an organic character closely in tune with their setting and were free from references to historical styles.

Davis built his summer home, Wildmont, along the same mountain ridge (fig. 3.34; colorplate 50). The house was built in stages; originally designed as a cottage in 1856, it became a villa with later additions. The final oval floor plan (1878) was unique among Davis's designs. The house was a central square block with semicircular ends, each containing a bay window. On the rear elevation, the principal focus was a Gothic gable adjacent to a stair tower with a conical roof. The front elevation contained another gable with a bay window. The entrance was off center to the left on this facade. The building had a rock foundation but was constructed of wooden vertical boarding and stuccoed brick. Even though the house incorporated Gothic

3.32. E. W. Nichols, View of Llewellyn Park, showing Wildmont, Eyrie, and gate lodge, West Orange, New Jersey. Engraving, 1859, with additional watercolor and ink drawings, 5 7/8 x 9 15/16 in. Drawings & Archives, Avery Architectural and Fine Arts Library, Columbia University (1940.001.00406).

gables and pinnacles, it did not have the flavor of Davis's earlier Tudor designs. The stair turret with conical roof suggested the influence of the Norman style.[34]

The personality of his client influenced Davis's design process. He believed that the home was the mirror of a man's soul and the center of his family. In an 1845 letter, Davis wrote one client:

> It is impossible for me to tell what expression to give the exterior that will answer your own beau ideal unless I am better acquainted with your *temper*! That is, whether you read Shakespeare more than Thomson; Moore more than Collins; or Homer at all, either in the Iliad or Odyessy [sic]; or whether you read the great book of Nature . . .[35]

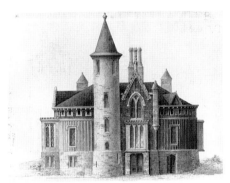

Wildmont reflected much of Davis's own philosophy. The Gothic style had always been his beau ideal; it symbolized the home of an artistic gentleman. Rounded floor plans had always fascinated him, and he had experimented with a number of small designs titled "Artist's Villa" which showed variations of circular plans.[36] Perched on a cliff overlooking Newark Bay, his home was situated above a romantic park that sought to embody the transcendental relationship of man and nature (fig. 3.35; colorplate 51).

Davis's career led the way for a new American architecture. From 1830 to 1870, he was responsible for more Gothic residences than any other American architect, most of whom had only one or two such designs to their credit.[37] Davis was the most successful synthesizer of the Picturesque, using the styles of the Gothic and Italianate with great talent. This new mode of building embodied the ideology of the country house with its inspiration taken from nature. Davis took the first steps to free the villa from its cubic restraints and develop organic buildings that responded to their settings. Country houses allowed for greater freedom to experiment than city dwellings, which were confined by lot size, formality, and social strictures. In the later years of the century, architects such as Henry Hobson Richardson and Frank Lloyd Wright created organic designs that were less dependent on historical ornament and had greater spatial daring but were still influenced by the Picturesque. In contrast, the Beaux Arts school of the late nineteenth century continued to promulgate designs from historical models, but with a renewed formality that rejected integration with nature. Davis's career provided an important link between the classicism of eighteenth-century rationalism and the open planning of late-nineteenth-century modernism.

"Being Sensible of the Value of Professional Services": Alexander Jackson Davis's Designs for the Interiors of Lyndhurst and Grace Hill

AMELIA PECK

In the spring of 1838, William Paulding (1770–1854), a former mayor of New York City, and his son Philip (?–1864) contracted with Alexander Jackson Davis to provide them with drawings and specifications for a country villa to be built in Tarrytown, New York. The house, which they named Knoll, is known today as Lyndhurst (fig. 4.1; colorplate 44). Originally, they probably intended to hire the architect only to deliver a basic set of drawings, paying him $100. However, contrary to their initial plans, and much to the house's benefit, Philip Paulding continued to work with Davis over the course of the next nine years. Davis supervised much of the ornate exterior detailing of the Gothic Revival villa, as well as the interior decoration. In addition, at Philip Paulding's request, Davis made fifty designs for furniture for the house, many of which were executed, and some of which still survive at Lyndhurst today. Furthermore, when Knoll was sold in 1864,[1] George Merritt (1807–1873), the house's new owner, asked Davis to design a large addition. As with Philip Paulding, Davis worked closely with Merritt on both the exterior and interior design of the new section of the house, and designed more furniture.

Davis's supervision of almost every aspect of the design of Knoll/Lyndhurst (and Grace Hill, which will be discussed later in this essay) was very much the exception to the usual role of an architect in nineteenth-century America. Especially in 1838, when Knoll was begun, but even as late as 1864, when it was expanded, architects were rarely responsible for the interior and furniture designs of the houses they built. In fact, most pre-Civil War American houses were not architect-designed at all. In the early decades of the nineteenth century, the architectural profession was practically nonexistent in America.[2] The first professional organization for architects, the American Institute of Architects, of which Davis was a founding trustee, was not formed until 1857, and the first American architecture school, at MIT, did not come into being until 1865. Apparently, anyone who put up a building could call himself an architect. Andrew Jackson Downing (1815–1852), the landscape designer and architectural theorist, who was Davis's close friend, in his additional notes to the first American edition of George Wightwick's *Hints To Young Architects* (1847), commented upon this troublesome phenomenon.

> We ought, perhaps, in strict justice to remark, *en passant*, that every one who calls himself an *architect* in our cities, is by no means entitled to that appellation. Some are mere builders of "three story bricks," and others have assumed the title and commenced business with only a knowledge of the rudiments of their art.[3]

Perhaps even more disturbing to the budding profession were the many prospective country house owners who tried to design their houses themselves,

4.1. Knoll for William and Philip R. Paulding, Tarrytown, New York, 1838. South and east (front) elevations. Watercolor and ink on paper, 14¼ x 10³⁄₁₆ in. The Metropolitan Museum of Art, Harris Brisbane Dick Fund, 1924 (24.66.70).

without benefit of any professional help. As late as 1863, architect Henry Hudson Holly (1834–1892) inveighed against this practice to the house-building public.

> Having selected the site and chosen the material, the next step is to procure a design best suited to the wants and conveniences of your family. . . . Can you furnish this design yourself? Decidedly not unless you have spent years in study and practice. Or, possessing good ideas yourself, can a carpenter or a mason carry them into a successful realization? We think not, for such men, however excellent their workmanship may be, cannot be supposed to sympathize with your more refined notions of domestic elegance and comfort. . . .
>
> The planning of a country house is something so peculiar and intricate, and demands careful study of so many outlying considerations, that none but an architect can do it justice.[4]

If architects were not hired as a rule to build country houses (or city houses, for that matter) as late as the 1860s, who oversaw the design of the interiors? There was no interior decoration profession as we know it today. Nevertheless, there were a number of different options a person could pursue when setting out to decorate his or her house. For families of limited means, who built what Downing would have classified as country cottages rather than country villas, pattern books were probably the main source of decorating advice. Before the 1850 publication of Downing's *The Architecture of Country Houses*, which included extremely detailed chapters on both interiors and furniture, the most widely read books were John Claudius Loudon's *Encyclopaedia of Cottage, Farm, and Villa Architecture and Furniture* (London: Longman, Brown, Green and Longmans, 1833; with supplement, 1842), a book from which Downing borrowed liberally, and Thomas Webster and Mrs. William Parkes's *Encyclopedia of Domestic Economy* (first American edition, New York: Harper & Brothers, 1845). An American source book, Catharine Beecher's *Treatise on Domestic Economy* (1841), was the first book to be written by an American woman that, at least in part, addressed practical architectural issues. All of these books attempted to educate the reader about different styles of architectural and interior design, discussing which furniture, fabrics, and colors were appropriate to which rooms in the house and which household objects would correctly communicate the personality and moral stance of the owner.

Decorating was also a topic that became popular in the American press toward the mid-century. Godey's *Lady's Book* began to publish curtain designs as early as 1839, and even started a buying service in 1852 that assisted families living outside urban centers in purchasing furniture, draperies, wallpapers, and so on by mail order from the New York and Philadelphia merchants extolled in the magazine's pages.[5]

Another important source for people who didn't use architects (as well as for those who did) were the newly created department stores. The first great dry goods store, A. T. Stewart's "marble palace," opened its doors in 1846. Located on Broadway between Reade and Chambers streets in New York City, Stewart's offered such items as rugs and carpeting, both furnishing and dress fabrics, laces, and linens. Documentation exists suggesting that for projects that entailed decorating entire houses outside the New York area, the store had a special decorating service as well. If the homeowner visited Stewart's store and chose a large quantity of textiles and carpeting for his home, Mr. Stewart would oversee—perhaps for a percentage of the overall cost of the objects—the construction and upholstery of suites of furniture by cabinetmakers such as John Henry Belter, the sewing of the stylish draperies made from the fabrics the homeowner had selected, and the fabrication of the carpeting.[6]

The most traditional approach to house decoration for people wealthy enough to be building villas on the scale of Lyndhurst and Grace Hill was to hire a series of contractors, often under the supervision of an upholsterer, to complete the interiors. The upholsterer was certainly the ultimate authority on house furnishing during the eighteenth century and may have continued as a power in England far into the nineteenth century. In America, the upholsterer's role as decorator seems to have been supplanted by large cabinetmaking firms around the middle decades of the century. Downing does discuss interior decorators in *The Architecture of Country Houses* (1850), saying

> . . . in villas of considerable importance, *interior decorators*, who devote themselves to this branch of the profession, are called in to complete the whole, as the builder leaves it. Some of these, like Mr. George Platt, of New York (who is at present the most popular interior decorator in the country), possess talent enough to take an apartment or a suite of apartments, design and execute the decorations, and colour, and furnish them throughout in any style.[7]

George Platt seems to be an interesting hybrid; he was a designer and manufacturer of high-style furniture at the time Downing wrote about him (fig. 4.2), yet he started out as a decorative painter, a craftsperson who was often referred to in both pattern books and business directories as a "decorator" at the time. In 1868, he was indeed working in the capacity of what we in the twentieth century would consider an interior decorator, designing and furnishing the grand Renaissance Revival dining room of LeGrand Lockwood's mansion in Norwalk, Connecticut. Gustave Herter, another important New York furniture maker, is similarly associated with the interior decoration of the Morse-Libby Mansion (1858–62) in Portland, Maine. But before 1865, such professionals were truly the exceptions to the rule.

4.2. ". . . furniture from the warehouse of [George] Platt, 60 Broadway, New York," fig. 242 from Andrew Jackson Downing's *The Architecture of Country Houses*, 1850.

In America, pattern books and articles in the press encouraged the public to include their architect in the design of the interiors of their houses and even, perhaps, in the design of the furniture for those houses. Downing stated that

> . . . it will readily be seen that the province of the architect does not cease with designing the general plan and exterior of any building, but that he should carry out the same spirit or style in all parts of the edifice. A building in which this is done throughout, has a great advantage over one where the style is only manifested on the outside; that advantage, in short, which everything in art or nature has, where we find unity and harmony persuading every portion of the entire work, and where we see that there is clearly no surface delusion but an intelligent unity reigning over the whole.[8]

In their 1856 pattern book, *Village and Farm Cottages*, Cleaveland and Backus put forth a somewhat different argument supporting the inclusion of the architect in the decisions made about the interiors of the house.

> The immediate duties of the architect are performed, when he has completed the house and its apartments. As however, he is often required to adapt his work to particular articles of predestined furniture, he may, perhaps, be allowed to suggest that the additions subsequently made in the way of decoration and furnishing, ought in their character and expression, to bear some correspondence to his rooms. There are many, and sometimes glaring violations of taste and propriety in this respect. After the architect comes the painter, paperer, upholsterer, and cabinetmaker, and these later often mar, if they do not spoil the best designs of the former.[9]

Given that there was a concerted effort in books and in the press during the period to encourage home builders to employ architects to design both the exteriors and interiors of their houses, and assuming that, in some cases, a family did decide to use an architect on all facets of its proposed home, an interesting question arises concerning which member of the family was in charge of directing the work. From most entries in Davis's Journal, it seems that he was initially engaged to design a house by the man of the family. In commissions where the relationship continued past the completion of the basic set of drawings, Davis seems to have corresponded and met primarily with the man. (There is one exceptional case worth noting, however. Davis maintained a working relationship with two women clients, Mrs. Edward Livingston and her daughter, Coralie Livingston Barton of Montgomery Place, over a period of thirty years.) But when it came to designing the interiors of the house, it seems that the man, although he was certainly in charge of the family's finances, did not always have the final say. Certain rooms, such as the drawing room (or "best parlor"), were traditionally considered the woman's domain, and it often fell to her to supervise their decoration. When architect Calvert Vaux (1824–1895) wrote about the appearance and use of a parlor in 1857, it was clear that he expected the woman of the house to be most concerned with that room.

> A best parlor ought to express, in its proportions, colors, and arrangement of furniture, an agreeable, hearty social welcome. The lady who studied her room when her guests had departed, after a lengthened and agreeable visit, so as to learn how the furniture had accommodated itself, as it were, to suit the social convenience of her friends, and who then modified her previous ideas accordingly, had the true artistic eye for beauty of arrangement, and certainly deserved to have a pleasant circle of acquaintance. There are but few strictly architectural features in a drawing-room that call for illustration. Good proportions can be supplied; but the lady of the house is the most important architect here.[10]

If, indeed, the lady of the house was the arbiter of fashion in the parlor, it meant that she was charged with the decoration of what was generally the grandest room in the house. Also, the furniture found in a parlor, usually a suite in the Rococo Revival style, was likely to be the most expensive purchased for the new house.

In some cases, it was suggested that the woman should be consulted about the actual planning of the entire house. In one of a series of articles entitled "The Architects and Architecture of New York," published in 1843 in the newsweekly *Brother Jonathan*, it was stated that the woman of the house's ideas on planning were as important as the architect's. This is hardly surprising, since the author of the unsigned series may quite possibly have been Mrs. Ann Stephens (1813–1886), wife of Edward Stephens, one of the publishers of *Brother Jonathan*. Ann Stephens was among the best-known women writers and editors of her day.[11] Davis recorded that he took her to see the progress being made on Knoll on July 4, 1843, and a very complimentary description of Knoll (called Paulding Manor in the article) appeared in the July 15, 1843, issue. In 1854, Mrs. Stephens used Davis's Waddell villa (1844) (fig. 4.3; colorplate 52) as the setting for her novel *Fashion and Famine* and mentions Davis as the architect of the house. On the subject of the woman's role in the design of the house, Mrs. Stephens states:

> . . . When the plan is furnished and the elevations and sections all presented for inspection to the proprietor, there is much yet to be done. The mistress of the mansion is to be consulted, the tastes of all its destined occupants must be known and respect-

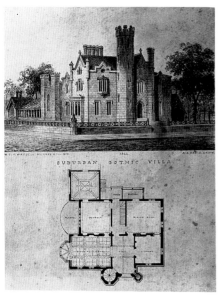

4.3. House for William C. H. Waddell, New York City, 1844. Perspective and plan. Watercolor and ink on paper, 13 ¼ x 9 ⅞ in. I. N. Phelps Stokes Collection, Miriam and Ira D. Wallach Division of Art, Prints and Photographs, The New York Public Library, Astor, Lenox and Tilden Foundations.

ed—there must be a room here and a pantry there—this dressing [sic] must be made larger—this bedroom must look out in this direction and the drawing room in that. In short, neither the architect nor the proprietor can tell what he wants till the lady, and perhaps her daughters or nieces have seen the plans.[12]

Mrs. Stephens was advocating a policy that surely made sense, as radical as it may have been considered in the early 1840s. In the case of Knoll/Lyndhurst and Grace Hill, Philip Paulding was a bachelor when Knoll was built, and Mrs. Merritt remains a shadowy figure in the history of Lyndhurst. However, as will be discussed later, there is clear evidence that Mrs. Litchfield was involved with the planning of the interiors at Grace Hill.

Davis's first meeting with William Paulding took place in May 1838, when he visited the rolling hillside along the Hudson River in Tarrytown upon which Paulding wished to build.[13] He returned to Tarrytown for the period between July 12 and July 16, 1838, and met with both William and his son Philip Paulding. During the days between July 16 and August 2, his next recorded visit, Davis worked on the drawings for a "Country Mansion in Pointed Style, near Tarrytown for Wm. Paulding, and son Philip R. Paulding." His charge for "Visiting the grounds and making a portfolio of plans sections, elevations, sections[sic]. &c." was $100.[14]

Davis's specifications for Knoll still exist in the collection of the New York Public Library. It is assumed that they were written to accompany the set of drawings made for the Pauldings in 1838. However, they have only Philip Paulding's name as client on them, and he, not his father, signed off on the title page. The Paulding family owned an older house in Tarrytown, where William Paulding eventually resettled, leaving Philip to work with Davis on his own after 1839. According to Davis's entries in his diaries, William Paulding continued to pay the bills for Davis's services, although Philip alone eventually occupied the house.

On the front page of the specifications, Davis listed the drawings that were included in the portfolio as follows:

1. Foundation and Cellars PLAN
2. First Floor. PLAN
3. Second floor. PLAN
4. Attic floor. PLAN
5. Section, North to South.
6. 2 Sections East to West.
7. View of East Front
8. Elevation of West (river) front
9. Elev. South end.
10. Elev. North end.
11. Elev. & both sides front door.

From this list, and lists of initial sets of drawings for other houses in Davis's Day Books and Journal, it seems that this rather basic set was all Davis supplied to his clients at the first stage of a project, for the initial fee. However, he did refer to "working drawings" and drawings "drawn on large scale" within the body of the specifications. On pages 5 and 6 of the specifications, Davis described his ideas for the interior detailing of the principal first-floor rooms. Drawing 2, the first-floor plan; drawing 5, the north-to-south section; and drawing 6, which seems to have encompassed two east-to-west sections, were referred to. Davis often included small-scale detailing indicating the interior architecture in his sections. The plan may have had

RESIDENCE OF PHILIP R PAULDING. ESQ. NEAR IRVING LANDING, HUD. RIV.

FIRST FLOOR.   SECOND FLOOR.

4.4. Knoll for William and Philip R. Paulding, Tarrytown, New York, 1838. Probably drawn 1862. West (rear) facade and two plans. Watercolor, ink, and graphite on paper, 14⅜ x 10¼ in. The Metropolitan Museum of Art, Harris Brisbane Dick Fund, 1924 (24.66.795).

indications of ceiling treatments; Davis also commonly drew reflected ceiling designs on his plans. (See Lyndhurst floor plan, fig. 4.25; colorplate 57.)

Knoll had a relatively simple floor plan (fig. 4.4). The entrance hall was slightly off center, as was the hallway that traversed the north-south axis. The drawing room, which covered the full width of the building on the south, was to the left as one entered. It was oriented to the south, with the central focus of the room the eighteen-foot-wide bay window. The saloon (or reception room) was directly ahead of the entrance hall, with western exposures to the river view. The dining room was to the right of the saloon and across the hall from the office. Instead of being located in the center of the house, the stairs to the second floor were innovatively placed at the building's north end, enclosed in a tower with a stepped cornice.

The first room Davis discussed in the specifications was the entrance hall.

Entrance Hall to be ribbed in stucco on proper furring, as shewn by plan and sections Nos. 2, 5, 6, the ribs to start from the heads of 3 inch octagon wood columns, 11 ft. high and be arched crosswise (but not lengthwise) upon a ceiling formed thus: [two small sketches, one of arch, one of side wall elevation] of 2 inclined planes rising one foot from the side wall. The manner will be further explained by architect.

There was little further information written by Davis regarding his conception of the appearance of an entrance hall in 1838. Drawing 11 of the list on the first page was an elevation of the front door, and "both sides" may refer to drawings made of both the exterior and interior features of the door. In more general terms in the same document, he did specify that the floors of all the principal rooms on the first floor be made of clear white pine planks, not more than five inches wide, tongue and grooved and blind nailed. It is also quite possible that the columns and other wooden architecture elements in the entrance hall were painted and grained (or perhaps even marbleized, as was a common treatment for entrance halls), since on page 15 he specified "The whole of the joiner's work internally, except for floors, shelves, and treads, to be primed, and painted three times, with best Eng. white lead in oil, and left for fancy imitation oak, or other wood."

The next room described in the specifications was the drawing room.

> Drawing room to be ribbed like hall, and have columns, each composed of three shafts of wood, 2 inches diameter, forming a "clustered column," [small sketch of horizontal section of clustered column] 11 ft. high; the rib springing from the capital of the column, 5 inches diameter: [sketch of section of rib] is to curve over, as shewn by red lines on plans, Nos. 2-5-6, enclosing a square on the flat ceiling, and spandrels at the four corners, flat and solid on furring, having only the under part, wedge, & bracket like, as in the rib—dropped down; thus in section: [sketch of section of spandrel] In the corners, the ribs to *die* on corbels, The corbels will be *masks of Shakespeare, Milton,* &c. furnished by Proprietor.

In addition to the corbels in the form of masks of famous men (which were probably never placed in this room), on the back of page 11, written in pencil, Davis has noted, "Material furnished by Proprietor:/ Cut stone/ Mantels/ Corbels/ Grates and iron railing." In other words, at this point in the process, Davis has left the purchase of some of the items that most affected the final appearance of the room to the discretion of the owner.

The saloon was next on Davis's list.

> Saloon ribbed in same manner, but with the ribs lying against the vertical wall, forming an *arch with soffit,* finishing with corbels, instead of columns. *Corbels furnished* by owner.

A saloon is not a room found in the houses of today. (The term "saloon" seems to have lost favor by 1864, because when Davis redid the plans of Lyndhurst to show the new addition, he changed the name of this room to "reception room.") According to Loudon, a saloon was "generally a sort of vestibule to the living-rooms"[15] which was often used as a music room. At Knoll, it falls between the drawing room and the dining room and would have been where a guest was led after leaving the entrance hall. There is mention on page 8 of the specifications of a drawing "in large scale" of the highly carved sliding doors between the entrance hall and the saloon.

The dining room is the only room in the house for which a highly finished perspective drawing remains. This drawing is not specifically mentioned in any of Davis's diaries, but it seems likely that it was made after the house was well under way, since the ornamental ceiling illustrated in the drawing is quite close to its present form (fig. 4.5; colorplate 53). Interior perspectives by Davis are quite rare; however, one of Davis's best-known works is a highly finished drawing of a room. Davis made a design for imaginary classical double parlors in about 1830, furnishing the parlors with tables and chairs obviously derived from the designs of Thomas Hope (fig. 4.6; colorplate 54). The Lyndhurst drawing is unfortunately unfurnished.

According to Davis's specifications, the dining room was originally to have had a flat ceiling with a bracketed or battlemented cornice.

> Dining room to have brackets instead of stucco cornice, formed thus: [sketch of side elevation of bracket 9″ high by 8″ across] 4 inches thick and placed regularly about 18

4.5. Dining room at Knoll, ca. 1840. Perspective. Watercolor, ink, and graphite on paper, 13½ x 20⅛ in. The Metropolitan Museum of Art, Harris Brisbane Dick Fund, 1924 (24.66.867).

4.6. Study for double parlors in the classical style, ca. 1830. Perspective. Watercolor and ink on paper, 13¼ x 18¼ in. Drawings Collection, The New-York Historical Society, Gift of Daniel Parish, Jr., 1908 (1908.28).

4.7. Study for the dining room mantelpiece at Knoll, 1839. Elevation. Ink, wash, and graphite on paper, 26 x 20¼ in. The Metropolitan Museum of Art, Harris Brisbane Dick Fund, 1924 (24.66.56).

in. from centers, apart: to be cast in stucco. [Sketch of front elevation of proposed bracketed cornice]

Or, instead of above brackets, a battlemented cornice thus: [sketch of section and elevation of battlemented cornice] may be substituted: the bead under to continue, but the cornice to have portions omitted as above.

The bay window to dining room to be arched with brick, with splayed jambs, and finish like the jambs and arch of entrance, (door & side lights.) The ceiling of the bay: flat with a battlemented cornice as above, in angle.

[in pencil below:] (Altered to groining)

The only other principal room on the first floor was the office, which Davis dismissed with the simple sentence that referred back to the finish of the dining room: "Office to be finished as last described."

The most spectacular room in the house was the soaring second-story library. For unknown reasons, this room was not specified for at all. On page 6 Davis notes: "Second Story to be lathed and plastered same as first floor, but without ribs or cornices, of any kind, except Library, [next part in pencil] the finishing of which is to be left out of contract." It is possible that Davis intended to contract for this part of the house separately; if there was a second contract or a set of specifications for the library, they have not survived.

The Pauldings set to work with the basic information provided by Davis's drawings and specifications, hiring James N. Wells and James W. Smith to be the project carpenters. However, less than a year later, on June 27, 1839, William Paulding sent Davis a somewhat desperate note stating, "Philip and myself wish to see you immediately as we cannot proceed in erecting our house, without previously consulting you."[16] This cry for help must have pleased Davis; in his Journal he describes what he found at Knoll after he visited the site July 1 through 3. "The work had progressed, without Mr. P's being sensible of the value of professional services. The consequence was, that the mullions of the windows were made too small by nearly one half; the drip stones and copings incorrect and vulgar." From this point on, Davis was involved with all aspects of the building; however, most of the entries in his diaries regarded aspects of his work for the interior of the house.

Davis began work by enriching the windows, which were originally to be, for the most part, plain casement windows. This new detailing enhanced the appearance of both the exteriors and interiors of the rooms. On page 13 of the specifications Davis did mention that he had planned tracery for the heads of some of the windows. Philip Paulding wrote to him on September 18, 1839, saying that he would like to visit Davis's rooms in order to "look at some of your books, select some tracery for the windows and get you to make a drawing of it. I think it will be a great addition to the appearance of the house to add some more details to the windows."[17] Davis noted in his Day Book that on December 10 he was paid $25 for "Working details for windows./ Paulding 2 set./ (doors inside and out.)/" and an additional $25 for drawings of "Chimney Pieces 3 kinds." In his Journal he expanded on this information under the same date heading. Here he said, "It was resolved to add tracery to the window heads, and arch the ceiling."[18] He also noted that the working drawings for tracery were for the drawing room and saloon windows only. On December 21 he recorded a study for the ceiling of the drawing room, presumably now arched, as well as other drawings for "ribs and stucco" and for "Stairs. Newel, verge &c."

On February 25, 1840, Davis noted, "Went with P. R. Paulding to Chimney Piece Manufacturers." One of these was likely to have been Underhill & Ferris (372 Greenwich Street, New York City), who we know eventually manufactured the mantels from Davis's designs (fig. 4.7). They were ready for inspection by November 16, 1841, when Philip Paulding sent the following humorous note to Davis: "You will much oblige me by calling at Underhill and Ferris as soon as possible (they were to be sent up this week) and inspecting the mantels before they are sent up. If you see any thing offensive to your gothick eye (you don't *squint* so no offence) put your veto upon it. They are extremely elegant and I wish them to be correct specimens of the style. How the ladies will *dote* on them—"[19]

Throughout the year of 1840, and into early 1841, Davis continued to visit the site, and recorded that he was paid for drawings of ceiling designs, working drawings for various details, and the "Library ceiling of open timber work; and gallery."

4.8. Study for a timbered library by Edward Buckton Lamb, fig. 2012 from J. C. Loudon's *Encyclopaedia of Cottage, Farm and Villa Architecture*, 1833.

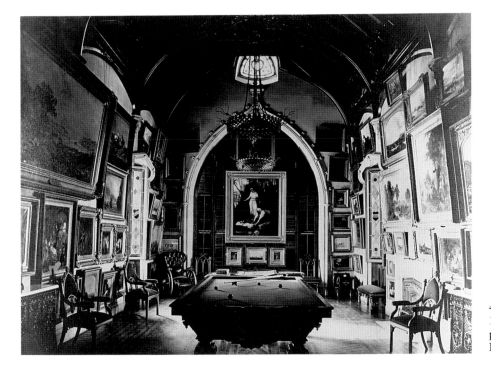

4.9. Knoll library during the Merritt era, ca. 1870. Archival Collection, Lyndhurst, a property of the National Trust for Historic Preservation.

The dramatic second-floor library was the room to which both Davis and Philip Paulding paid particular attention. A library was considered absolutely essential to the home of any nineteenth-century gentleman. Downing wrote that a library, the room "devoted to intellectual cultures," was as important to a villa as the dining room and the drawing room. The library at Knoll was an unusually monumental room, soaring two stories in height to an open timbered ceiling, lit by a central skylight (fig. 4.9). There was a great stained-glass window at the west end, with a musicians' gallery facing it at the east end. Its design was based on a medieval hall, yet it also included features, such as its timber roof supports, that were more commonly found in English country churches than in other domestic libraries in America at the time. Davis may have drawn his inspiration for the room from a plate in Loudon (fig. 4.8) of a library in the Gothic style designed for the book by British architect Edward Buckton Lamb (1803–1869). The great stained-glass window at the end of the room, facing west out upon the Hudson River, was the subject of many drawings (and at least two letters) between June 1841 and March 1842. The aforementioned letter dated November 16, 1841, from Philip Paulding to Davis is a revealing source about the original design for the window, which was replaced during the 1880s.

> I will thank you also as soon as you can possibly do it, to make designs for all the windows of the library. $250. must be the highest mark for these windows; Two hundred must do it if possible— The side windows may be quite plain; a little patch or two of colour and the outside tracery followed in lead and colours will be all sufficient. Rich colours will tell well in the small windows above the big one, having regard to its western aspect and the defect of light thereby. Here expense may be incurred. The big window should be a nonpareil. I should like also to have a flat coloured light to put at the bottom of the lantern but if it cannot be included in the $250 let it go— I leave this entirely to your taste and Mr. Gibsons; you can consult with him and get his ideas as to colours and prices. When you have made the drawings, I will have them put into the hands of Mr. Wells to make the best bargain with him that he can.[20]

All that remains of Davis's designs for the window are two small sketches (fig. 4.10). The National Trust for Historic Preservation, Lyndhurst's owners since 1966, has an enlarged detail of an exterior photo made during the Merritts' ownership that gives some idea of the window's composition (fig. 4.11). A series of stained-glass designs for unknown projects by Davis, in the Metropolitan Museum's collection (fig. 4.12),

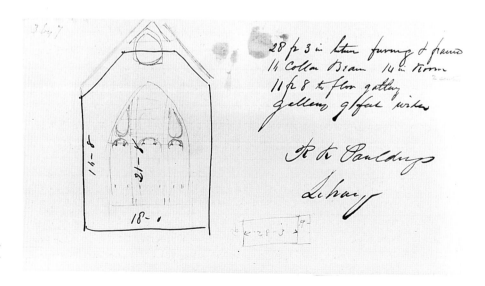

4.10. Study for the great west window in the Knoll library, 1841. Ink and graphite on paper, 5 5/16 x 7 3/4 in. A. J. Davis Collection, The New-York Historical Society (582).

4.11. Exterior of the west facade of Lyndhurst for George Merritt, ca. 1867. Archival Collection, Lyndhurst, a property of the National Trust for Historic Preservation.

is enlightening as to the character of Davis's designs. The great window seems to have included heraldic shields, as well as an innovative series of figures, which were uncommon in domestic stained glass of the day.

The "Mr. Gibson" mentioned in Philip Paulding's letter was William Gibson (1809–1884), one of the first stained-glass artists working in New York. According to his obituary in the March 20, 1884, issue of the *Crockery & Glass Journal,* "He was born in Edinburgh in 1809, and was there educated in glass staining and decorative work. In 1833 he came to New York and established the business here. He was the first to introduce artistic glass staining into this country." A receipt from Gibson to Davis for work on an unidentified house, dated December 1839, is in the New York Public Library's Davis papers. At this time, Gibson's address was 548 Pearl Street in New York City. Interestingly, the receipt covers only decorative painting work, such as graining a Gothic table and "painting 3 slabs for bookcase imitation jasper." It is likely that Gibson had few clients interested in including pictorial stained glass in their homes in the 1830s. However, as the decades went by, decorative stained glass became almost the norm in many newly built homes. Gibson did some of the stained-glass work at Grace Hill in 1857, and sometime in the 1870s published a flyer advertising his work in stained glass as well as his "Gallery of Architectural Decorative Art" at Nos. 374 & 376 Broadway. In the advertisement he called himself a "Decorative Artist" and offered to "make designs and furnish estimates for every department of *Architectural Furnishing* and embellishment of appropriate style. . . ."[21]

Gibson's stained-glass work seems to have been a very much appreciated innovation. In the description of Knoll published in *Brother Jonathan,* it was given special notice.

4.12. Study for a stained-glass window, ca. 1840. Elevation. Watercolor and ink on paper, 14½ x 10⅜ in. The Metropolitan Museum of Art, Harris Brisbane Dick Fund, 1924 (24.66.1042).

> There is one thing in this villa which we would not omit to mention. Every window is of enameled glass, and the panes made of the small diamond shape. The coloured light thrown into the rooms when the sun shines upon the windows, carries back the association to the olden times. There is, too, something aristocratic, in the best sense of the word, (which we take to be gentlemanly) in these gorgeous windows of enameled glass. . . .[22]

4.13. Study for furniture for Knoll, 1841. Graphite on paper, 4¼ x 6⅝ in. Drawings & Archives, Avery Architectural and Fine Arts Library, Columbia University (1940.00.00441).

Although the article may have exaggerated somewhat to say that every window at Knoll was of enameled glass, it did point out how notably and effectively the colored glass was used in the house.

During the autumn of 1841, Davis also noted that he made drawings for the interior woodwork of various rooms, i.e "tracery for interior doors," designs for the wainscot in both the office and the library, and on October 5, he first mentioned "Designing for Furniture for P." The subject of Davis's furniture designs has been extensively researched and written about elsewhere, and some of the pieces that still exist at Lyndhurst can be accurately assigned to the Paulding era.[23] There is an important point that should be made about the role Davis's furniture designs played within the context of the Knoll interiors. The furniture was considered to be an integral part of the design of the interior; it was not thought of as objects that should, or could, be viewed outside of the context of Knoll's environment (fig. 4.13). Contemporary commentators were well aware of the importance of Davis's innovations. In the same article in *Brother Jonathan* in which Knoll is discussed, the author first mentions Davis's villa for Joel Rathbone and its furnishings.

> The whole interior beautifully corresponds in the finishing and embellishments, and the same architect (A. J. Davis) that designed the villa has designed every piece of furniture. This is as it should be. Every piece of furniture should seem to be a part of the house, and who can tell so well as the architect what will correspond with the design, and be appropriate in the details.

The author has the following to say about the furniture at Knoll.

> This [the house] is a perfect specimen of the most beautiful of the pointed styles, and the whole interior is in keeping with the style. Mr. Davis has designed every article of furniture, so that every chair and every table would appear to a guest in the house to be *at home* in its place—as if belonging to the room or the spot, and as a necessary part of the whole.[24]

The concept of a totally integrated design for a house's exterior, interior, and furniture preceded by fifty years the work of Frank Lloyd Wright, who is generally thought to be the innovator of the concept in this country.

Although the interior architecture of Knoll's rooms still exists in fairly unchanged condition today at Lyndhurst, it is hard to imagine how exciting the coherent design of the interiors must have been in 1842, when the rooms were furnished in Davis's designs and had their original surface decorations intact. Clearly, Knoll was one of Davis's best works, and it helped establish his reputation as an architect on the cutting edge of residential design.

After the house was completed in 1842, Davis continued his relationship with Philip Paulding until at least 1847. He recorded further designs for furniture, including bookcases, tables, bedposts, and fire grates. He also recorded social evenings in Paulding's company, such as November 17, 1847, when he and Paulding went "to Palmo's to see the Model Artistes." After this date, Davis's ties with Knoll and the Pauldings seemed to have come to an end. Philip Paulding married in 1851, but the union was not a success. After his wife left him in 1855, he moved out of Knoll, renting it fully furnished to a C. Yale, Jr.[25] Davis was not to renew his association with the house until about fifteen years later.

One of Davis's most important commissions of the 1850s was Grace Hill, a house that is known today as Litchfield Villa (fig. 4.14; colorplate 55). Located in Brooklyn's Prospect Park, it still stands today, some of its interior detailing intact, and is used as offices by the New York City Parks Department. Davis started work on the project in November 1853, and by May 1854 he had submitted a "Set of plans, elevation, sections, &c. for a Dwelling house upon the Greenwood height, Brooklyn, Ninth Avenue" to Edwin Clark Litchfield (1815–1885), for which he charged $300. Litchfield was a successful investor in railroads and Brooklyn real estate, and a very different type of client from Philip Paulding. Whereas Paulding, then a bachelor, apparently wanted a house that spoke of repose and retirement from the city, Litchfield was building a grand home for his wife and four children that faced the burgeoning city from its hilltop site. Paulding chose a Tudor Gothic-style house, with its aristocratic references to English society as well as its associations with the great universities at Oxford and Cambridge. The most imposing room at Knoll was the timbered library. Downing explained that a Gothic-style villa expressed the taste of "a man or family of domestic tastes, but with strong aspirations after something higher than social pleasures."[26] For Litchfield, Davis designed elevations in two different styles; a "Villa in [the] American Style of Italian" was chosen over a "Villa in [the] Castleated [sic] Style of Gothic"[27] (fig. 4.15). According to Downing, the Italianate was not as well suited to a rural site as the Gothic, but was

4.14. Grace Hill for Edwin C. Litchfield, Brooklyn, New York, 1854. Front elevation. Watercolor, ink, and graphite on paper, 20¹⁵⁄₁₆ x 27⅞ in. The Metropolitan Museum of Art, Harris Brisbane Dick Fund, 1924 (24.66.67).

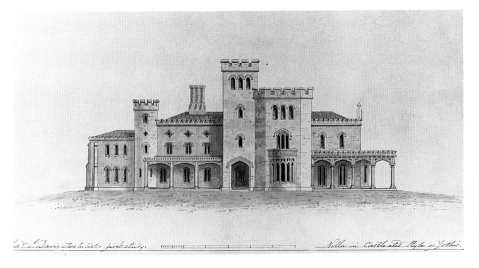

4.15. "Villa in Castleated Style of Gothic," study for Grace Hill for Edwin C. Litchfield, Brooklyn, New York, 1853–54. Front elevation. Watercolor and ink on paper, 8½ x 14 in. Drawings & Archives, Avery Architectural and Fine Arts Library, Columbia University (1940.001.00529).

. . . remarkable for expressing the elegant culture and variety of accomplishment of the . . . man of the world . . . it is also very significant of the multiform tastes, habits, and wants of modern civilization. On the whole, then, we should say that the Italian style is one that expresses not wholly the spirit of country life nor of town life, but something between both, and which is a mingling of both.[28]

In other words, the Italianate seemed to be the perfect style for a modern man of the world like Edwin Litchfield, and for the Brooklyn site, which was, at the time, a suburban location.

The floor plan at Litchfield was in keeping with many of the residential floor plans Davis designed in the 1850s and 1860s (figs. 4.16a & b). Davis was strongly influenced by the writings of eighteenth- and early-nineteenth-century French rationalist architects, and was particularly fond of the works of Jean Nicolas Louis Durand (1760–1834), whose *Précis des Leçons d'Architecture données à l'École Polytechnique* (2 vols., Paris, 1802–05) helped form his ideas about planning. Durand explained a design process based on simple geometric forms that could be combined, overlapped, or subdivided in order to create a rational plan, well suited to public buildings. Davis took these ideas and translated them for use in his villa designs; the plan of Grace Hill was a rather rigid composition of octagons, circles, and squares, totally symmetrical on the north-south axis and balanced on the east-west axis. Because each of the individual rooms was unique in form (except for the dining room and parlor, which were mirror images of each other), the house was not experienced as being as tightly laid out as it appeared on the plan.

Unlike his experience at Knoll, Davis seems to have been integrally involved with the building process at the Litchfield villa from very early on. (Although Edwin C. Litchfield's house is known as Litchfield Villa today, Davis referred to the house as "Ridgewood" in his diaries. After the family moved in, however, the Litchfields

4.16a & b. Grace Hill for Edwin C. Litchfield, Brooklyn, New York, ca. 1855. First floor plans. Ink and graphite on paper, 15 x 10¼ in. each. A. J. Davis Collection, The New-York Historical Society (275N).

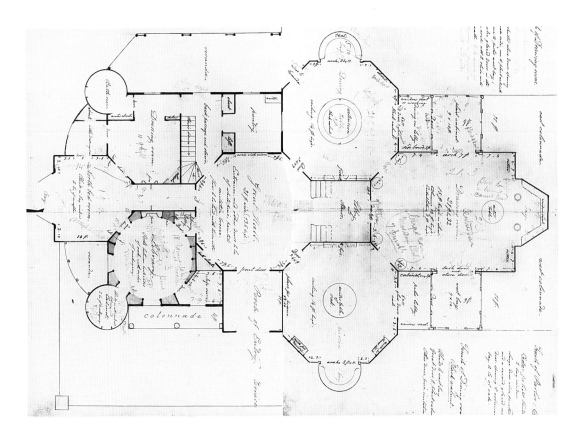

called the house Grace Hill, a play on Mrs. Litchfield's maiden name, which was Grace Hill Hubbard.) According to Davis's own short chronology of the building of the house,[29] by June 1854, "Work commenced under the superintendence of C. B. Bilgieu, Mason. Mr. Davis not undertaking the superintendence of the work, but furnishing working details only, the days-work method requiring constant watchfulness." By April 1855, George Nichols had been hired "to superintend the carpenter's work and act as Clerk of the Works."[30] Finally, in April 1856, Davis himself took over "the general superintendence and auditing accounts." However, in a note in Avery Library's Davis collection (Hl-3v), Davis stated that he was actually superintending from May 1854 to April 1856. The house was not completed until October 1857, so Davis worked as the superintendent for at least a year and a half. The reason that the issue of superintendence was so important was that the client was not on the site for most of the time the house was being built. Edwin Litchfield and his family left for a tour of Europe in October 1855 and did not return until spring 1857, when the house was almost completed. In his Journal, Davis recorded one hundred visits to the site between June 1854 and December 31, 1856, and noted that starting with January 1, 1857, "Many details and visits made after this date are not itemized."

Davis began to work on the designs for the interiors early in the building process. At the end of October 1854, according to the Journal, Davis was concentrating on the "sections + plans of rooms," including plans of the circular library and the drawing room, as well as "Cornices. Details for floors, . . . sliding doors." On five days in January 1855, Davis recorded in his Day Book working on "Interiors for Litchfield" and "Details for Litchfield. Interior finish of house." During the spring and into the summer, Davis worked on numerous drawings of ceilings, cornices, and other details of the rooms.

On August 7, 1855, Davis visited the site "to meet Mrs. L. & other ladies." Although it is unclear how much involvement Mrs. Litchfield had with the design of the house, it seems likely that she did make her ideas about the interiors known. Much later in the process, in June 1857, after her return from Europe, Davis noted meeting with her on the 2nd, when the "Painters (were) at work," on the 23rd, "1 to 6 with ladies," and on the 25th, when he met Mrs. Litchfield in New York City to shop. Instead of visiting upholsterers or furniture makers, as might be expected, Davis and Mrs. Litchfield visited William Gibson, the stained-glass decorator mentioned in connection with Knoll; John M. Thatcher (434 Broadway), from whom they ordered the house's furnace; Thomas Goadby (213 Grand), who made fire grates and fenders; the marble works of Fisher, Bird & Co. (287 Bowery and 460-65 Houston); W. J. Hanington (820 Broadway), another stained-glass decorator; and two other merchants not yet conclusively identified.

Although Davis seems to have corresponded only with Mr. Litchfield during the time the family was in Europe, Mrs. Litchfield was clearly interested in all aspects of the appearance of the interiors. A set of specifications concerned primarily with the interiors of the house does exist in the collection of the New-York Historical Society. On the front page, in Davis's hand, is written: 'SPECIFICATION OF THE MATERIALS AND WORKS REQUIRED FOR BUILDING A DWELLING HOUSE *on Long Island [Brooklyn], 9 & 10 av. 3 to 5th.* FOR *Mrs. Edwin C. Litchfield.* ACCORDING TO THE ACCOMPANYING DRAWINGS, AND THE CONDITIONS SUBJOINED."[31] On October 3, 1855, Davis noted having worked on a set of "Specifications for interior at Litchfields" in his Day Book. This may refer to the same set that he prepared for Mrs. Litchfield. (Davis's own set of specifications for the house is in the Metropolitan Museum's col-

4.17. Drawing room at Grace Hill, ca. 1876–86. Photo courtesy of The New York Genealogical and Biographical Society.

4.18. Parlor at Grace Hill, ca. 1876–86. Photo courtesy of The New York Genealogical and Biographical Society.

4.19. Library at Grace Hill, ca. 1876–86. Photo courtesy of The New York Genealogical and Biographical Society.

lection. It includes less information about interior work, but bound into it are lists of the contractors and merchants who worked on the building.)

Mrs. Litchfield's specifications were very detailed and included directions for finishing or painting each room. The drawing room, which was the most richly detailed room in the house,[32] was to be painted white and gold, a color scheme that was very popular for formal drawing rooms of the day. Downing recommended white and gold for drawing rooms, saying that the wall color should be "decidedly light, so that brilliancy of effect is not lost in the evening"[33] (fig. 4.17). In the specifications, Davis had also suggested finishing the woodwork in the room in mahogany (either real or grained), but the Litchfields chose the lighter painted finish. The Litchfields brought a gilt Rococo Revival suite of furniture home from Paris with them for the drawing room. By the 1850s, Rococo Revival drawing room suites were *de rigeur,* no matter what style of house one owned. Downing did not show any interiors designed in "the modern French style," since he considered its curved and flowing lines a modification of Italianate design, and he seemed to have preferred the Italianate. He did not condemn Rococo Revival furniture, but he thought it should be confined to the areas of the house that were traditionally the preserve of the ladies. He reported that "*Modern French furniture,* and especially that in the style of *Louis Quatorze,* stands much higher in general estimation in this country than any other. Its union of lightness, elegance and grace renders it especially the favorite of ladies. For country-houses we would confine its use, chiefly, to the drawing-room or boudoir. . . ."[34]

The woodwork in the parlor (which was used as the family sitting room) was to be finished in oak (fig. 4.18), the dining room woodwork in black walnut, and the library in mahogany and oak (fig. 4.19). The Great Hall was finished rather grandly, according to information gathered from both sets of specifications. Davis's instructions were to "paint and course off (the walls) in imitation polished granite." The ceiling was "to be sky blue, between ribs of stone" (fig. 4.20). The doors were to be painted imitation bronze. The floor was laid with ornately patterned tiles; these are some of the few features of the original decoration that still exist today in the house. Another unusual feature of Mrs. Litchfield's specifications was that Davis went so far as to draw in suggestions for furniture placement on the plans (see figs. 4.16a & b).

Davis sent a set of plans to Mr. Litchfield in Europe, so that he might refer to them in light of the letters he and Davis were sending back and forth. Unfortunately, only one letter regarding the interiors seems to have survived.[35] It is very revealing of the nature of the client-architect relationship between Davis and Litchfield, especially with respect to decisions made about the interiors. Davis was clearly coming up with the ideas for the decorations, but even from Europe, Litchfield exercised strong control. Although the date of this letter has been interpreted by some as July 5, 1857, the handwriting is hard to read, and Davis's Day Books recorded meetings with Litchfield in New York by July. From evidence within the body of the letter, the date is probably *February* 5, 1857. In it, Litchfield responded to questions put to him by Davis in letters written on the 4th and 30th(?) of December. He discussed a variety of subjects, such as floor finishes, i.e "The *porch under the great tower,* may be laid with *marble tile:* and the Hall with *Garnkirk*[36] tile. . . . The *dining room* floor may be of plank—as we shall carpet it." In discussing the tile floor for the hall, it is clear that Litchfield wanted to make the final decision on the choice of design.

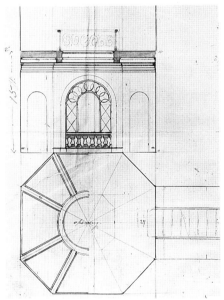

4.20. Center hall at Grace Hill, ca. 1855. Elevation and ceiling plan. Ink on paper, 15 x 10¼ in. A. J. Davis Collection, The New-York Historical Society (275N).

I have not had any special opportunity for examining *Garnkirk* tile in England.

If therefore it is necessary to order it long in advance, in order to get it, I must leave the matter to you. If the selection could be left until my return without involving a delay beyond a few days—that is if the tile can at any time be found in New York of suitable patterns + in sufficient quantities, I would prefer to leave it.

But if it is necessary to order it made + sent from Europe—then I [d_____] as follows:

(1) Select some pretty design, in style of finish + [n_____] corresponding properly with the building—*neither exceeding nor falling short of that controlling point*—then ascertain the cost of providing the quantity required for the Hall.
(2) Send me a *sketch* (so as to give me a *notion* of it) showing how it will look in the Hall—that is *the figure* + the combination of it proposed by you.
Also specify the cost.
(3) Upon receiving this, if I approve it, I will at once return it to you +[_____] you to [_____] for it. This (if you write me promptly) will find ample time to buy it and get it from Europe, before my return in the Spring.

The mantels are another issue about which Mr. Litchfield seemed to have misgivings. He approved spending the enormous sum of $550 for the Rococo Revival mantel that Davis chose, which still stands in the parlor today. It is white Carrara marble, decorated with foliage, fruit, flowers, and birds, and includes a three-foot-high female figure on each pier, one holding a spyglass and a globe, the other a cross and a Bible. However, Litchfield couldn't seem to make up his mind whether Davis should buy the mantels for the other rooms at the marble dealers in New York, or whether he should look for some to purchase himself during his visit to Italy. Litchfield approved of Davis buying a mantel for the library (in addition to the aforementioned parlor mantel) only if waiting for Litchfield's return would delay the room's completion. All in all, he preferred that Davis wait to make any choices until his return. Davis may well have waited, because he mentioned spending the day "with E. C. Litchfield & brother at Ridgewood" on May 17, 1857 (proving Litchfield was back from Europe by then), and major activity surrounding the ordering of mantels took place on May 16 ("Chim. pieces + painting. Engaged Gori on mantels. 5") and May 20 ("Mantels for Litchfield of Gori 5 & Fer. & Tab. 1"). The "Gori" from whom Davis purchased five mantels was Ottaviano Gori (897 Broadway), listed in the 1857 New York City directory as "Sculptor and manufacturer of marble work," who was probably best known for the ornamental capitals symbolizing Commerce and Plenty that he carved for A. T. Stewart's store. It seems possible that he sculpted the parlor mantel. "Fer. & Tab." were Ferris & Taber (386 Greenwich), marble dealers. The Mr. Ferris of Ferris & Taber was probably the same Ferris involved with Underhill & Ferris, the company that provided the mantels for Knoll.

Another facet of the interiors of the house that Davis directed was the design of the decorative painting. All of the principal rooms had elaborate painting schemes, like that previously mentioned pertaining to the Great Hall. Davis seems to have made basic sketches showing the type of decoration, figures, etc. he wanted, but he left the final designs to the artists (fig. 4.21). The trellis ceiling in the main drawing room was a reworking of the ceiling he designed for fig. 176, "Dining Room.—Italian Style," in Downing's *Architecture of Country Houses* (1850) (fig. 4.22). A one-page specification in Davis's hand that is in the collection of Avery Library (Hl-30) may be a draft of a document Davis intended to have a painter use as a guide.

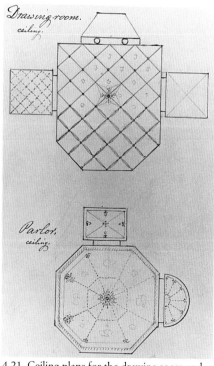

4.21. Ceiling plans for the drawing room and parlor at Grace Hill, ca. 1857. Ink and graphite on paper, 9 7/16 x 6 in. Drawings & Archives, Avery Architectural and Fine Arts Library, Columbia University (1940.001.00532).

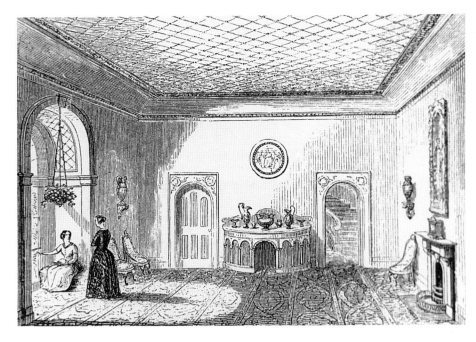

4.22. "Dining Room.—Italian Style.," fig. 176 from Andrew Jackson Downing's *The Architecture of Country Houses,* 1850.

Specification for painting the room known as *the parlor* in E. C. Litchfield house Brooklyn. May, 1857

1. The ceiling to be in style similar to a drawing submitted by [blank space]
2. The cornice to be painted and gilded as directed. Some of the moldings to be foliated
3. The side walls to be plain painted, and tinted neutral as directed
4. The architraves to be marbled as directed.
[in pencil] They are white with gilt molding
5. The doors painted and grained in imitation of rich old oak, varnished with copal root oak
[in pencil] (They are painted plain oak)
6. Sashes imitation bronze, inside and out.

An unusually large group of painters was hired to complete the work. On May 22, 1857, Davis noted that the painters were at work, and they were still working on the project on September 1. Some of the painters who did the work were H. Nowlan & Kearney (18 Amity), who specialized in marbleizing and graining and earned $1,782 on the project, more money than any of the other contractors; Heinrich Bossard (address unknown), "painter of parlor ceiling, cupids &c."; W. Hamilton (185 W. 25th Street), who "painted Litchfield's library"; Primo Boretti (address unknown), who "Painted statues in stair vestibule, 2nd story." Guiseppi Guidichini (24 Irving Place), whose name has also been associated with the Morse-Libby Mansion in Portland, Maine, may have done the spectacular ribbon ceiling and other decoration in the drawing room.

Except for the built-in bookcases in the circular library, Davis apparently did not design any furniture for the Litchfield family. As early as September 18, 1855, he mentioned work on "furniture for library," and again on December 20, when he was busy "on Litchfield's library bookcases." Later (June 10, 1856) he mentioned working "on Litchfield plans for furniture," but the only cabinetmakers mentioned in any of the journals or specifications were Burns & Trainque (453 Broadway), who were used on March 4, 1857, "for polishing & repairing blinds," and Burns alone, who was paid on October 2, 1857, "for varnishing bookcases, polishing &c. bay windows."

4.23. Second-floor hall at Grace Hill, ca. 1876–86. Photo courtesy of The Brooklyn Historical Society.

An Italianate house like Grace Hill did not call for its own architect-designed furniture the way Knoll did; one reason for this was that there was no specific Italianate-style furniture. The rooms at Knoll were all designed in a unified Gothic style; the period photographs for Grace Hill show rooms in which both the architecture and furniture were more eclectic. The Litchfield family was well established; they furnished the house with objects that ranged from "homey" to high style, from the rather modest empire chairs of the 1830s that appear in a photo of the upstairs hall and may have come from a previous home (fig. 4.23), to the grand Parisian drawing room suite, certainly purchased in Europe specifically for the new house. Even if Davis had little to do with the design of the furniture (though he had recommended its placement in his specifications for Mrs. Litchfield), he noted the end of the project with apparent pleasure: "October 13 Went to Litchfields. The family had moved into the new house, and were placing the furniture."

George Merritt's needs as a client fell somewhere in between those of Philip Paulding and Edwin Litchfield. Merritt started his career as a merchant but made his real wealth from his ownership of a patent for a railroad-car spring. He probably had many reasons for wanting to expand Knoll into Lyndhurst; he was a married man with a number of children, and the house as it stood may have been too small to comfortably accommodate his family. However, the most important reason he had to enlarge Knoll to almost twice its original size was to own a house that would accurately express his social position (fig. 4.24; colorplate 56). The ambitions of a gentleman of 1838 and those of a gentleman of 1864 were considerably different; the changes that took place in the house as Knoll became Lyndhurst well illustrate this point. There is nothing awkward or disturbing about the joining of the new wing to Knoll; Davis's designs for both the exterior and interior of the addition were extremely skilled. However, the new rooms all have a heavier, more grandiose quality,

4.24. Lyndhurst for George Merritt, Tarrytown, New York, 1865. West (rear) elevation and plan. Watercolor, ink, and graphite on paper, 18 ⅞ x 26 ⅜ in. The Metropolitan Museum of Art, Harris Brisbane Dick Fund, 1924 (24.66.14).

both spatially and ornamentally, than the rooms from 1838–42. The Merritt dining room is an early example of the type of opulent decoration that characterized the homes of the wealthy during the post-Civil War years. In the Merritt plan, the dining room, a room designed for entertaining, became the focus for the house; during Paulding's era, the library and all it symbolized had been preeminent. Merritt dismantled Paulding's great library and turned Knoll's finest room into a billiard room/picture gallery (see fig. 4.9).[37] By the time Merritt became the owner of the house, collecting pictures had overtaken collecting books as an indicator of well-to-do culture. The accessibility of mass-produced books to the middle and lower classes by mid-century may have made a large library seem less desirable or too commonplace; however, art collecting was only within the reach of the very rich. In a series of decisions that Davis and Merritt must have worked on together, the old square dining room was changed to the library, with an additional cabinet room appended to the north through the bay that had once been Paulding's serving area, while the monumental new dining room, with its own entrance lobby (called the "postern" by Davis), was situated on the far northern end of the house (fig. 4.25; colorplate 57).

Merritt was first mentioned in Davis's Day Book on October 5, 1864, when Davis sent him a letter regarding plantings, presumably at Lyndhurst. On the morning of November 5, 1864, Davis went to Tarrytown to see Merritt, "and visited the Paulding house, with view to additions." By November 7, he was hard at work on "Plans, elevations, sections for G. Merritt." During the following February, Davis spent a number of days on Merritt's plans, which were adopted on February 27. For the ten drawings he had completed by March 1, 1865, he was paid $100. The in-depth work began on March 8, 1865, when Davis "Went with Geo. Merritt to Tarrytown to examine details of Paulding House, and engaged all week upon plans, working drawings &c." Of the many drawings Davis made at this time, at least eighteen showed details of the interior. These included a "Section long N. & South. shewing interior finish," "Inside of bay window opening, shewing columns," "Sections and details of ceilings, dining room &c.," "Inside of dining room, backed with

4.25. Lyndhurst for George Merritt, Tarrytown, New York, 1865. First floor plan. Watercolor, ink, and graphite on paper, 25 ¼ x 54 ⅛ in. The Metropolitan Museum of Art, Harris Brisbane Dick Fund, 1924 (24.66.42).

4.26. Dining room at Lyndhurst, ca. 1900. Archival Collection, Lyndhurst, a property of the National Trust for Historic Preservation.

flooring above," and a variety of drawings of interior doors and windows. He continued to work on drawings for Merritt through March and April; by the middle of April, Austin H. Briggs, the head carpentry contractor, had been hired.

As the work on the exterior structure of the building began, Davis continued to work on the interior detailing, especially that of the new dining room. On April 17 and 18 he made a drawing of the beamed dining room ceiling, and on the 21st he completed two drawings of Merritt's "Dining room finish in color, outlined for work." This points to the fact that the rich reds and rusts of the dramatic decorating scheme in the dining room were to Davis's specifications (fig. 4.26).

Davis spent much of the summer designing the new tower that was to rise over the postern and library cabinet room. At the end of August he began to concentrate on the new downstairs library (fig. 4.27). In May he had made a note in his Day Book that the library was to be grained; he probably hoped that changing the appearance of woodwork in the Knoll dining room from stone color to wood would give the room a warmer, more inviting appearance befitting a library. On August 24 and 25 he recorded making four elevations of the library which he sent to Merritt. In his Journal, among other drawings, he noted plans for library cases on the same dates. Perhaps this refers to the placement of the bookcases in the converted library; Davis may have planned to reuse the bookcases from Paulding's upstairs library at this point, since he did not note designing new bookcases until January 24, 1866. The bookcases that currently stand in the room have details, such as the incised gold line decoration also found in the Merritt dining room suite (also assumed to be designed by Davis, but unmentioned in his diaries), that clearly indicate that they were designed in the 1860s; their manufacturer is unknown, but Davis did refer in his Day Book to a Mr. Hudson working on the bookcases in December 1866.

In the fall Davis worked on details of both the library and the dining room. On September 5 he designed the "Tracery for side and closets Merritt dining room," and on the 14th went to the site to work out more details in the dining room. He completed another drawing of the library on October 5, of "4 sides and plan," and was continuing to make studies for the library on November 1, 8, 10, and 14. On November 17 he stated (finally) that he had "Finished Merritt's Library."

In December, aside from designing the floors of the dining room and entry on December 11, Davis spent much of his time designing corbels, bosses, and other molded plaster decorations for many of the rooms of the house. When Paulding's Knoll was built, rooms were not enriched with the level of decoration planned for the Merritt wing. In order to create visual continuity between the two generations of the house, Davis embellished many of the Paulding rooms with additional plasterwork. In April and May of 1866 Davis worked on a formal list of these corbels and other plaster decorations, and on May 17 he accompanied Merritt to New York City, where they ordered $175 worth of work from Thomas Coffee, a sculptor whose shop was located at 148 Tenth Avenue.[38] Plasterwork was ordered for the old rooms as well as the new. Additional plasterwork was ordered for the reception room (Paulding's old "saloon"), the office, and the billiard room (Paulding's old library), for which Davis also designed new arch spandrels along the side walls under the trussed roof.[39] Two of the primary Paulding bedrooms were added to as well; the state bedroom received fourteen corbels and a ceiling boss, and the south bedroom's ceiling was decorated with six corbels, one central boss, and six additional bosses. Four decorative window and door hoods were also added to the room.

All of this plasterwork helped give the completed house a coherent appear-

4.27. Library at Lyndhurst, ca. 1870. Archival Collection, Lyndhurst, a property of the National Trust for Historic Preservation.

4.28. Drawing room at Lyndhurst, ca. 1870. Archival Collection, Lyndhurst, a property of the National Trust for Historic Preservation.

4.29. Reception room at Lyndhurst, ca. 1870. Archival Collection, Lyndhurst, a property of the National Trust for Historic Preservation.

ance. For many years, it has been assumed that Davis left the interior detailing of Knoll intact, just as it was in the Paulding days, and added the new Merritt wing without changing the earlier rooms at all, except for the addition of fancy painting. The evidence now points to greater changes to the rooms than was assumed. The drawing room and the entrance hall are the only two principal rooms in the house in which the original architectural detailing from the Paulding era was left unchanged. The drawing room, however, was completely redecorated by the Merritts. True to the prevailing customs of the day, Paulding's Gothic drawing room was made over in the "French Style," complete with Rococo Revival furniture, wall-to-wall carpeting, and crystal chandeliers (fig. 4.28).

A great deal of progress was made on the house in the summer of 1866. In an undated letter, possibly written in the early fall of that year, George Merritt supplied Davis with a somewhat disgruntled progress report:

> The mantels are being put up and Coffin the plasterer is through. Briggs thinks he can complete the tower this week. Mr. Sharp the Glass Stainer has been up and I have arranged with him to make some specimens before he takes the work in hand. The painters get along slowly I am not satisfied with the way Nolan manages and may be obliged to employ another painter.[40]

The mantels for the dining room and new bedrooms that were being put up were designed by Davis in June and ordered from Fisher, Bird & Co., 287 Bowery, on June 22. The contractors mentioned in the letter, who have not been previously identified, are Alfred Coffin, 243 Front Street, plasterer, and Henry E. Sharp, 164 Ninth Avenue, glass stainer. Davis mentioned "Drawing borders for window glass" in his Journal on August 8, 1866. The "Nolan" that Mr. Merritt seemed so annoyed by was probably H. Nowlan, who did the graining and marbleizing at Grace Hill. Strangely absent from Davis's Day Book and Journal is any mention of the artists who worked on the wonderful painted decorations in many of the rooms. The ceiling in the reception room is of special note; the design depicts figures representing the hours of the day and night, painted in the style of Italian frescoes of the early sixteenth century (fig. 4.29). A subject reminiscent of the Italian masters was probably particularly appealing to the Merritts, who had spent time touring Italy. The reception room during their tenure seemed to be used in part as a display area for the objects they had collected on their European travels. The only mention Davis made of the reception room ceiling was that, on August 8, 1866, the "Fresco [is] underway in Reception room."

Although as late as October 1866 Davis still recorded making elevations and sections of the library, by November the work was drawing to a close. All that Davis had left to do was to complete his catalogue for Merritt's new library. He visited the site a few final times during the next month, advising Merritt on picture frames and chandeliers. He made his last recorded working visit to his masterpiece on April 2, 1867.

Knoll, Grace Hill, and Lyndhurst were all exceptional commissions for Davis. They were very rare opportunities to superintend all aspects of a building's design and construction. In working on these houses, he was blessed with receptive clients who were willing to respect his vision, and wealthy enough to allow his ideas to become reality. And because Lyndhurst and Grace Hill are among the few great Davis villas that still stand, we are able to witness Davis's inspiring gift for designing some of the finest domestic exteriors and interiors of the nineteenth century.

Works and Projects

COMPILED BY JANE B. DAVIES

T his selected list contains the majority of Davis's documented works and projects, both executed and unexecuted. It attempts to include all of his documented works that are known to be extant, including minor ones. The designs omitted from the list were probably not executed; many of these were ambiguously or incompletely entered in Davis's records and lack known related drawings. Some minor alterations were also omitted. Studies and conceptual designs for unspecified buildings were excluded.

Information for the entries has been culled chiefly from Davis's record books (Day Books and office Journal), drawings, memoranda, and letters by clients, as well as from personal attempts to locate structures. Additional information has been derived from numerous local sources with the help of many persons.[1]

Arrangement is approximately by date of design, following the order in which the design was recorded by Davis within the year, with dates of construction added when they have been ascertained.[2]

1828–29 Designs for altering the Park Theatre, Park Row, New York City. Roman and Gothic Revival styles. Not executed.

1828 Design for altering the Alms House, Chambers Street, New York City. Greek Revival. Not executed.

1829 Design for a City Hall, New York City. Greek Revival portico of ten columns. Not executed.

1829–31 James A. Hillhouse House, Highwood (later Sachem's Wood), head of Hillhouse Avenue, New Haven, Conn. Greek Revival portico of two Ionic columns between two square piers. Also ice house and children's playhouse (1835); farmer's house (1839, Gothic cottage). Demolished (house in 1943). (See figs. 3.2–3.4; colorplates 36, 37.)

1829 Design for a Mercantile Library, Nassau Street, New York City. Federal and Greek Revival. Not executed. (See fig. 2.21.)

1829 Clinton Hall, Beekman and Nassau Streets, New York City. Town & Davis. Greek Revival. Executed with modifications. Demolished.[3]

1829 Ralph Ingersoll House, 143 Elm Street, New Haven, Conn. Town & Davis. Greek Revival. Extant (now Yale University offices); loss of exterior stucco or paint; some interior details survive.

1829–30 Groton Monument, Groton, Conn. Town design with some Davis details. Egyptian obelisk. Extant; in 1881 the height was raised eight feet.

1829 Competition design for a City Hall, Albany, N.Y. Greek Revival. Not executed.

1829–30 South Congregational Church, Main and Crescent Streets, Middletown, Conn. Town & Davis. Greek Revival, Doric distyle-in-antis recess portico with flanking antae; ca. 1840 a cupola was added (not Town & Davis). Demolished 1867. (See fig. 6.)

1829 Samuel Russell House, High Street, Middletown, Conn. Designed by Town, 1828; some details by Davis. Greek Revival. Extant (now Wesleyan University Honors College).

1829 Samuel Whitmarch House, near Northampton, Mass. Town & Davis. Greek Revival, hexastyle with one-story wings. Demolished.

1829 Thomas Lord House, New York City. Doorway. Town & Davis. Greek Revival. Demolished.

1829, 1830 [Roderick?] Curtis Houses, New York City. Doorways and interior details. Town & Davis. Greek Revival. Sites not identified (Lafayette and/or Bleecker Streets?). Demolished.

1830–32 Designs for Astor Hotel, Broadway, New York City. Town & Davis. Greek Revival. Not executed. (See fig. 30; colorplate 21.)

1830 William W. Montgomery Stores, Magazine and Canal Streets, New Orleans, La. Greek Revival. Demolished.

1830–34 Aaron N. Skinner House, 46 Hillhouse Avenue, New Haven, Conn. Davis (and perhaps Town). Greek Revival, Ionic tetrastyle temple with side wings. Extant; altered and enlarged.

1830–33 General Hospital, New Haven, Conn. Town & Davis. Greek Revival. Demolished.

1831–33 Samuel Ward House, The Corner, Bond Street and Broadway, New York City. Town & Davis. Greek Revival, modified in construction. Demolished 1873.

1831 Luman Reed House, 13 Greenwich Street, New York City. Town & Davis. Greek Revival. Demolished.

1831 Designs for the Bank of America, Wall Street, New York City. Town & Davis. Greek Revival. Not executed.

1831–32 Trinity Church, Wall Street, New York City. Pulpit, alterations, and marble communion table (executed by Ball Hughes). Gothic Revival. Church replaced; communion table survives at Calvary Episcopal Church.

1831–32 Courthouse and Town Hall, Middletown, Conn. Town & Davis. Greek Revival. Demolished.

1831 Robert Donaldson House, 15 State Street, New York City. Front entrance to existing house. Town & Davis (ornaments executed by John Frazee). Greek Revival. Demolished.

1831–32 West Presbyterian Church, Carmine Street at head of Varick Street, New York City. Town & Davis. Greek Revival, Doric distyle-in-antis recess portico with flanking antae and pseudoperistyle. Demolished ca. 1865 when Varick Street was extended.

1831 Design for a country house for [William Ferris?] Pell, Ticonderoga, N.Y. Greek Revival, tetrastyle Ionic. Not executed.

1831 Designs for the Trumbull Gallery, Yale College, New Haven, Conn. Town & Davis. Greek Revival. Not executed, but probably influenced Trumbull's design. (See fig. 1.16.)

1831 First Presbyterian Church, Fayetteville, N.C. Town & Davis. Greek Revival. Extant; much altered, although the Town lattice-truss roof framing survives.

1831–34 Église du Saint Esprit (French Protestant Church), Church and Franklin Streets, New York City. Town & Davis. Greek Revival, tetrastyle Ionic portico and high dome. Demolished 1864 (dome destroyed by fire 1839). (See figs. 28, 29; colorplates 17, 18.)

1831–32 Designs for New York University. Several designs in Greek Revival style. Not executed. (See fig. 2.17; colorplate 30.)

1831–35 Indiana State Capitol, Indianapolis, Ind. Town & Davis. Greek Revival, Doric octastyle with pseudoperistyle and tall dome. Replaced by new capitol of 1878–88. (See fig. 2.1.)

1832–33 Designs for a hotel, Louisville, Ky. Town & Davis. Greek Revival. Apparently not executed.

1832–35 LeGrand Cannon Stores (Cannon Place), Washington Square (now Monument Square), Troy, N.Y. Town, Davis, & Dakin. Greek Revival. Extant (now Cannon Building); much altered.

1832 Second Avenue Presbyterian Church, Second Avenue, New York City. Dakin, Davis, and James Gallier. Greek Revival. Later Church of the Nativity, Roman Catholic. Demolished 1968.

1832–33 La Grange Terrace (Colonnade Row), Lafayette Street, New York City. Details for Seth Geer. Dakin and Davis. Greek Revival. Partially extant; altered.

1832 Design for two stores for Anthony Rasch, New Orleans, La. Greek Revival. Apparently not executed.

1832 Design for a house for John Turner, Bracebridge Hall, William and Ann Streets, New York City. Greek Revival. Not executed.

1832 Joseph White Moulton House (later owned by Alden J. Spooner), Henry Street near Red Hook, South Brooklyn, N.Y. Gothic Revival cottage villa. Demolished when Summit Street was extended (1840s?).

1832–34 Three projects for a Patent Office, Washington, D.C. Town & Davis. Greek Revival. Not executed. (See figs. 2.5–2.8; colorplates 24, 25.)

1832–34? Robert Gilmor III House, Glen Ellen, Towson, Md. Town, Gilmor, and Davis. Gothic Revival villa. Also on the estate, a small Doric tetrastyle temple for entertaining. Demolished (house in 1930s). (See fig. 3.18; colorplate 42.)

1832–33 Competition design for Girard College, Philadelphia, Pa. Town, Davis, & Dakin (chiefly Town). Greek Revival. Not executed.[4]

1833–42 U.S. Custom House, Wall Street, New York City. Town & Davis, John Frazee, and others. Greek Revival, Doric octastyle with pseudoperistyle. Extant (now Federal Hall Memorial); modified in execution by others, including omission of dome and reduction of porticoes' depth. (See figs. 2.2, 2.3; colorplate 23.)

1833–40 North Carolina State Capitol, Raleigh. Town & Davis, William Nichols, Jr., and David Paton. Greek Revival. Extant. (See fig. 2.4.)

1833 Design for St. John's College, Annapolis, Md. Greek Revival. Not executed.

1833 Design for a villa for Edmund H. Conway. Tuscan Revival. Proposed site unknown; no evidence of execution. (See fig. 3.10; colorplate 39.)

1834 Robert C. Johnson House, Tioga Terrace (later Vesper Cliff), Owego, N.Y. Additions across front and on sides. Greek Revival. Extant.

1834 Designs for a villa for Robert Donaldson, for a Hudson River site near Fishkill Landing (now Beacon), N.Y. Gothic Revival. Not executed. (See fig. 3.19; colorplate 43.)

1834 Design for a church for Edwin J. Peck, Ohio. Town & Davis. Greek Revival. Perhaps Second Presbyterian Church (now Historic Madison, Inc.), Madison, Ind., on Ohio River; built 1834–35 by Edwin J. Peck, extant, and said to have a Town lattice roof truss.

1834 Design for a house for William Wolcott Wadsworth, Geneseo, N.Y. Town & Davis (probably Davis). Greek Revival. Not executed.

1834–36 Nathan Whiting House, Hillhouse Avenue, New Haven, Conn. Town & Davis. Greek Revival. Demolished 1890s.

1834 Exchange Bank, 30 (later 76) State Street, Hartford, Conn. Town & Davis. Greek Revival. Demolished.

1834 Designs for a country house for Gardiner G. Howland, near Flushing, N.Y. Greek Revival. Not executed.

1834–35; 1837–39 Pauper Lunatic Asylum, Blackwell's Island, New York City. Designed 1834–35; partially built 1837–39, 1847–48, with modifications by others. Tuscan Revival (changed to Greek Revival in construction by others), with Davisean windows. One octagon extant but damaged by fire and neglect. (See figs. 3, 2.12.)

1834 Design for a Roman Catholic Chapel (for Judge William Gaston), New Bern, N.C. Gothic Revival. Not executed.

1834? or 1835? Design for the American Institute, New York City. Egyptian Revival. Not executed. (See fig. 2.23; colorplate 32.)

1835 J. D. Stevenson, Tobacco Inspection Warehouse, Clinton, Water, and South Streets, New York City (copy of the design also made for Stevenson for Philadelphia). Town &

Davis. Greek Revival. Demolished; execution of Philadelphia design unknown.

1835 Competition design for Halls of Justice and House of Detention ("The Tombs"), Elm and Centre Streets, New York City. Greek Revival front on Elm Street, Egyptian Revival front on Centre Street. Not executed, but awarded a premium; influential on the final design by John Haviland. (See fig. 2.11; colorplate 27.)

1835–36 Lyceum of Natural History (later New York Academy of Sciences), 561 and 563 Broadway, between Prince and Spring Streets, New York City. Town & Davis. Greek Revival, with Davisean windows and metal shopfronts (by Town). Demolished. (See fig. 2.22.)

1835 Design for a house for Herman B. Potter, Buffalo, N.Y. Town & Davis. Greek Revival. Execution unknown.

1835 Mechanics Hall (hotel), Broad and William Streets, Newark, N.J. Davis and Russell Warren. Greek Revival. Demolished.[5]

1835–37 New York University Chapel interior (at center of the University building), Washington Square, New York City. Gothic Revival. Building demolished 1894. (See figs. 2.18, 2.19; colorplate 31.)

1835–37 Dutch Reformed Church, Grand Street, Newburgh, N.Y. Davis and Russell Warren. Greek Revival, Ionic tetrastyle portico and high dome. Extant; dome removed ca. 1850; enlarged by George Harney; now in bad disrepair.

1835 Competition designs for a City Hall, Brooklyn, N.Y. Eleven designs in Greek, Gothic, and Egyptian Revival styles, in various shapes including circle and hexagon. Not executed. (See figs. 2.29, 2.30; colorplate 34.)

1835 Competition design for the City (later United States) Hotel for the Boston and Worcester Railroad, Beach and Lincoln Streets, Boston, Mass. Greek Revival. Not executed.

1835 Cyrus Durand House, Elmwood, Irvington, N.J. Tuscan Revival, with Davisean windows. Enlarged in 1880s; demolished 1925.

1835–37 Elizabeth Apthorp House, 56 Hillhouse Avenue, New Haven, Conn. Tuscan and Egyptian Revival. Extant; enlarged (Davis added one story in 1855 for Joseph Sampson, but later additions are by others) and very much altered, including the shortening of the Egyptian porch columns.

1835–38 First Congregational (now First Unitarian) Church, Union and Eighth Streets, New Bedford, Mass. Davis and Warren. Gothic Revival. Extant; interior changes.

1835–37 Abigail Salisbury and Edward E. Salisbury House, Church and Wall Streets, New Haven, Conn. Tuscan Revival with Davisean windows and portico of two giant columns. Demolished 1934.

1835–40 New York Orphan Asylum, west of Broadway, between Seventy-third and Seventy-fourth Streets, New York City. Designed by Town; details and chapel by Davis, with some superintendence by Warren. Gothic Revival. Demolished.

1835 Design for a villa for Nathaniel Jocelyn, New Haven, Conn. Roman Revival. Not executed.

1835 Design for a house for David Codwise, near New Rochelle, N.Y. Villa or cottage orné "of an Oriental character," with ornamental veranda. Not executed. (See fig. 3.6; colorplate 38.)

1835–36 Designs for Bristol College, Bristol, Pa. Pennsylvania, Clifton, Milnor, and White Halls. Warren and Davis. Greek Revival for the first three, Gothic Revival for the last (by Davis). Only Pennsylvania Hall (designed by Warren?) was built, in modified form; demolished.

1836 Designs for ten villas and a chapel, for Ravenswood (now part of Queens), N.Y. Greek, Tuscan, and Gothic Revival. Not executed. (See fig. 3.13.)

1836 Design for the Merchants' Exchange, Wall Street, New York City. Greek Revival, with six Corinthian columns and low dome. Not executed. See 1862 for later design for a Commercial Exchange at Nassau, Cedar, and Pine Streets, New York City.

1836 Chapel and Sunday School Building for Mercer Street Presbyterian Church, New

York City. Greek Revival. Demolished.

1836–37 Christ Church, Broad Street, Belleville, N.J. Gothic Revival. Unfinished building was burned in 1837 by an incendiary, rebuilt in modified form, and now replaced.

1836 Wyllys Warner House, Howe Street, New Haven, Conn. Greek Revival, with elaborate veranda. Demolished ca. 1920.

1836–51 Robert Donaldson estate, Blithewood, Annandale-on-Hudson, N.Y. Remodeling of house into bracketed cottage orné with decorative veranda (1836, rear addition 1842); Gothic Revival gatehouse (1836); bracketed gatehouse (1841); Egyptian Revival tool house; ornamental spring house; and other estate structures. Only the bracketed gatehouse is extant (now part of Bard College). (Veranda, see fig. 20, colorplate 12; Gothic Revival gatehouse, fig. 3.24, colorplate 46; bracketed gatehouse, fig. 21.)

1836 Design for remodeling St. Marks-in-the-Bowery Church, New York City. Greek Revival. Not executed.

1836 Charles H. Roach House, Ravenswood (now part of Queens), N.Y. Tuscan Revival villa. Demolished. (See fig. 3.11; colorplate 41.)

1836 Design for a villa for James Smillie, Rondout (now part of Kingston), N.Y. Italianate. Construction started but discontinued. (See fig. 19; colorplate 11.)

1836 Double house for Mr. Dean, 501 George Street, New Haven, Conn. Greek Revival. Extant but very much remodeled.[6]

1836–39 Henry Whitney House, Belmont, 405 Whitney Avenue, New Haven, Conn. Greek Revival (preliminary design for a Gothic villa was not executed). Demolished 1924. (See fig. 1.)

1836 Isaac Lawrence House, Maple Cottage, 85 Trumbull Street, New Haven, Conn. "Suburban Villa" patterned after the David Codwise design in *Rural Residences*. Now remodeled beyond recognition.

1836 Design for additions to villa of William Ferris Pell, The Pavilion, Ticonderoga, N.Y. Greek Revival? Execution unknown.

1836–37 Mary Prichard House, 35 Hillhouse Avenue, New Haven, Conn. Greek Revival. Extant; additions toward rear, some roof details lost.

1836? Design for a house for William C. Rhinelander, Washington Square and Fifth Avenue, New York City. Probably 1836, Davis; but possibly 1834, Town & Davis. Greek Revival. Not executed. (See fig. 4; colorplate 2.)

1837 Competition design for Illinois State Capitol, Springfield, Ill. Town and Davis (jointly but not as firm). Greek Revival, Doric hexastyle with pseudoperistyle and dome. Not executed. See 1867 for later competition design.

1837 Design for a hotel for Henry W. Warner on Constitution Island, Hudson River (across from West Point), N.Y. Gothic Revival. Not executed. (See fig. 7.)

1837 Country church and schoolhouse for Isabella Donaldson, Annandale-on-Hudson, N.Y. Bracketed. Demolished. (See figs. 2.20a, 2.20b.)

1837 Design for a house for Mr.(?) Vail, near Morristown, N.J. Greek Revival? Site and execution unknown.

1837 Design for a city house for Mr. Bissell, Toledo, Ohio. Greek Revival. Not identified.

1838–40 Henry Sheldon House, Millbrook, near Tarrytown, N.Y. Gothic Revival cottage villa. Demolished. (See figs. 3.23, 3.26.)

1838 Alfred Hall House, 245 Main Street, Chatham (now Portland), Conn. Greek Revival. Extant (now Liberty Bank for Savings); altered, entrance steps changed, stucco and details lost.

1838–42 William and Philip R. Paulding House, Knoll (later Lyndhurst), including furniture, near Tarrytown, N.Y. Gothic Revival villa. Extant; see 1864–67 for enlargement by George Merritt. (See figs. 3.20, 4.4; colorplate 44.)

1838 Henry H. Leeds Cottage and design for a villa, near Ossining, N.Y. Gothic Revival. Cottage apparently built but now demolished; villa design not executed.

1838–39 Designs for the University of Michigan, Ann Arbor. Gothic Revival. Not executed. (See fig. 2.14; colorplate 28.)

1838–39 Nathan B. Warren House, Mt. Ida, Troy, N.Y. Gothic Revival cottage villa. Later much enlarged (not by Davis). Demolished.

1838 Design for a villa for William P. Van Rensselaer, Albany, N.Y. Greek Revival. Not executed.

1839 Oliver Bronson House, Hudson, N.Y. Ornamentation of existing house exterior; stable/barn. Bracketed. Extant (now under the State Prison Authority), but house in disrepair. See 1849 for later addition.

1839 Designs for Ohio State Capitol, Columbus, Ohio. Revision of competition designs and an original design. Greek Revival. Not executed, but probably influenced final design by other architects.

1839 Design for a villa for Henry W. T. Mali, Manhattanville, N.Y. Roman Revival. Not executed. (See fig. 3.7.)

1840 Samuel M. Fox House, Throgs Neck (now Bronx), N.Y. Gothic Revival cottage villa. Probably built. Demolished.

1840 Designs for houses and other buildings for Samuel B. Ruggles, Union Square, New York City. Greek Revival. Not executed.

1841 Design for a villa for John B. James, Rhinebeck, N.Y. Gothic Revival. Not executed. (See fig. 16; colorplate 8.)

1841 Dr. Federal Vanderburgh Cottage, Linwood Hill, Rhinebeck, N.Y. Gothic Revival cottage. Demolished. (See fig. 31.)

1841 Samuel T. Jones Cottage, greenhouses, and stable, New Brighton, Staten Island, N.Y. Gothic Revival cottage and bracketed stable. Demolished between 1924 and 1937.

1841 Robert Adam House, Annandale-on-Hudson, N.Y. Cottage orné. Demolished.

1841–60 Mrs. Edward Livingston House, Montgomery Place, Annandale-on-Hudson, N.Y. Additions to existing house, coach house, and estate structures. Classical. Addition and coach house extant; estate structures demolished (some designs not executed). For later work at Montgomery Place, see 1861–73 Coralie Livingston Barton. (See fig. 3.8.)

1842–44 Wadsworth Atheneum, Hartford, Conn. Town & Davis and Henry Austin. Gothic Revival. Extant; large additions and interior changes. (See fig. 1.17.)

1842–49 Joel Rathbone House, Kenwood, farmhouse, gate lodge, and some furniture, south of Albany, N.Y. Gothic Revival. Villa demolished, gate lodge extant (remodeled?), and farmhouse possibly extant. (See figs. 25, 3.21; colorplates 15, 45.)

1842–44 Francis J. Huntington House, Sycamores, West Hartford, Conn. Davis (and Town?). Gothic Revival cottage villa. Demolished ca. 1927.

1842 Design for a house for Dr. Morgan, New London, Conn. Town & Davis. Classical? Execution not determined.

1842 Schoolhouse for Mary Garretson, Rhinebeck, N.Y. Gothic Revival? Probably extant.

1842–44; 1847–48 Samuel E. Lyon House, Lyon Place and Waller Avenue (later moved to 7 Lyon Place), White Plains, N.Y. Gothic Revival cottage villa; rear addition, 1847; gardener's house, 1851. Demolished (house 1948).

1842–44 John Angier House, 129 High Street, Medford, Mass. Davis and Angier, in consultation with A. J. Downing. Gothic Revival cottage villa, with bracketed eaves. Extant; some details apparently lost.

1843 Design for an Astor Library, New York. Classical, with Davisean windows. Not executed. (See fig. 2.25; colorplate 33.)

1843 Designs for houses for Elihu Townsend, Gramercy Park, New York City. Classical. Not executed.

1843–44 Church of the Holy Cross (including organ case and stalls), Eighth Street, Troy, N.Y. Davis and Nathan B. Warren. Gothic Revival. Extant; much altered, with additions by Richard Upjohn and Henry Dudley.

1843 Norman White Houses, Gramercy Park, New York City. Verandas, ornamental and classical. Partially extant.

1843–44 Henry H. Elliott and Robert C. Townsend Houses, Fifth Avenue at Thirty-eighth Street, New York City. Bracketed, with ornamental porches and Davisean, bay, and oriel windows. Demolished. (See fig. 13.)

1843 Designs for rows of houses, four for St. Marks Place and eight for Union Square, New York City. Davis and Seth Geer. Classical? Not executed.

1843 Edward Huntington House (rear addition 1854), 35 Liberty Street, Rome, N.Y. Gothic Revival, with Davisean windows. Demolished, but influential on the extant Nathaniel Mudge House, now First Church of Christ Scientist, Rome, N.Y.

1843–44 Bunker House, New Brighton?, Staten Island, N.Y. Gothic Revival villa. Later R. C. Wetmore House; perhaps enlarged by Charles G. Carleton. Demolished.

1844 Henry Delamater House, 44 Montgomery Street, Rhinebeck, N.Y. Gothic Revival cottage. Extant (now Beekman Arms guest house).

1844–45 University of North Carolina, Chapel Hill, N.C. Additions to Old East and Old West buildings. Bracketed, with Davisean window. Extant; some changes now under restoration. Designs for alteration of South Building and chapel and for a Botanic Garden not executed. See 1849–52 for later work at the university.

1844 John M. Morehead House, Blandwood, 447 West Washington Street, Greensboro, N.C. Remodeling, additions of front section and dependencies. Italianate villa. Extant.

1844 Design for a house for Dr. David Weir, Greensboro, N.C. Gothic Revival villa. Not executed.

1844 Dr. T. F. Bartlett House, Cricket Lawn, Old Lyme, Conn. Cottage orné. Extant; some changes.

1844 Rankin House, Fishkill [Beacon?], N.Y. Remodeling. Davis and A. J. Downing. Executed but unidentified.

1844 Henry H. Chamberlin House, Worcester, Mass. Gothic Revival cottage. Demolished.

1844 Design for the Boston Athenaeum, for proposed site at Tremont and Court Streets, Boston, Mass. Greek Revival, with Davisean windows. Not executed.

1844–45 William Coventry H. Waddell House, Murray Hill at Fifth Avenue and Thirty-seventh Street, New York City. Gothic Revival villa. Demolished 1856 due to the leveling of Fifth Avenue. (See fig. 4.3; colorplate 52.)

1844 Designs for John Quincy Adams House, Quincy, Mass. Additions of library and veranda. Classical. Library design not executed, veranda design apparently executed and perhaps extant.

1845–47 John Cox Stevens House, College Place and Murray Street, New York City. Classical, with curved Corinthian portico and Davisean windows. Demolished. (See fig. 5; colorplate 3.)

1845 Burial sarcophagus of Judge William Gaston, New Bern, N.C. (for Robert Donaldson). Classical. Extant.

1845 Design for a block of houses for William Torrey, Twenty-third Street between Ninth and Tenth Avenues, New York City. Greek Revival. Basis of London Terrace. Demolished ca. 1930.

1845 Design for the Church of the Holy Apostles, Ninth Avenue and Twenty-eight Street, New York City. Gothic Revival (octagonal). Not executed. (See figs. 2.27, 2.28; colorplate 35.)

1845–47 Designs for a mansion, Mt. Wollaston, for Charles Francis Adams and John Quincy Adams, Quincy, Mass. Italianate villa. Not executed despite many later revisions and enlargements.

1845–47? William J. Rotch House, 7 Orchard Street (now 19 Irving Street), New Bedford, Mass. Gothic Revival cottage villa. Extant; a few changes; moved ca. 1910 to corner of the estate. (See fig. 3.25; colorplate 47.)

1845 William Walsh House, Nut Grove, and gatehouse, south of Albany, N.Y. Greek Revival villa. Later Hospital for Incurables. Demolished.

1845–48 Philip St. George Cocke House, Belmead, double cottage, and smoke house, on James River, Powhatan County, Va. Gothic Revival villa. House extant (later St. Emma's Military Academy, now Blessed Sacrament High School); some details lost.

1845 Henry Graham Thompson House, Prospect Street, Thompsonville, Conn. Gothic Revival cottage villa. Extant (now owned by State of Connecticut); shape of central and dormer windows may have been changed during construction.

1845 Design for a cottage for William H. Drake, Hartford, Conn. Gothic Revival. No evidence of execution.

1845–47 Charles B. Sedgwick House, 742 James Street, Syracuse, N.Y. Gothic Revival cottage villa. Later rear addition by another architect. Demolished 1962.

1845 Joshua Richmond House, New Bedford, Mass. Tuscan Revival. Not identified.

1845 Design for a house for Charles C. Alger, West Stockbridge (or Berkshire), Mass. Gothic Revival villa. Not executed.

1845–47 Henry A. Kent House, Ravenswood, barn/stables (1848), and addition (1864), Gowanus Bay (Bay Ridge), Brooklyn, N.Y. Gothic Revival villa. Demolished.

1846–47 Charles Augustus Davis House, East Twentieth Street and Gramercy Park, New York City. Classical, with Davisean windows. Demolished 1912.

1846–50 Henry K. Harral House, Walnut Wood, and coach house/stable, Golden Hill Street, Bridgeport, Conn. Gothic Revival villa. Demolished 1958. Some architectural fragments were removed and have been incorporated in a restored room in the Barnum Museum, Bridgeport, and others are preserved in the Smithsonian Institution, Washington, D.C. Design of addition for library and office proposed 1853, not executed. For cemetery monument to Harral, see 1854. (See fig. 15; colorplate 7.)

1846–47 Henry Wood House, Brambleworth Cottage, Croton Lake Road, Bedford Hills (near Mt. Kisco), N.Y. Gothic Revival cottage. Extant; finials replaced, inconspicuous rear addition, and minor interior changes.

1846 Designs for triple town house for Philip Kearney, Sr., for Twenty-second Street between Fourth Avenue and Broadway, New York City. Classical, with Davisean windows. Not executed.

1846–47 Judge John Vanderbilt House, 560 Flatbush Avenue at Lincoln Road, Brooklyn, N.Y. Gothic Revival villa. Demolished ca. 1907?

1846 William Emerson House and stables, New Brighton, Staten Island, N.Y. Greek Revival (Gothic Revival design not executed). Demolished.

1846; 1851–55 Charles Green House, South Windsor, Conn. Gothic Revival cottage villa. Designed 1846; design revised and enlarged, adding tower, and constructed, 1851–55. Extant (vergeboard apparently never built).

1846–47 Charles E. Butler House, coach house/stable, and icehouse, Clifton, Staten Island, N.Y. Tudor Revival villa. Designs for addition, 1849 and 1852, not executed. Burned.

1846 Daniel Cony Weston House (later J. H. Manly), Augusta, Me. Bracketed. Later much remodeled; extant?

1846–47 Lewis G. Morris House, Mount Fordham, Bronx, N.Y. Remodeling. Italianate villa. Demolished. For later work at Mount Fordham, see 1862–78.

1847 Presbyterian Church, Chapel Hill, N.C. Tuscan Revival. Burned 1919.

1847 Design for remodeling George Beach, Jr., House, Hartford, Conn. Italianate villa. Apparently not executed.

1847–48 James W. Phillips and Charles C. Taber Houses, 138 and 140 Twelfth (later 12 and 14 West Twelfth) Street, New York City. Italianate. Demolished 1958. (See fig. 12.)

1847–49 Dr. Amos G. Hull gatehouse, gate, and watch turret, Liberty Street, Newburgh, N.Y. Norman Romanesque. Gatehouse and gate demolished in 1960s; watch turret extant; design for a Norman Romanesque villa not executed. (See fig. 18; colorplate 10.)

1847 John Hartwell Cocke Temperance Spring Temple for Bremo, Fluvanna County, Va. Greek Revival. Extant; moved on the estate; central blocking lost.

1847–49 Julia Jackson Davis House, Kirri Cottage, 13 (later 32) Warren Street, Newark, N.J. Tudor Revival cottage. Additions 1854 and 1857. Demolished ca. 1897. (See fig. 17; colorplate 9.)

1847 Plan and sketch of a cottage for Frederick Law Olmsted, Sachem's Head, Staten Island, N.Y. Not executed.

1847 Design for a house for B. Phelps, for a site near Springfield, Mass. Gothic Revival cottage villa. Davis in consultation with A. J. Downing. Not executed.

1847 Trinity Episcopal Church, Nichols (Trumbull), Conn. Gothic Revival. Burned 1960s.

1848 Rome Academy (for Edward Huntington), Rome, N.Y. Classical, with Davisean windows. Demolished.

1848 Lewis B. Brown House, coach house/stable, and plan for grounds, Rahway, N.J. Tuscan Revival (later called by Davis his "American style"). Demolished. (See fig. 24.)

1848–49 Powhatan County Courthouse, Powhatan, Va. Greek Revival, Doric distyle-in-antis. Extant.

1848 Stuart Perry and William W. Swezey Houses, Newport, N.Y. Twin Italianate villas. Extant; some alterations.

1848 Joseph Hartwell Williams House, Oak Trees, Augusta, Me. Bracketed. Demolished.

1848 Cemetery monument to Henry Erskine (for Charles Scott Gay), Old Stone Presbyterian Church Cemetery, Lewisburg, Va. Classical. Extant.

1848 Charles E. Miller House, Chalk Level, Pittsylvania County, Va. Gothic Revival cottage. Extant; small side addition.

1848–49 Methodist Church, Church and Market Streets, Red Hook (then called Scrabble), N.Y. Gothic Revival. Built by Jonathan Beers of Bridgeport, Conn., where it was framed; transported to site by water and overland. Replaced by larger church in 1893.

1848 Design for a house, Newport, R.I. Davis and A. J. Downing. Italianate. Not identified and execution unknown.

1848–50 Design for a villa for Charles G. Carleton, Staten Island, N.Y. Gothic Revival. Apparently not executed.

1848–61 Virginia Military Institute buildings, Lexington, Va. Gothic Revival. Extant: barracks, one professor's house, and superintendent's house (the first two rebuilt after 1864 burning, the last two rebuilt several hundred feet back by Bertram Goodhue, 1914–15, barracks now enlarged and veranda lost on the professor's house). Demolished: mess hall (rebuilt after Civil War, burned 1904, and replaced); one professor's house, 1960s; western porter's lodge, 1912. Designs not executed: barracks extension (Claytor Hall, 1859–60), hospital additions, and eastern porter's lodge. For post-Civil War unexecuted projects, see 1869–70. (See fig. 2.16.)

1848–50 Jonathan Prescott Hall House, Malbone, Malbone Road, Newport, R.I. Gothic Revival villa. Extant; wing added, veranda replaced.

1849 Robert R. Stevens Office, Hoboken, N.J. Greek Revival. Demolished.

1849–50 Design for a house for Thomas Hunt, Gowanus Bay, Brooklyn, N.Y. Italianate villa. Not executed.

1849 Design for a house for W. L. Vandenbergh, Fultonville, N.Y. Greek Revival. Execution unknown.

1849–51 George Washington Penney House, Oakwood, Newport, Ohio. Gothic Revival cottage villa (modified version of the design for B. Phelps, 1847–48). Extant; some details lost.

1849 Rev. George Whipple House, Morningside, River Road, Belleville, N.J. Gothic Revival cottage. Extant ca. 1975 but in bad disrepair and distinguishing details lost.

1849 Dutch Reformed Church, Hastings-on-Hudson, N.Y. Gothic Revival. Core extant, but much remodeled.

1849 John Clarkson Jay estate, Boston Post Road, Rye, N.Y. Summerhouse. Gothic Revival (bracketed). Demolished 1960s.

1849–50 Niles Higinbotham House, Cottage Lawn, and summerhouse, 435 Main Street, Oneida, N.Y. Gothic Revival cottage villa. Extant (now Madison County Historical Society); veranda cresting lost?, wall color darkened.

1849–50 J. Smith Ely House, Edie Street, New Brighton, Staten Island, N.Y. Gothic Revival villa. Demolished.

1849 Oliver Bronson House, Hudson, N.Y. Towered addition across the riverfront. Italianate villa. Extant (now under the State Prison Authority); in disrepair. See 1839 for earlier work on this house.

1849–52 University of North Carolina, Smith Hall (also called Alumni Hall, Assembly Hall, and Library), Chapel Hill, N.C. Greek Revival, with four corn-and-wheat Corinthian capitals. Extant (now Playmakers Theatre); exterior slightly altered, interior much altered. See 1844–45 for earlier work at the University.

1849 Competition designs for a Washington Monument, Richmond, Va. Two Roman and one Gothic Revival. Not executed.

1849 Designs for a chapel and gatehouse, Evergreen Cemetery, Brooklyn, N.Y. Davis in collaboration with A. J. Downing. Romanesque Revival. Execution uncertain.

1849–50 William Chamberlain Cottage at Maizefield, West Market Street, Red Hook, N.Y. Classical, with Davisean windows. Extant; interior alterations.

1849 Edwin M. Holt House, Alamance County, N.C. Design based on the elevation of the L. B. Brown House published in *The Horticulturist,* January 1849, with floor plans by Davis. Tuscan Revival or "American style." Extant.

1849 Design for a cottage for W. F. Jones (carpenter), Auburn, N.Y. Gothic Revival. Probably addition to house on Van Anden Street, now demolished; may also have been the Sherwood House.

1849–50 Designs for an agricultural college for New York State. Davis and A. J. Downing. Classical. Not executed.

1850 Anthony Constant Cottage, Hastings-on-Hudson, N.Y. Swiss. Demolished 1960s.

1850–52 Francis Key Hunt House, Loudoun, Castlewood Park, Lexington, Ky. Gothic Revival villa. Extant; veranda and much interior detailing lost.

1850 Design for a villa for James Chambers, Highland Villa, for a site near West Point, N.Y. Davis in consultation with A. J. Downing. Italianate. Not executed.

1850–52 North Carolina Hospital for the Insane, Raleigh, N.C. Tuscan and Roman Revival. Partially extant (center section demolished); much altered, including additions and roof alteration. (See fig. 2.13.)

1850–53 Daniel H. Brooks House, stable, summerhouse, and grounds plan, near Port Chester, N.Y. Italianate. Demolished.

1850–51 E. R. Johnes House, Colden and South William Streets, Newburgh, N.Y. Remodeling, with addition of tower. Italianate. Demolished.

1850–52 Llewellyn S. Haskell House, Belmont (later owned by Dr. J. V. D. Berier), opposite Belleville, N.J. Italianate villa. Demolished.

1850–51 Design for a villa for Charles Scott Gay, Richmond, Va. Italianate. Not executed.

1850 Designs for a villa and cottage for Dr. Blanchard Fosgate, Auburn, N.Y. Italianate villa and Gothic Revival cottage. Execution unknown.

1850 E. Reuel Smith House, 11 West Lake Road, Skaneatales, N.Y. Gothic Revival cottage villa. Extant; some alterations and loss of details.

1850–52 New York City Armory, Elm and White Streets, New York City. Gothic Revival. Demolished.

1851–52 William S. Archer House, Elk Hill, Amelia County, Va. Remodeling. Elizabethan Revival villa, with corn-and-wheat capitals on veranda. Burned during the Civil War.

1851–52 Richard Lathers House, Winyah (addition 1856–57), and coach house/stable

(1863), New Rochelle, N.Y. Italianate villa. Demolished.

1851 Lewis B. Brown House, West Chester, N.Y. Italianate villa. Demolished?

1851 Designs for remodeling William Alexander Graham House, Montrose, Hillsborough, N.C. Gothic Revival and Italianate. Not executed.

1851 Design for a villa for Daniel Devlin, Craigmore, Manhattanville, N.Y. Italianate. Execution uncertain: either executed with substantial changes or superseded by a design by another architect. Demolished.

1851 Design for a villa for H. D. Wells, Hartford, Conn. Italianate. Apparently not executed.

1851–52 Samuel F. B. Morse House, Locust Grove, South Road, Poughkeepsie, N.Y. Remodeling. Davis and Morse. Italianate villa. Extant; later addition.

1851–54 Richard O. Morris House, Hawkwood, Green Springs, Louisa County, Va. Italianate villa. Shell extant; severely damaged by fire in 1982. (See fig. 3.14; colorplate 40.)

1851 Design for a villa and gardener's house for Charles Thorne Cromwell, Manursing Island, Rye, N.Y. Italianate. Execution uncertain: either executed with changes or superseded by a design by another architect. Demolished.

1851 Designs for a villa for Henry F. Spaulding, Manhattanville, N.Y. Italianate. Probably not executed but possibly influenced design of Spaulding's villa, Oaklawn (now part of Riverdale Country Day School), by Thomas S. Wall at Riverdale.

1851–53 Yale College Alumni Hall, New Haven, Conn. Gothic Revival (1881 proposal to raise one story higher not executed). Demolished 1911; the two towers were rebuilt at Weir Hall.

1852 Alexander Hammond House, Skaneateles, N.Y. Tuscan Revival or "American Style." Extant (clapboarding was used instead of board-and-batten).

1852 Christopher Reeve House, Detroit, Mich. Italianate villa. Demolished.

1852 Design for a villa for Charles B. Sedgwick, Syracuse, N.Y. Italianate. No evidence of execution.

1852–53 Design for a villa for Robert R. Raymond, Syracuse, N.Y. Italianate. No evidence of execution.

1852–53 Design for remodeling of Jesse H. Lindsey House, Greensboro, N.C. Bracketed. Not executed.

1852–56 John Cox Stevens House, South Amboy, N.J. Remodeling, greenhouse, garden structures, and landscaping. Classical. Demolished.

1852 Archibald Gracie King House, Weehawken, N.J. Gothic Revival cottage villa. Burned.

1852–56 Charles C. Alger House, Downing Place, Liberty Street, Newburgh, N.Y. Remodeling (of A. J. Downing's villa) and coach house/gardener's house. Gothic Revival villa. Demolished.

1852–55 William P. Chapman House, Whitby, Boston Post Road, Rye, N.Y. Gothic Revival villa. Extant (now Rye Country Club); addition and alterations (Davis's design of billiard room addition [1871] not executed). (See fig. 26; colorplate 16.)

1853 Designs for buildings for Raritan Bay Union, Perth Amboy, N.J. Italianate and classical. Not executed.

1853–54 Llewellyn S. Haskell House, Eyrie, Eagle Rock, Orange Mountain, West Orange, N.J. Remodeling of a farmhouse (addition 1856) and Gothic Revival observatory tower (1853–56). Rustic villa. Demolished 1920s. (See fig. 3.33.)

1853–63 Robert Donaldson House, Edgewater, Barrytown, N.Y. Classical additions to existing house, octagonal Gothic Revival and Italianate cottages, Italianate chapel, schoolhouse, boathouse, and rustic temple. Extant except the final two; chapel tower altered.

1853–54 Cocke Family Monument, Mount Pleasant, Surry County, Va. A prism. Extant.

1853 Design for stores with a dwelling above for Henry Lind, Porto Cabello (Puerto Cabello, Venezuela?). Style, site, and execution not traced.

1853–54 Courthouse and Town Hall, Bridgeport, Conn. Tuscan Revival, with Davisean windows. Shell extant; drastically altered 1903, when style was changed to Greek Revival; interior gutted and two stories made into three.

1853–56 Bela Hubbard House, Vinewood, 260 Vinewood, Detroit, Mich. Italianate villa. Demolished 1933.

1853–57 John Alsop King, Jr. House, The Point, King's Point, Long Island, N.Y. Italianate villa. Extant (revised version built, without tower); minor additions and changes.

1853 Design for a house for Col. H. B. Tomlin, Old Church, Hanover County, Va. Classical, with Davisean windows. Execution not traced.

1853–56 John C. Baughman House, Fort Street, Detroit, Mich. Italianate villa. Demolished.

1853 Salem Female Seminary, Salem, N.C. Elevations. Greek Revival. Extant (now Salem College); Davis's design was presumably followed.

1853–58 Edwin Clark Litchfield House, Grace Hill, coach house, greenhouse, and chicken house, Brooklyn, N.Y. Italianate villa. House extant (now New York City Department of Parks headquarters, Prospect Park); exterior stucco and many interior details lost. (See figs. 4.14–4.16b; colorplate 55.)

1854–57 Alexander E. Outerbridge House, Echo Hill, and coach house/stable, Holmesburg, Tacony (now part of Philadelphia), Pa. Italianate villa. Demolished.

1854–57 Edwin B. Strange House, Ingleside, gardener's house, and greenhouse, Broadway, Dobbs Ferry, N.Y. Gothic Revival villa. Extant (now main building of St. Christopher's School); veranda crudely replaced, many exterior and interior details lost; gardener's house altered; greenhouse gone.

1854–55 John Munn House, 1 Rutger Park, Utica, N.Y. Italianate villa. Extant (now Dowling Nursing Home); veranda partially enclosed; some interior changes.

1854–57 Jacob R. Shotwell House and coach house, Esterbrook Avenue and Elm Street, Rahway, N.J. Italianate villa. Demolished.

1854–55 Benjamin N. Huntington House and addition (1870), Rome, N.Y. Tuscan Revival. Demolished.

1854–57 John G. Lamberson House, Alsop Street, Jamaica, Long Island, N.Y. Italianate villa. Demolished or completely altered.

1854–56 Benjamin C. Webster House, Harrison Street, East Orange, N.J. Gothic Revival. Demolished.

1854 Monument to Henry K. Harral, Bridgeport Cemetery, Bridgeport, Conn. Gothic Revival. Extant.

1854–57; 1858–59 Ellwanger and Barry Mt. Hope Nursery Office, Mount Hope Avenue, Rochester, N.Y. Gothic Revival. Extant (now owned by the University of Rochester); 1858–59 addition (with tower) by Davis, 1892 addition not by Davis.

1855–56 Remodeling of several houses for Llewellyn S. Haskell, Llewellyn Park, West Orange, N.J. Apparently all demolished.

1855–70 Edward Kent House (additions 1869–70) and coach house/stable (1865), near Fort Hamilton, New Utrecht (now Brooklyn), N.Y. Gothic Revival villa. Demolished.

1855–59 John J. Herrick House, Ericstan, and furniture designs, Tarrytown, N.Y. Gothic Revival castellated villa. Demolished 1944; some furniture extant. (See figs. 3.28, 3.29; colorplate 49.)

1855–56 D. C. Foot House, Broadway, Dobbs Ferry, N.Y. Italianate villa. Demolished 1970.

1855–57 Augustus C. Richards House, Woodcliff, and round coach house, near Fort Tryon site, New York City. Gothic Revival castellated villa. Demolished 1939.

1855 Anna Grimke Frost House, Llewellyn Park, West Orange, N.J. Bracketed. Extant; much remodeled.

1856–59 Alexander J. Davis summer lodge, Wildmont, above Llewellyn Park, West Orange, N.J. Gothic Revival cottage, later villa. Additions 1860s and 1878; the latter enlarged the cottage into a villa, incorporating fragments from Waddell's villa, stored since 1856. Burned 1884. (See figs. 3.34, 3.35; colorplates 50, 51.)

1856 James Donaldson Gatehouse, New Hamburg, N.Y. Italianate cottage (Gothic Revival version not executed). Extant; altered.

1856–57 Designs for alterations to Old South and to the chapel and for small dormitories, University of North Carolina, Chapel Hill, N.C. Classical. Not executed.

1856–60 Davidson College campus, Davidson, N.C. Tuscan Revival, with Davisean windows. Of the extensive design only Chambers Hall was built, in a shortened version; burned 1924. (See fig. 2.15.)

1856–57 Oneida Seminary, Oneida, N.Y. Bracketed, with Davisean windows. Demolished.

1857 Gate lodge and gate, Llewellyn Park, West Orange, N.J. Rustic. Extant; some alterations. (See fig. 3.32.)

1857–66 Designs for park structures for Llewellyn S. Haskell, Llewellyn Park, West Orange, N.J. Rustic. Kiosk executed and demolished; temple, schoolhouse, lyceum, conservatory, and two additional gate lodges, execution unknown, but none extant.

1857 Designs for four villas as investment houses for Llewellyn S. Haskell, Llewellyn Park, West Orange, N.J. Italianate and Gothic Revival. Not executed.

1857–59 Joseph Howard House, Castlewood, and coach house, Mountain Avenue, Llewellyn Park, West Orange, N.J. Gothic Revival castellated villa. Extant; alterations (north wing not built and 1865–66 designs of addition for Haskell not executed). (See fig. 3.31; colorplate 48.)

1858 Investment stone cottage for Llewellyn S. Haskell, West Bloomfield (now Montclair), N.J. Executed, but not described or identified.

1858 Designs for additional investment cottages for Llewellyn S. Haskell, West Bloomfield (now Montclair), N.J. One Swiss, style of the others unknown. Execution unknown.

1858–59 Investment house for Llewellyn S. Haskell, Arcade Villa (first called Virginia House; also called Arcade Cottage, or Arcadia), and coach house/stable, Glen Avenue, Llewellyn Park, West Orange, N.J. Italianate villa. Demolished.

1858–59 Thomas B. Merrick House, Tyrdyn Terrace (later called The Terraces), and coach house/stable, Mountain Avenue, Llewellyn Park, West Orange, N.J. Italianate villa. Extant; much altered.

1858–59 Block of eleven houses unified in one comprehensive design for George Higgins, House of Mansions, Fifth Avenue between Forty-first and Forty-second Streets, New York City. Northern part became Rutgers Female Seminary. Gothic Revival. Demolished. (See fig. 11.)

1858 Robert Dabney House, Elmington, Powhatan County, Va. Italianate villa. Extant; only the towerless half of the house was built, in modified form.

1858–59 Designs for a house for Harriette L. Rimmer (or Reimer), Tarrytown, N.Y. Gothic Revival villa and cottage. Not executed.

1858 Designs for a villa for George Ellwanger, Rochester, N.Y. Italianate and Gothic Revival. Not executed.

1858–75 Designs for houses (single, double, and blocks) and a church for Edwin Clark Litchfield for his properties in Brooklyn, N.Y. Gothic Revival and other styles. Execution unknown.

1858–63 Villas and cottages for Richard Lathers and his friends, Lathers' Hill and Winyah Avenue, New Rochelle, N.Y. Two or three Gothic Revival villas and two Gothic Revival cottages were built, including villas for Charles M. Thurston (later A. G. Hemingway) and E. D. Griffin, and a cottage later owned by Frederic Remington. Demolished (four extant 1909; some alterations). Several designs (including for J. S. Ely) of various styles, not executed.

1858–59 Edward W. Nichols Cottage, Oak Bend, Llewellyn Park, West Orange, N.J. Gothic Revival. Extant; proposed addition by Davis (1866) not executed, but discreet rear addition made later (perhaps by Charles Follen McKim).

1859–60 Lawrence M. Davenport Cottage, Sans Souci, and coach house, Davenport Neck, New Rochelle, N.Y. Gothic Revival cottage. Extant; wing added by Davis for W. W. Evans, 1871–74; further additions later by others; coach house demolished.

1859 Design for Brooklyn Academy of Music, Brooklyn, N.Y. Classical. Not executed.

1859–61 I. Smith and Shepard Homans House and coach house/stable, Englewood, N.J. Italianate cottage villa. Demolished. See 1863 for remodeling for David Hoadley.

1859–60 Designs for White Sulphur Springs Hotel, Va. (now W. Va.) Additions, new hotel, and bath house. Classical and Gothic Revival. Not executed.

1859–60 Design for an Episcopal church, White Sulphur Springs, Va. (now W. Va.). Gothic Revival. Not executed.

1859–62? Investment house for Llewellyn S. Haskell, Bloomfield Villa (purchased 1860 and finished by Samuel Wilde, later purchased by D. T. Warren), 12 Eagle Rock Road, West Bloomfield (now 84 Llewellyn Road, Montclair), N.J. Italianate villa. Extant; much altered.

1860 Jesse Williams House, Llewellyn Park, West Orange, N.J. Remodeling. Bracketed. Extant; much altered.

1861–73 Coralie Livingston Barton House, Montgomery Place, Annandale-on-Hudson, N.Y. Additions to mansion (1863–64), farm cottage (1861), and house (1867). Classical, Italianate, and Swiss (house). Extant. Proposed gate lodge (1868) and mansion addition (1872–73) not executed. For earlier work at Montgomery Place, see 1841–60 Mrs. Edward Livingston.

1862; 1864–65 Oneida Valley National Bank, Oneida, N.Y. Italianate. Demolished 1918.

1862 Design for a Commercial Exchange, Nassau, Cedar, and Pine Streets, New York City. Classical, with Davisean windows (also Gothic Revival design?) Not executed. (See fig. 8.)

1861–65 John G. Baker House, Greyhurst, Perry Lane, South Orange, N.J. Gothic Revival cottage villa. Demolished ca. 1920?

1862 Store for Niles Higinbotham, Oneida, N.Y. Italianate. Extant 1970 (probably the Olin Electronics store, Madison Street between Maine and Williams Streets); alterations, including removal of cornice, remodeling of ground floor.

1862–70 Lewis G. Morris House, Mount Fordham, Bronx, N.Y. Alterations (1862 and 1870), coach house, gatehouse, and windmill tower. Italianate and Gothic Revival (windmill tower). Demolished. Several designs for cottages apparently not executed. For earlier work at Mount Fordham, see 1846–47.

1863–66 Edwards Pierrepont House, Hurstpierrepont, and gate, Garrison-on-Hudson, N.Y. Gothic Revival villa. Extant; altered and details lost. Design for billiard room addition (1866) not executed.

1863 David Hoadley House, Englewood, N.J. Remodeling of Homans House into Italianate towered villa. Demolished. For Homans House, see 1859–61.

1863; 1872; 1891 Designs for Abram Hewitt estate, Ringwood Park, N.J. Addition to house, gates, bridge, gardens, landscape gardening, village. Execution very doubtful.

1864 Designs for the Congregational Church of the Messiah, Fourth Avenue, New York City. Gothic Revival and other styles. Not executed.

1864 Design for Branch Bank of the State of Indiana for James B. Howe, Lima, Ind. Style, site, and execution not traced.

1864–67 George Merritt House, Lyndhurst, Tarrytown, N.Y. Remodeling of Paulding's Knoll. Gothic Revival villa. Extant. For earlier work at Knoll, see 1838–42 William and Philip R. Paulding. (See figs. 3.22, 4.25; colorplates 56, 57.)

1866 Design for a National Military Asylum. Gothic Revival. Not executed.

1867 Competition designs for U.S. Post Office, New York City. Greek and Roman Revival, with Davisean windows (designs revised and redrawn 1882). Not executed. (See fig. 2.26.)

1867 Edward S. Davis House, Danbury, Conn. Greek Revival. Not identified.

1867 Competition designs for Illinois State Capitol, Springfield, Ill. Greek and Roman Revival. Not executed. See 1837 for earlier competition design by Town & Davis.

1867 Design for the Institution for the Deaf and Dumb of Iowa, Council Bluffs, Iowa. Classical. Not executed.

1867–69 Many designs for houses for Llewellyn S. Haskell for Llewellyn Park, West Orange, N.J. Various styles; recapitulations and modifications of earlier designs and also new designs. No evidence of execution.

1868 Llewellyn Frost Haskell Cottage, Llewellyn Park, West Orange, N.J. Designed by Llewellyn Frost Haskell, revised by Davis. Second Empire. Extant; much altered.

1868 Mrs. Elwood Byerly House (built by David E. Green), Llewellyn Park, West Orange, N.J. Second Empire. Extant; discreet addition and alterations.

1869 Designs for houses in Huguenot Park, New Rochelle, N.Y. Various styles. Execution unknown.

1869 Design for a villa for W. R. Bergholz, Huguenot Park, New Rochelle, N.Y. Second Empire. Execution uncertain; not located.

1869–70 Designs for the Virginia Military Institute, Lexington, Va. Barracks extension, Claytor Hall, Memorial Chapel. Gothic Revival. Not executed. For earlier work at the Institute, see 1848–61.

1870 Design for the New-York Historical Society, New York City. Classical. Not executed.

1870 Designs for a Female Orphan Asylum, Lynchburg, Va. Greek Revival. Apparently not executed.

1870–73 Samuel Wilde House, 58 Fullerton Avenue, Montclair, N.J. Gothic Revival villa (first design, 1868–69, not executed). Demolished 1948.

1871–73 Lawrence M. Davenport House, Davenport Neck?, New Rochelle, N.Y. Italianate villa (earlier Italianate designs for Davenport apparently not executed). Executed, but not located.

1874–75 Augustus C. Richards House, Ridgeview (later Cedar Lawn), Broadway, Irvington, N.Y. Designed by Richards, "assisted" by Davis (preliminary design for Richards, 1871–72, not executed). Gothic Revival villa. Remodeled into a castle ca. 1906 by Isaac Stern. Demolished ca. 1963.

1875–76 Robert D. and Isabel Donaldson Bronson House, St. Augustine, Fla. Tuscan Revival. Extant; much altered.

1877 Competition designs for Long Island Historical Society, Montague Street, Brooklyn, N.Y. Classical. Not executed.

1880 Designs for remodeling store for Louise L. Hunt, 751 Broadway, New York City. Gothic Revival. Not executed.

1883–84 Design for a villa for Edward H. Litchfield. Gothic Revival castellated villa. Not executed.

1885–91 Designs for rebuilding Alexander J. Davis House, Wildmont, West Orange, N.J. Gothic Revival villa. Not executed. For Wildmont, see 1856–59 Alexander J. Davis summer lodge.

Notes

The major A. J. Davis collections are in the Metropolitan Museum of Art (cited in the notes as MMA); the Avery Architectural and Fine Arts Library, Columbia University (Avery); the New-York Historical Society (NYHS); and the New York Public Library (NYPL). The first volume of Davis's Day Book, dating from February 1828 (with earlier information recorded retrospectively) through September 1853, is in the New York Public Library; the second, dating from October 1853 through December 1869, is in the Avery Library. His office Journal is in the Print Department of the Metropolitan Museum of Art.

Introduction

1. As a mature architect, Alexander Jackson Davis rarely used his full middle name, but used only his middle initial. In the early years of his career he had used the full name.

2. Talbot Hamlin, "The Rise of Eclecticism in New York," Journal of the Society of Architectural Historians 11 (May 1952), p. 3.

3. Hamlin, Greek Revival Architecture in America (London, New York: Oxford University Press, 1944), p. 132.

4. Davis's use of the term "Tuscan" is confusing, since he used it in different ways: classical Vitruvian Tuscan (influenced by Inigo Jones's St. Paul's, Covent Garden) for monumental public designs, and Picturesque Tuscan (from country vernacular) for some of his Italianate villas.

5. On the modification of the Greek anta form, see Hamlin, Greek Revival Architecture, pp. 346–47. On Town & Davis usage, see Jane B. Davies, "A. J. Davis' Projects for a Patent Office Building, 1832–1834," Journal of the Society of Architectural Historians 24 (October 1965), pp. 239–40; Town had used a pseudoperistyle of shallow pilasters on his Hartford City Hall, 1828–29.

6. Davis, Journal, p. 20 (March and June 1831), MMA; and Day Book, pp. 95, 109, 123, 493, 495, NYPL. See also Davis's draft of an enlarged version of the Davis entry in William Dunlap's History of the Rise and Progress of the Arts of Design in the United States, Davis Collection (F-2), Avery.

7. Davis, Day Book, p. 273 (February 1, 3–7, 1845), NYPL. A photograph of the row as built is reproduced in Nathan Silver, Lost New York (New York: Houghton Mifflin, 1967), p. 134.

8. Edith Wharton, A Backward Glance (New York: D. Appleton-Century, 1934), p. 2; she was writing of Fifth Avenue during her childhood, in the 1860s.

9. Documentation on the verandas is not precise, but Davis's Journal, p. 73 (May 5, 1843), MMA, records: "Design. Veranda for Norman White," who built the houses; see also Davis's Day Book, p. 243 (May 5, 1843), NYPL. He had previously sketched a design with ornamental porches for houses on the west side of Gramercy Park for other clients; this sketch is reproduced in Stephen Garmey, Gramercy Park: An Illustrated History of a New York Neighborhood (New York: Balsam Press, 1984), p. 56.

10. Davis, Rural Residences (New York: The Author, 1837 [i.e., 1838]; reprint, New York: Da Capo Press: 1980), p. [3].

11. Davis, "Address" (draft for an introduction to a proposed later edition of Rural Residences), Davis Collection (G-1), Avery.

12. An unexecuted design for John B. James at Rhinebeck, 1841, influenced several designs. Downing called it "my old favorite . . . perhaps . . . as good a thing as can be produced by any living or dead man!" Downing to Davis, March 5, 1849, Davis Collection, MMA. He published a revised version as Design XXX in his The Architecture of Country Houses (New York: D. Appleton and Company, 1850; reprint, New York: Da Capo Press, 1968), p. 338.

13. The Horticulturalist 1 (October 1846), and The Architecture of Country Houses, p. 316 (with the latter, Downing also published an adaptation that he designed himself, p. 312).

14. Samuel H. Davis, "Obituary," Republican, Winchester, Virginia, May 26, 1831, Davis Collection (Q-1a), Avery. The author was a half-brother of A. J. Davis and the editor of the newspaper.

15. Davis, "Principal Works of Alex J. Davis," vol. 8 (24.66.1407), leaf 6, Davis Collection, MMA. Internal evidence indicates that this was probably written about 1863 or 1864.

16. Davis, Day Book, p. 13, NYPL; on p. 41 he remarked that the book was "borrowed of Ithiel Town Arch't."

17. William H. Pierson, Jr., American Buildings and Their Architects: Technology and the Picturesque (Garden City, New York: Doubleday & Co., 1978), pp. 278–79.

18. Davis, Day Book, pp. 63 (December 29,

1828) and 65 (January 5, 10–17, and 21, 1829), NYPL. Drawings of Hillhouse's proposed design for his house, drafted by Davis, together with proposed designs by other architects and friends, are in the Hillhouse Family Papers, Sterling Library, Yale University.

19. Davis, Day Book, p. 68 (February 1, 1829), NYPL.

20. Davis drew the illustrations directly on the whitened woodblocks, ready for the engraver. The joint work was usually based on rough sketches by Downing with revisions (often major), details, and landscape settings by Davis; the plans were by Downing, rectified by Davis. For a study of the relationship of Davis and Downing, see Jane B. Davies, "Davis and Downing: Collaborators in the Picturesque," in *Prophet with Honor: The Career of Andrew Jackson Downing, 1815–1852*, ed. George B. Tatum and Elisabeth Blair MacDougall (Washington, D.C.: Dumbarton Oaks, 1989), pp. 81–123.

21. [Montgomery Schuyler,] "Study of a New York Suburb, New Rochelle," *The Architectural Record* 25 (1909), p. 246.

Chapter 1

1. Davis, draft for an essay "On Architecture," 1834, Davis Papers, NYPL.

2. Davis's Journal, MMA, includes many references to the time he spent organizing his papers and sketches. Davis wrote the sketch of his life that was published anonymously in William Dunlap, *History of the Rise and Progress of the Arts of Design in the United States*, 2 vols. (New York: George P. Scott, 1834), 2, pp. 408–11. Dunlap's correspondence and meetings with Davis about his autobiography are documented in Dunlap's diary. See Dorothy C. Barck, ed., *The Diary of William Dunlap (1766–1839)* (New York: New-York Historical Society, 1931), pp. 768, 770, 774, 792, 795, 821, 823. Parts of Davis's draft for Dunlap can be found in Avery (F-2), MMA (pocket notebook 46.114.82), and NYHS (miscellaneous manuscripts Davis and miscellaneous manuscripts Dunlap).

3. Davis's papers include many jotted-down quotes that he presumably believed in or admired. These are from a miscellaneous notebook, Davis Papers, NYPL.

4. Davis, miscellaneous notebook, Davis Papers, NYPL.

5. Davis, draft for an essay "On Architecture."

6. Joseph B. Davis, draft for "Obituary. Alexander Jackson Davis," Davis Collection (F-2), Avery.

7. Davis, draft for Dunlap, MMA.

8. For illustrations of work by these artists, see Corcoran Gallery of Art, Washington, D.C., *Views and Visions: American Landscape before 1830*, exhib. cat. by Edward Nygren et al. (1986).

9. Davis, draft for Dunlap, MMA.

10. Dunlap, *Rise and Progress of the Arts of Design*, 2, p. 409.

11. Ibid.

12. Edward Lind Morse, *Samuel F. B. Morse: His Letters and Journals*, 2 vols. (Boston and New York: Houghton Mifflin Company, 1914), 1, p. 251.

13. [Edward Livingston], "Academy of Arts," New York *Morning Courier*, January 22, 1803. For further information on the American Academy of the Fine Arts, see Carrie Rebora, "The American Academy of the Fine Arts," Ph.D. diss., City University of New York, 1991.

14. See American Academy of the Fine Arts minutes, August 7, 1824, NYHS. See also "Academy of Arts," New York *American*, June 18, 1824, which includes a description of the "new Studio."

15. The sketch is inscribed "made while a student Am. Acad. Fine Arts—1826." The date is incorrect and the inscription is not in Davis's hand.

16. Andrews to his patron, Philip Schuyler, April 8, 1825, giving an account of his studies the previous autumn, NYHS.

17. For further information on the formation of the Association of Artists, see Rebora, "The American Academy of the Fine Arts," chapter 6, "Two Academies of Art."

18. National Academy of Design Archives. See also *National Academy of the Arts of Design. Instituted Jan. 19, 1826* (New York, 1826), p. 6, for a published list of association members.

19. *National Academy of the Arts of Design*, p. 6.

20. Ibid., p. 7.

21. On Cole's New York debut and the rise of American landscape painting, see Ellwood C. Parry III, "Thomas Cole's Early Career: 1818–1829," in Corcoran Gallery of Art, *Views and Visions*, pp. 161–87.

22. Draft for Dunlap, MMA. Peale's advice is not documented, but most logically dates from 1826 or 1827, when Peale was frequently in New York. Peale and Davis both lived at Julien House, owned by Lydia Vose, in late 1827. See Davis's Day Book, NYPL.

23. Davis, draft for Dunlap, Avery.

24. Gulian C. Verplanck, *Address, Delivered Before the American Academy of Fine Arts* (New York: Charles Wiley, 1824; reprinted 1825). See also "Verplanck's Address," New York *Evening Post*, May 26, 1824; "The Fine Arts," *Atlantic Magazine* 1 (June 1824), pp. 150–55.

25. Verplanck, *Address, Delivered Before the American Academy*, pp. 8–13.

26. I. N. Phelps Stokes, *The Iconography of Manhattan Island: 1498–1909*, 6 vols. (New York: Robert H. Dodd, 1918), 3, pp. 603–4.

27. *National Academy of the Arts of Design*, p. 8. See also *Constitution and By-Laws of the National Academy of Design* (New York: D. Fanshaw, 1826), p. 4.

28. Bartlett Cowdrey, comp., *National Academy of Design Exhibition Record: 1826–1860*, 2 vols. (New York: New-York Historical Society, 1943), 1, p. 114.

29. [D. Fanshaw], "The Exhibition of the National Academy of Design, 1827. The Second," *The United States Review and Literary Gazette* 2 (July 1827), p. 263.

30. Ibid., pp. 244–45.

31. Ibid., p. 261.

32. Davis provided drawings for ten issue frontispieces between 1826 and 1830. Between 1831 and 1833, he contributed six relatively unembellished views of buildings. All sixteen drawings accompanied essays on the pertinent buildings. Between 1831 and 1833, he also contributed six small

vignettes of New York buildings for a steel engraver.

33. Cowdrey, comp., *National Academy of Design Exhibition Record*, p. 114.

34. Davis, draft of letter, May 1828, Davis Collection (pocket notebook 46.114.82), MMA.

35. Ibid.

36. Eliot Clark, *History of the National Academy of Design: 1825–1953* (New York: Columbia University Press, 1954), p. 252.

37. [Fanshaw], "The Exhibition of the National Academy of Design," p. 245.

38. Davis to the Council of the National Academy of Design, November 1828, draft in Davis Collection (pocket notebook 46.114.82), MMA.

39. National Academy of Design minutes, November 17, 1828, NAD Archives, note that Davis's offer was accepted and that John Neilson, Jr., the instructor in perspective, was assigned to contact Davis.

40. *Constitution and By-Laws of the National Academy of Design* (New York: Clayton and Van Norden, 1829). Davis's copy is in the Thomas J. Watson Library, MMA.

41. Cowdrey, comp., *National Academy of Design Exhibition Record*, p. 114.

42. Davis to the National Academy of Design Committee on Lectures, 1830, Davis Papers, NYPL. See also National Academy of Design minutes, March 22, 1830, NAD Archives.

43. John C. Donoghue, "Alexander Jackson Davis, Romantic Architect, 1803–1892," Ph.D. diss., New York University, 1977, p. 396.

44. See Rebora, "The American Academy of the Fine Arts," chapter 6, "Two Academies of Art."

45. Davis, draft of toast, Letterbook, Davis Papers, NYPL.

46. Day Book, NYPL, and Journal, MMA, include numerous references to his art collection.

47. American Academy of the Fine Arts minutes, September 12, 1832, NYHS.

48. *Catalogue of Paintings and Statuary, Exhibited by the American Academy of the Fine Arts, May 1832. The Fourteenth Exhibition* (New York: William A. Mercein, 1832), cat. nos. 52, 112.

49. American Academy of the Fine Arts minutes, January 14, 1834, NYHS.

50. Davis, draft for an essay "On Architecture."

51. Day Book, NYPL.

52. See Rebora, "The American Academy of the Fine Arts," chapter 8, "Bees in the Carcase of the Dead Lion: The Academy After Trumbull."

53. Davis to Trumbull, February 24, 1839, American Academy of the Fine Arts Papers, NYHS.

54. "The Architects and Architecture of New York," *Brother Jonathan*, vol. V, no. 3 (May 20, 1843), p. 62.

55. National Academy of Design constitution. See also Durand to Davis, May 23, 1836, Davis Collection (N-13-e), Avery.

56. Prospectus, Davis Collection (50-6), Avery. Morse's landscape painting embellished the prospectus.

57. Miscellaneous manuscripts, Davis Collection, NYHS.

58. Davis, "Vitruvius and Soane on Patronage. With some original remarks on the Profession of Arch't'r and the Importance of the Arts of Design,"

lecture delivered before the Apollo Association, March 1, 1841, Davis Collection (58-1), Avery. See also the notice and advertisement in the New York *Evening Post,* March 15, 1841, p. 2.

59. For information on the National Academy's 1861 competition for a new building and P. B. Wight's winning design, see Art Institute of Chicago, *P. B. Wight: Architect, Contractor, and Critic, 1838–1925*, exhib. cat. with essay by Sarah Bradford Landau (1981), pp. 16–19. The academy's building committee invited Leopold Eidlitz, Jacob Wrey Mould, Richard Morris Hunt, and P. B. Wight to enter the competition.

60. Davis, "Address before the New-York Historical Society," 1874, American Academy of the Fine Arts Papers, NYHS.

61. Davis to T. Addison Richards, June 18, 1881, Letterbook, Davis Papers, NYPL.

Chapter 2

1. Davis, "Alexander Jackson Davis—Architect," unpublished manuscript, undated, Davis Collection, NYHS. This is one of several drafts Davis prepared for the biographical sketch that William Dunlap published in his *History of the Rise and Progress of the Arts of Design in the United States*, 2 vols. (New York: George P. Scott, 1834).

2. Davis, "Fragments, Scraps, etc.," unpublished manuscript, undated, Davis Collection, NYHS.

3. Henry-Russell Hitchcock and William Seale, *Temples of Democracy: The State Capitols of the USA* (New York: Harcourt Brace Jovanovich, 1977), p. 113.

4. As late as January 1882, Davis recorded in his Journal, p. 322, MMA, that he was reading Stuart and Revett's *Athens.*

5. For a discussion of the Custom House, see Talbot F. Hamlin, *Greek Revival Architecture in America* (London, New York: Oxford University Press, 1944), pp. 154–56.

6. Jane B. Davies, *A. J. Davis and American Classicism*, exhib. cat. (New York: Sleepy Hollow Press, 1989), p. 11. Thomson resigned from the Custom House job in a dispute over wages in 1835. He was succeeded as superintending architect first by his son, William Archibald Thomson, and later by sculptor John Frazee, who saw the building through to completion in 1842. For more on Thomson see Geoffrey Carter, "Samuel Thomson: Prolific New York Builder," *Preservation League of New York State Newsletter* XVII (Fall 1991), pp. 4–5.

7. Hamlin, *Greek Revival Architecture*, p. 324.

8. Excerpt from Davis's draft, Davis Collection (F-2), Avery, for his biography in Dunlap (see n. 1), quoted in Roger Hale Newton, *Town and Davis, Architects: Pioneers in American Revivalist Architecture 1812–1870* (New York: Columbia University Press, 1942), p. 85.

9. Davis, "Abuses in Architecture," unpublished manuscript, undated, p. 2, Davis Collection, NYHS.

10. Ibid.

11. Hitchcock and Seale, *The State Capitols*, pp. 83–84.

12. Davis, Journal, p. 21, MMA.

13. Davies, *Davis and American Classicism*, p. 7. Jane B. Davies has also pointed out that Town had used pilasters on the exterior of his Hartford City Hall and Market House, designed in 1828–29, before his formal association with Davis. These, however, were shallower than the bold antae that appear on the Indianapolis capitol and other buildings by Town & Davis, as well as on buildings Davis designed alone. This leads Davies to think that Davis had the leading hand in developing the dramatic potential of the pilastrade.

14. Hitchcock and Seale, *The State Capitols*, p. 87.

15. Davis, Journal, p. 103, MMA.

16. For a full account of this project, see Jane B. Davies, "A. J. Davis' Projects for a Patent Office Building, 1832–1834," *Journal of the Society of Architectural Historians* 24 (October 1965), pp. 229–51. Also instructive is Wilcomb E. Washburn, "Temple of the Arts, The Renovation of Washington's Patent Office Building," *AIA Journal* X (March 1969), pp. 8–16.

17. Davies, "Patent Office," p. 245.

18. Davis, "Abuses in Architecture," p. 2.

19. Ibid.

20. Davis, "Fragments." For Davis's position within the Egyptian Revival movement in the United States, see Richard G. Carrott, *The Egyptian Revival, Its Sources, Monuments and Meaning, 1808–1858* (Berkeley: University of California Press, 1978). In Appendix III, "The New York City Halls of Justice and House of Detention (the 'Tombs')," Carrott details the history of the design competition held for that building and explains Davis's role in it.

21. Davis, Journal, p. 44, MMA.

22. Davis had apparently been given plans and elevations of the Hanwell hospital by James MacDonald, director of the Bloomingdale Asylum. Davis illustrated Hanwell together with plans of his Blackwell's Island and Raleigh, North Carolina, asylums in "Asylums, London, New York, Raleigh from Alex. J. Davis, Architect," unpublished portfolio, 1883, Prints and Drawings Department, NYHS. For a nearly contemporary discussion of Hanwell, which was the largest public asylum in Great Britain, see Pliny Earle, *A Visit to Thirteen Asylums for the Insane in Europe* (New York, 1841), pp. 1–9.

23. Davis, text for business advertisement, Davis Collection, NYHS.

24. Quoted in Albert Deutsch, *The Mentally Ill in America* (New York: Columbia University Press, 1949), p. 145.

25. Davis, "Davis." The architect mentions this in his list of buildings included with the autobiography.

26. Davis, Journal, p. 115, MMA.

27. Ibid.

28. Wayne Andrews, *Architecture, Ambition and Americans: A Social History of American Architecture* (New York: Harper, 1964), p. 120.

29. Deutsch, *The Mentally Ill,* p. 303.

30. For a discussion of Davis's work in this field, see Paul Venable Turner, *Campus, An American Planning Tradition* (New York and Cambridge: Architectural History Foundation and MIT Press, 1984), pp. 124–25.

31. For a detailed discussion of the New York University building, see Arthur Scully, Jr., *James Dakin, Architect: His Career in New York and the South* (Baton Rouge: Louisiana State University Press, 1973), pp. 17–22.

32. Scully, *James Dakin*, p. 21, points out that Dakin owned an engraving of the interior of Oxford Cathedral.

33. Turner, *Campus*, p. 124.

34. *Rural Residences* was reprinted, with an introduction by Jane B. Davies, by Da Capo Press in 1980.

35. Ibid.

36. I am indebted to Jane B. Davies for this information. The drawings are in the Davis Collection, NYHS.

37. See Jane B. Davies, "The Wadsworth Atheneum's Original Building: I. Town & A. J. Davis, Architects," *Wadsworth Atheneum Bulletin* V (Spring 1959), pp. 7–18.

38. Specifications for the Lyceum are in MMA.

39. Davis, Journal, p. 278, MMA.

40. Davis, text for business advertisement.

41. Quoted in Davies, *Davis and American Classicism*, p. 19.

42. Davis, note, Davis Collection, NYHS.

43. "Artist's Villa," *The Horticulturist* 4 (December 1854), pp. 563–64 and frontispiece.

44. Davis, note, Davis Collection, NYHS.

45. Davis, Journal, p. 71 (January 15, 1843), MMA.

46. Davis, ms. beginning "1834–1880. After an interval . . .," p. 9, Davis Collection, NYHS.

47. Davis, Journal, p. 288, MMA.

48. "An Old Architect on Modern Architecture," New York *Sun*, October 28, 1878, p. 1. The date of September 1877 at the end of the letter must be a misprint.

49. Davis even found the park landscape somewhat disappointing. After a visit there in June 1870, he wrote in his Journal, p. 239, MMA, "I am always glad to get home; not so at Wildmont. Probably wild nature [is] more lasting in the enjoyment it affords, than art of man."

Chapter 3

1. There is a thoughtful analysis of Davis's floor plans and their relationship to the works of J. N. L. Durand in Patrick A. Snadon, "A. J. Davis and the Gothic Revival Castle in America, 1832–1865," Ph.D. diss., Cornell University, 1988.

2. Ibid., p. 10.

3. "The Architects and Architecture of New York," *Brother Jonathan*, vol. V, no. 15 (August 1843), p. 422. This article goes on to enumerate the criteria for selecting a site for a country house. The passage is a close paraphrase of John Claudius Loudon's advice in his *Encyclopaedia of Cottage, Farm, and Villa Architecture and Furniture* (London: Longman, Brown, Green, and Longmans, 1833; with supplement, 1842), pp. 763–66.

4. Davis, *Rural Residences* (New York: Da Capo Press, 1980; reprint of 1838 edition with introduction by Jane B. Davies).

5. Davis, Day Book, p. 222 (October 5, 1864), Avery.

6. Typescript, Lyndhurst Archives. Davis ad-

vised several clients, including Philip St. George Cocke and John J. Herrick, on the purchase of books on taste, including those on architecture, art, poetry, literature, and landscape gardening.

7. A. J. Downing, *Victorian Cottage Residences* (New York: Dover, 1981; reprint of 1873 edition of *Cottage Residences*), p. 5.

8. *The Diary of Philip Hone*, ed. Allan Nevins, 2 vols. (New York: Dodd, Mead & Co., 1927), 2, p. 550.

9. In *Cottage Residences* Downing suggests a design for a house, "each department of the house being complete in itself, and intruding itself but little on the attention of the family or guest when not required to be visible, which is the ideal of domestic accommodation" (p. 3). After Downing's death in 1852, his eloquent advocacy of romantic styles waned, and critics once again saw Davis's floor plans as cramped. "Our New York Letter," *American Builder and Journal of Art*, December 1868, published this scathing remark: "Mr. Davis is still meditating vast designs which have their end getting us all shut up again snug and uncomfortable in the feudal box."

10. Charles Brownell's "In the American Style of Italian, The E. C. Litchfield Villa," master's thesis, University of Delaware, 1970, p. 194, gives an excellent account of the origins and use of what Davis called scientific bricklaying:

This system provides a continuous series of vertical ducts in the core of the wall for the sake of 'proper ventilation and . . . dryness' (Davis coll., Met., Vol. XV, p. 9). Urging the adoption of this method in *The Architecture of Country Houses* (p. 59), Downing noted that to the best of his knowledge, hollow walls had first been introduced into the United States from British practice by Ithiel Town, Davis's late partner. Following Downing's death this bricklaying method was again recommended to the American public, by John Bullock in *The American Cottage Builder* (New York, 1854; pp. 18–21; see also pp. 186–88); by D. H. Jacques, who cited Downing, in *The House* (New York, 1858; p. 159); and by Samuel Sloan, who followed Downing's treatment quite closely in *Sloan's Homestead Architecture* (Philadelphia, 1861; pp. 34–36).

11. A. S. B. Culbertson to A. J. Downing, 1847, Davis Collection (24.66.1417), MMA. The letter was originally addressed to Downing, since Culbertson had admired Sheldon's villa in his *Treatise on Landscape Gardening*. Downing forwarded the letter to Davis.

12. Davis, Day Book, March 15, 1828, NYPL.

13. In an introduction to a series of classical designs in his scrapbooks, vol. 2, leaf 1, Davis Collection, MMA, Davis expounded on the merits of Greek architecture in what amounted to a paraphrase of Stuart and Revett:

We must ever acknowledge the Greeks of old our masters in style which bears their name, and whose Alphabet we adopt:—the ORDER, which originated in the East, and was appropriated, perhaps perfected in Greece. We therefore give precedence to a specimen of this Order, in its three degrees of comparison or styles: Doric, in

the "Parthenon of Athens", Ionic, in "the temple" on the Ilissus; and Corinthian, in "the Monument of Lysicrates" all from Athens.

14. [James A. Hillhouse], *Sachem's-Wood: A Short Poem, with Notes* (New Haven: B. & W. Noyes, 1838), courtesy New Haven Colony Historical Society. These selected passages illustrate Hillhouse's dedication to his father, who died in 1832, and the development of Hillhouse Avenue.

Farewell to "Highwood!" name made dear
By lips we never more can hear!
That came, unsought for, as I lay,
Musing o'er landscapes far away;
Expressive just of what one sees,
The upland slopes, the stately trees;
Oaks, prouder that beneath their shade
His lair the valiant Pequot made, . . .
. . . Now, from this bench, the gazer sees
Towers and white steeples o'er the trees
Mansions that peep from leafy bowers,
And Villas blooming close by ours; . . .

15. Davis, *Rural Residences*, n.p.

16. Ibid.

17. Four principal works of English landscape theory that influenced English and American design were Edmund Burke, *Philosophical Enquiry into the Origin of Our Ideas of the Sublime and Beautiful* (1757); Uvedale Price, *Essays on the Picturesque* (1794); Richard Payne Knight, *The Landscape* (1794); and Humphrey Repton, *Sketches and Hints on Landscape Gardening* (1795). Davis had copies of all of these treatises. Also see chapters 9 and 10 of James S. Ackerman, *The Villa, Form and Ideology of Country Houses* (Princeton, N.J.: Princeton University Press, 1990), for an excellent survey of the literary origins of the Picturesque and their influences on Downing. Mention is also made of the Davis/Downing relationship.

18. For a comprehensive discussion of A. J. Davis's contribution to Downing's publications, see Jane B. Davies, "Davis and Downing: Collaborators in the Picturesque," in *Prophet with Honor: The Career of Andrew Jackson Downing, 1815–1852*, ed. George B. Tatum and Elisabeth Blair MacDougall (Washington, D. C.: Dumbarton Oaks, 1989), pp. 81–123.

19. A. J. Downing, *Treatise on the Theory and Practice of Landscape Gardening* (New York: C. M. Saxton & Co., 1855, 5th edition), p. 385.

20. The interlinking of facades was common in other complex designs of this period, such as Ericstan and Lyndhurst. Davis also did a rendering of his own home, Wildmont, shown as one continuous facade.

21. Downing, *Landscape Gardening*, pp. 405–6.

22. As found in Snadon's "Gothic Revival Castle in America," MS 387, Travel Diary of Robert Gilmor III, vol. II, May 26–30, 1830, n.p., Robert Gilmor, Jr., Papers, Maryland Historical Society.

23. For a comprehensive analysis of Glen Ellen and Lyndhurst, see William H. Pierson, Jr., *American Buildings and Their Architects: Technology and the Picturesque* (Garden City, New York: Doubleday & Co., 1978), chapter 6, "Alexander Jackson Davis and the Picturesque."

24. Davis's first work for Robert Donaldson was

in 1831, when he designed railings, candelabra, and marble pedestals for his New York City residence. In addition to a city house, Donaldson owned a series of Hudson River estates. His first was Blithewood, where Davis remodeled an earlier house and designed a gatehouse and numerous garden structures. In the 1850s he purchased Silvania, and had Davis add an octagonal library to the house. Davis also made designs for a schoolhouse, greenhouses, gardeners' cottages, and a chapel on that estate.

25. Robert Donaldson to Davis, May 12, 1863, Davis Collection (2–4), Avery.

26. A. J. Downing, *Treatise on the Theory and Practice of Landscape Gardening* (New York: Wiley & Putnam, 1841, 1st edition), p. 323.

27. These elevations and plans are shown on two drawings at MMA, 24.66.1406(42) and 24.66.1406(44).

28. Davis's Journal, p. 208, MMA, recorded that he made designs on October 20, 1863, for Robert J. Dillon, "Studies for refitting Pauldings." Dillon was considering the purchase of Knoll, but the transaction never took place. Davis may have used these same designs for George Merritt when he purchased the property in 1864.

29. See Davies, "Collaborators in the Picturesque," for examples of bracketed-style houses by Davis and Downing.

30. Loudon, *Cottage, Farm, and Villa Architecture,* p. 777. Loudon is referring to G. L. Meason's *The Landscape Architecture of Great Painters of Italy* (London, 1827), which contained sixty illustrations of castles. Some of these were used by Loudon in the *Encyclopaedia.*

31. Avery contains most of the floor-plan drawings for Ericstan in the series 14–1 through 14–10. The evolution of the design can be traced through their examination.

32. There have been several articles written on the history of Llewellyn Park. The most recent is Susan Henderson, "Llewellyn Park, Suburban Idyll," *The Journal of Garden History,* vol. 7, no. 3 (July/September 1987). In the first footnote of Henderson's article, there is a complete bibliography of published articles.

33. Reuben Vose, "Wealth of the World Displayed," New York, 1859, clipping found in Avery (P1-1).

34. Several years earlier, Davis designed his only Norman/Romanesque commission (1847–49), for Dr. Amos Hull. The villa was never built, but a gatehouse and watch turret were constructed. In the drawing at MMA (24.66.71), the villa, which is seen on the hill above the gatehouse, resembled Wildmont, with the same turret and gable composition on the rear facade. The gatehouse showed a knowledgeable handling of the style and its related detailing. It displayed rounded arch windows, chevron decorations, and a small turret on the end of the portcullis. Davis never developed his work in the Romanesque as did architect Henry Hobson Richardson twenty years later.

35. Davis to Mrs. William Walsh, Albany, New York, May 1845, Letterbook (1821–90), 381d–382, NYPL.

36. There are examples of "Artist's Villa" designs in both NYPL and MMA.

37. On p. 17 of Snadon's "Gothic Revival Castle

in America," he states, "Between 1832 and 1857 Davis designed a total of fifteen Gothic Revival castles (which were built), an average of one every eighteen months for a quarter-century. By contrast, no other American architect designed over one Gothic castle in the course of a whole working career." He notes that his compilation does not include unexecuted designs, and it also does not encompass cottage villas.

Chapter 4

1. In 1862, a Robert James Dillon was considering buying Knoll. He commissioned Davis to make ten drawings for an addition; after the property was sold to Merritt in 1864, these drawings may have influenced Merritt's decision to add the new wing to Knoll.

2. *Brother Jonathan,* vol. V, no. 3 (May 20, 1843), p. 61. In 1843, one of a series of articles in the newsweekly *Brother Jonathan* entitled "The Architects and Architecture of New York" stated that "Architecture, in this city and State, has, within the last fifteen years, undergone a great and important change. Before that time nearly all buildings were designed by the carpenters and masons who constructed them, and the business of the architect was almost wholly unknown." These articles were highly complimentary to the work of Town & Davis.

3. George Wightwick, with additional notes by Andrew Jackson Downing, *Hints To Young Architects* (New York: Wiley & Putnam, 1847), p. xxviii.

4. Henry Hudson Holly, *Holly's Country Seats* (New York: D. Appleton and Company, 1863), pp. 29–30.

5. Gail Caskey Winkler, *Influence of Godey's Lady's Book on the American Woman and Her Home: Contributions to a National Culture (1830–1877),* Ph.D. diss., University of Wisconsin–Madison, 1988.

6. For an interesting investigation of A. T. Stewart's role as decorator, see *Remembering Father: James Brown Clay, Merchants, Materials and a New Ashland,* by Robert S. Spiotta, master's thesis, Cooper-Hewitt Museum and Parsons School of Design, September 1990.

7. Andrew Jackson Downing, *The Architecture of Country Houses* (New York: D. Appleton and Company, 1850), p. 405.

8. Ibid., p. 365.

9. Henry W. Cleaveland, William Backus, and Samuel D. Backus, *Village and Farm Cottages* (New York: D. Appleton and Company, 1856), p. 131.

10. Calvert Vaux, *Villas and Cottages* (New York: Harper & Brothers, 1857), pp. 85–86.

11. "Stephens, Ann Sophia (1813–Aug. 20, 1886)," *Dictionary of American Biography* (New York: Charles Scribners Sons, 1962), vol. IX, p. 576.

12. *Brother Jonathan,* vol. V, no. 5 (June 3, 1843), p. 121.

13. The dates referred to in this article, unless otherwise noted, have all been taken from Davis's own diaries.

14. Davis, Journal, vol. 1, p. 59, MMA.

15. John Claudius Loudon, *The Encyclopaedia of*

Cottage, Farm, and Villa Architecture and Furniture (London: Longman, Brown, Green, and Longmans, 1833; with supplement, 1842), p. 795.

16. Davis Collection (17–6), Avery.

17. Davis Collection (N–13g), Avery.

18. Although the decision to arch the ceilings was mentioned by Davis in such a seemingly casual manner, this redesign must have entailed a good deal of creative thinking for Davis and a good deal of extra work for the contractors of the building. The arched ceilings greatly enriched the appearance of the rooms; the interiors would be much duller if the ceilings had all remained flat. Even today, the ceilings of Lyndhurst are remarkable.

19. Lyndhurst Archives.

20. Ibid.

21. Downs Manuscript and Microfilm Collection, The Henry Francis du Pont Winterthur Museum, Winterthur, Delaware.

22. *Brother Jonathan*, vol. V, no. 11 (July 15, 1843), p. 301.

23. Jane B. Davies, "Gothic revival furniture designs of Alexander J. Davis," *The Magazine Antiques*, vol. CXI, no. 5 (May 1977), pp. 1014–27.

24. *Brother Jonathan*, vol. V, no. 11 (July 15, 1843), p. 301.

25. Knoll Inventory, 1855, Lyndhurst Archives.

26. Downing, *Country Houses*, p. 295.

27. Davis Collection (Hl-3d and Hl-3e), Avery.

28. Downing, *Country Houses*, p. 285.

29. Davis Collection (Hl-3z), Avery.

30. A conflicting document in Davis's hand, Davis Collection (Hl-3f), Avery, states that George Nichols "was engaged to visit the works, as superintendent," on January 18, 1856.

31. Davis Collection (275N), Print Department, NYHS.

32. Davis was an early recycler. When the Waddell villa was torn down in 1856, Davis incorporated two Corinthian columns from that house into the columnar screen in front of the bay window in the drawing room at Grace Hill. Unfortunately, they did not survive the current utilization of the house.

33. Downing, *Country Houses*, p. 403.

34. Ibid., p. 432.

35. Davis Collection (27–14), Avery.

36. This probably refers to tiles made by the Garnkirk Fire-clay Works, Garnkirk, Scotland. Statuary and fountains made from the company's buff-colored clay were much admired at the Great Exhibition in London, 1851. The elaborately decorated tiles that were actually laid in the hall have been identified as coming from Minton and Company.

37. The extent of Merritt's book collection at the time he moved into the house is unclear. He may not have had any books on design in the collection, but must have been an enthusiastic student, because he gave Davis $250 with which to buy books on the subject for him. In addition, Davis also supplied him with a "model catalogue," more than 200 titles long, of great books on architectural and landscape design. See Davis, Day Book, February 1 and 7, 1867, Avery. Davis entitled his catalogue "LIST OF BOOKS FOR G.M. FROM A.J.D. CLASS OF ARCHITECTURE, SCULPTURE, PAINTING & ENGRAVING and being the most valuable of this class existing upon the earth." It also included works on history, travel, nature, and poetry, complete with the books' prices. This document is in the Lyndhurst Archives.

38. The corbel list is in the collection of the NYPL.

39. Drawing attached to corbel list (see above). Also see Davis, Day Book, April 19, 1866, Avery.

40. Davis Collection (17–4), Avery.

Works and Projects

1. I am very grateful for the assistance rendered, over a long period of time, by the staffs of the Metropolitan Museum of Art; the Avery Architectural and Fine Arts Library, Columbia University; the New York Historical Society; and the New York Public Library, as well as by the staffs of other libraries, historical societies, and museums that struggled to answer my inquiries, and by the many individuals who aided in the search for evidence of the outcome, or traces, of Davis's designs. Davis himself left several lists of his works, but since they were compiled from memory, they are incomplete, full of errors (especially in dating), and often do not distinguish between executed and unexecuted works.

2. Some discrepancies in dating exist between this list and my shorter list in the *Macmillan Encyclopedia of Architects* (New York: Free Press, 1982), vol. 1, p. 513, since the editorial directive for the latter list specified dates of construction only.

3. For the periods of the Town & Davis partnerships (February 1, 1829–May 1, 1835, and May 1, 1842–July 13, 1843), the firm name is used if the work was not clearly by Davis alone (if clearly by Davis alone, no architect's name is specified). A few items that apparently were the work of Ithiel Town alone have been omitted.

4. The records for the period of the Town, Davis, & Dakin firm (May 1, 1832–November 1, 1833) are particularly confused, and it is especially difficult to determine the respective work of the three members except in instances when Davis specifically designated credit. If it is not clear who did the work, the firm name is used. For two periods (June 21–September 7, 1832, and January 20–May 21, 1833) Davis was away from the New York office, in Washington and Baltimore; therefore, the work recorded for the New York office during these periods has been omitted.

5. From August 1, 1835, until sometime in 1836, Davis and Russell Warren "joined interests." During that period some work was done jointly and apparently some work separately by each architect. Work that was done jointly or is not clearly attributable to one of the two architects is listed with both names. Work that seems clearly attributable to Davis alone is given without an architect's name, while work obviously by Warren is omitted.

6. Located by Elizabeth Mills Brown in *New Haven: A Guide to Architecture and Urban Design* (New Haven: Yale University Press, 1976), p. 80, no. G60.

Colorplates

COLORPLATE 1
Study for a church in the Egyptian style, ca.
1834. Front and side elevations. Watercolor and
ink on paper, 26 ¾ x 18 ¾ in. The Metropolitan
Museum of Art, Harris Brisbane Dick Fund,
1924 (24.66.443).

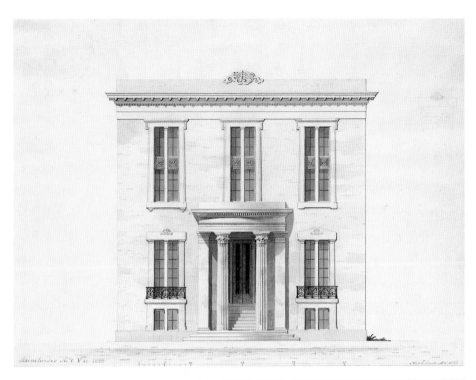

COLORPLATE 2
House for William C. Rhinelander, New York
City, 1836 (project). Front elevation and partial
section. Watercolor, ink, and graphite on paper,
17 ½ x 25 ¹¹⁄₁₆ in. The Metropolitan Museum of
Art, Arnold Bequest, 1954 (54.90.134).

COLORPLATE 3
House for John Cox Stevens, New York City,
1845. Front elevation. Watercolor, ink, and
graphite on paper, 15 ½ x 20 ½ in. Drawings
Collection, The New-York Historical Society,
Gift of Daniel Parish, Jr., 1908 (1908.27).

COLORPLATE 4
Study for two residential rows facing across a
court, New York City, ca. 1831. Perspective.
Watercolor and ink on paper, 9 ¾ x 26 ½ in. The
Metropolitan Museum of Art, Harris Brisbane
Dick Fund, 1924 (24.66.1291).

COLORPLATE 5
Study for a Greek Revival doorway, ca. 1831.
Elevation. Watercolor, ink, and graphite on
paper, 19¹³⁄₁₆ x 14⅜ in. The Metropolitan
Museum of Art, Harris Brisbane Dick Fund,
1924 (24.66.756).

COLORPLATE 6
Study for a double town house, ca. 1843. Front
elevation. Watercolor and ink on paper, 14 ½ x
20 ⁵⁄₁₆ in. The Metropolitan Museum of Art,
Harris Brisbane Dick Fund, 1924 (24.66.55).

COLORPLATE 7
Walnut Wood for Henry K. Harral, Bridgeport, Connecticut, 1846–50. Perspective. Watercolor and ink on paper, 14 5/16 x 20 in. Drawings & Archives, Avery Architectural and Fine Arts Library, Columbia University (1940.001.00038).

COLORPLATE 8
House for John B. James, Rhinebeck, New York, 1841 (project). Front elevation. Watercolor, ink, and graphite on paper, 13 1/4 x 19 3/8 in. Drawings & Archives, Avery Architectural and Fine Arts Library, Columbia University (1940.001.00042).

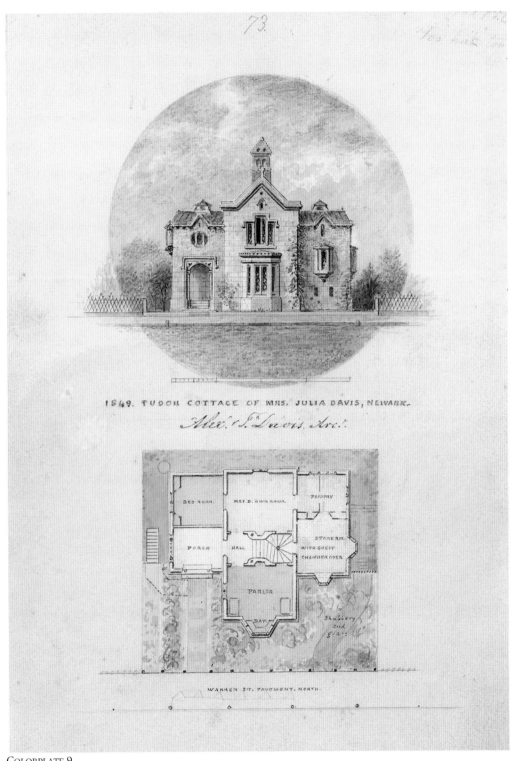

73

1849. TUDOR COTTAGE OF MRS. JULIA DAVIS, NEWARK.

Alex. J. Davis, Arch.

BED ROOM.   MRS. D. OWN ROOM.   PANTRY.

PORCH   HALL   STORE RM. WITH GUEST CHAMBER OVER.

PARLOR

BAY.

Shrubbery and Stair.

WARREN ST. PAVEMENT. NORTH.

COLORPLATE 9
Kirri Cottage for Julia Davis, Newark, New
Jersey, 1847–49 (later additions 1854, 1859).
Front elevation and plan. Watercolor, ink, and
graphite on paper, 10 x 6 $^{15}/_{16}$ in. The
Metropolitan Museum of Art, Harris Brisbane
Dick Fund, 1924 (24.66.789).

COLORPLATE 10
Gate lodge for Amos G. Hull, Newburgh, New
York, 1849. Front elevation. Watercolor, ink,
and graphite on paper, 14 ⅜ x 19 ¹³⁄₁₆ in. The
Metropolitan Museum of Art, Harris Brisbane
Dick Fund, 1924 (24.66.71).

COLORPLATE 11
Study for a villa for James Smillie, Rondout,
New York, 1836. Front elevation and two
plans. Watercolor, ink, and graphite on paper,
14 ½ x 10 ⅜ in. The Metropolitan Museum of
Art, Harris Brisbane Dick Fund, 1924
(24.66.1416 [49], vol. XVII, leaf 56).

VILLA IN THE ITALIAN STYLE, BY A. I. DAVIS

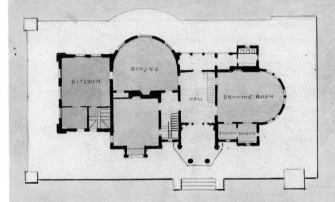

FIRST FLOOR

KITCHEN · DINING · HALL · DRAWING ROOM · CABINET BOUDOIR

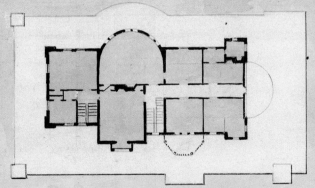

SECOND FLOOR.

water & sky lightest.   Hemlock   Pine   Pine   View N.W. at Blithewood

COLORPLATE 12
"View N. W. at Blithewood," Annandale-on-
Hudson, New York, ca. 1841. Watercolor, ink,
and graphite on paper, 7 ⅞ x 9 ¹⁵⁄₁₆ in. Drawings
& Archives, Avery Architectural and Fine Arts
Library, Columbia University
(1955.001.00059).

COLORPLATE 15
Preliminary design for Kenwood for Joel
Rathbone, south of Albany, New York, 1842.
Rear elevation. Watercolor and ink on paper,
13 ¾ x 19 ¹¹⁄₁₆ in. The Metropolitan Museum of
Art, Harris Brisbane Dick Fund, 1924
(24.66.22).

COLORPLATE 16
Library bay at Whitby for William P.
Chapman, Rye, New York, 1853. Elevation and
section. Watercolor and ink on paper, 17 ⅛ x
12 ½ in. The Metropolitan Museum of Art,
Harris Brisbane Dick Fund, 1924 (24.66.16).

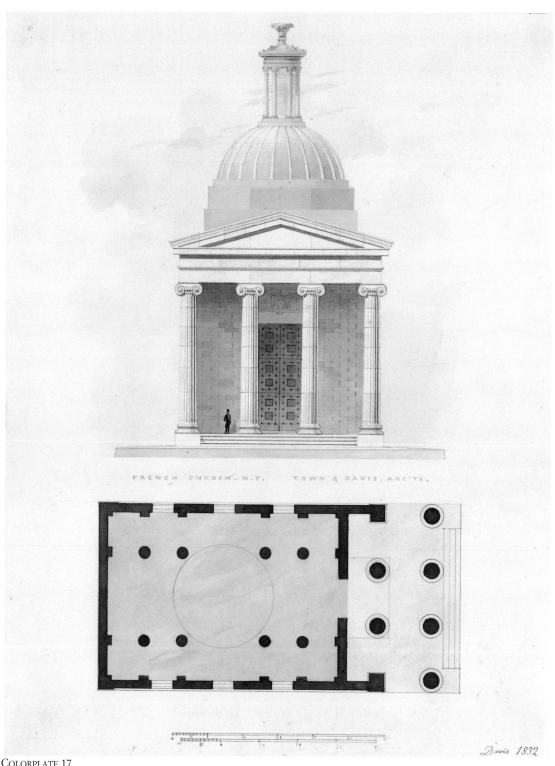

COLORPLATE 17
Église du Saint Esprit, New York City,
1831–34. Town & Davis. Front elevation and
plan. Watercolor and ink on paper, 11¾ x 8¹⁵⁄₁₆
in. The Metropolitan Museum of Art, Harris
Brisbane Dick Fund, 1924 (24.66.82).

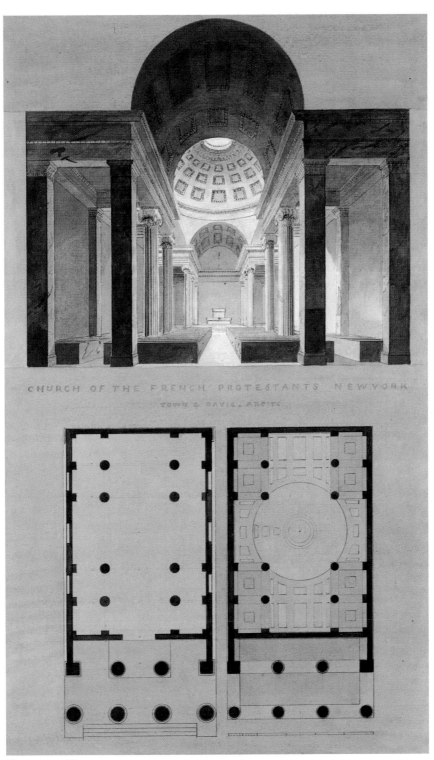

COLORPLATE 18
Église du Saint Esprit, New York City,
1831–34. Town & Davis. Section and two
plans. Watercolor and ink on paper, 21 ⅞ x
14 ⅜ in. The Metropolitan Museum of Art,
Harris Brisbane Dick Fund, 1924 (24.66.84).

COLORPLATE 19
"View of the Village of Florida, Orange Co.
N.Y. from the North-West," ca. 1820–22.
Watercolor and ink on paper, 16⅛ x 20¾ in.
The Metropolitan Museum of Art, Harris
Brisbane Dick Fund, 1924 (24.66.749).

View of St. Thomas Church (Josiah R. Brady,
architect), ca. 1827. Black ink, gray and brown
wash on paper, 8 x 10 in. Drawings Collection,
The New-York Historical Society, Foster Jarvis
Fund, 1953 (1953.201).

COLORPLATE 21
Astor Hotel, New York City, ca. 1830
(project). Perspective. Watercolor, ink, and
graphite on paper, 20 5/16 x 31 1/2 in. The
Metropolitan Museum of Art, Harris Brisbane
Dick Fund, 1924 (24.66.30).

COLORPLATE 22
View through a monumental Greek portico, ca.
1828–30. Watercolor, ink, and graphite on
paper, 17 ⅞ x 21 ¼ in. A. J. Davis Collection,
The New-York Historical Society (575).

COLORPLATE 23 (overleaf)
Custom House, New York City, 1833. Town &
Davis. Longitudinal section. Watercolor and
ink on paper, 13 ⅞ x 19 ½ in. Drawings &
Archives, Avery Architectural and Fine Arts
Library, Columbia University
(1940.001.00132).

A. J. DAVIS. del. for CUSTOM HOUSE. N. Y.

TOWN & DA

ONGITUDINAL SECTION. PREMIUM DESIGN.

ARCHITECTS

COLORPLATE 24
The Patent Office, Washington, D.C., designed
1832, drawn 1834 (first project). Town &
Davis. Perspective. Watercolor, ink, and
graphite on paper, 19½ x 27¾ in. The
Metropolitan Museum of Art, Harris Brisbane
Dick Fund, 1924 (24.66.423).

COLORPLATE 25
The Patent Office, Washington, D.C., 1834
(first project). Town & Davis. Transverse
section and two plans. Watercolor and ink on
paper, 25¾ x 17⅝ in. The Metropolitan
Museum of Art, Harris Brisbane Dick Fund,
1924 (24.66.448).

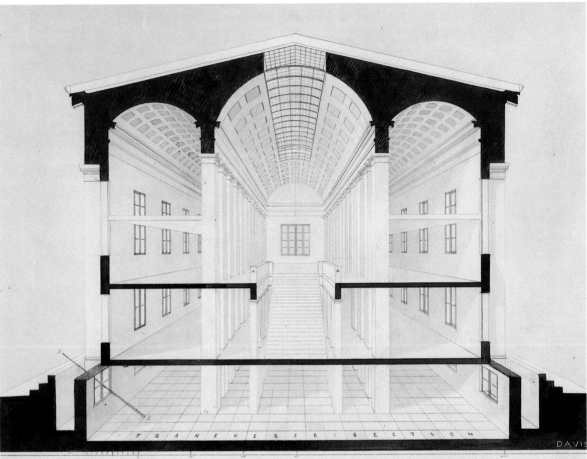

TRANSVERSE SECTION

DAVIS

SCALE.

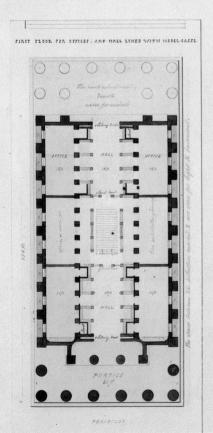

FIRST FLOOR FOR OFFICES, AND HALL LINED WITH MODEL-CASES.

PORTICO

PERISTYLE

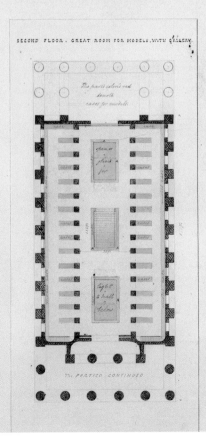

SECOND FLOOR, GREAT ROOM FOR MODELS, WITH GALLERY.

The PORTICO CONTINUED

ERMENT. (HERMONTHIS)

C<small>OLORPLATE</small> 26
Study of the Temple of Erment, ca. 1830.
Elevation and plan. Watercolor, ink, and
graphite on paper, 18 ¾ x 26 ¾ in. The
Metropolitan Museum of Art, Harris Brisbane
Dick Fund, 1924 (24.66.445).

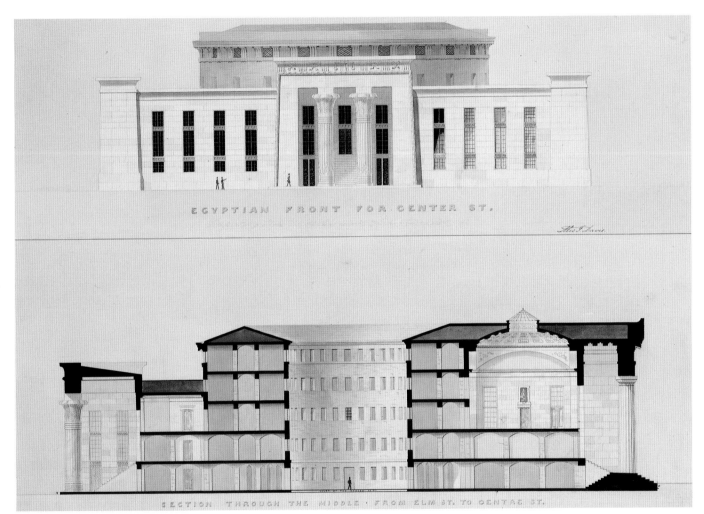

EGYPTIAN FRONT FOR CENTER ST.

SECTION THROUGH THE MIDDLE · FROM ELM ST. TO CENTRE ST.

COLORPLATE 27
Competition drawing for the Halls of Justice,
New York City, 1835. Centre Street elevation
and longitudinal section. Watercolor, ink, and
graphite on paper, 25 ½ x 31 ⅜ in. The
Metropolitan Museum of Art, Harris Brisbane
Dick Fund, 1924 (24.66.437).

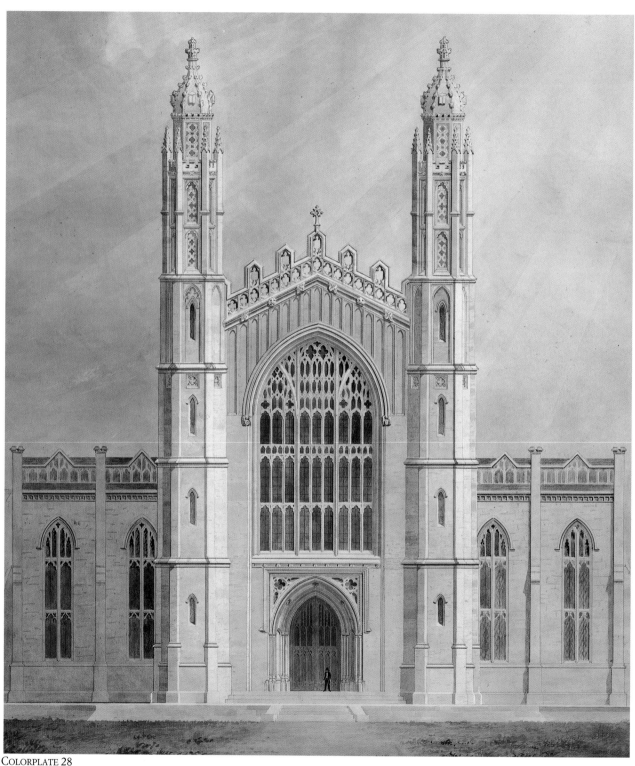

COLORPLATE 28
Library and Chapel, University of Michigan,
Ann Arbor, 1838–39 (project). Front elevation.
Watercolor, ink, and graphite on paper, 31⅜ x
26⅛ in. The Metropolitan Museum of Art,
Harris Brisbane Dick Fund, 1924 (24.66.41).

BIBLIOTHECA.

COLORPLATE 29
Study for a library, 1838. Front elevation.
Watercolor, ink, and graphite on paper, 25 ⁹⁄₁₆ x
17 ¾ in. The Metropolitan Museum of Art, The
Elisha Whittelsey Collection, The Elisha
Whittelsey Fund, 1949 (49.102.9).

COLORPLATE 30
New York University in the classical style, 1832
(project). Perspective. Watercolor, ink, and
graphite on paper, 14 ⅝ x 20 ⅝ in. A.J. Davis
Collection, The New-York Historical Society
(16).

COLORPLATE 31
Design for the interior of New York University
Chapel, 1835. Perspective. Watercolor, ink,
and graphite on paper, 25 ¹⁵⁄₁₆ x 19 ¼ in. A. J.
Davis Collection, The New-York Historical
Society (15).

FOR THE UNIVERSITY CHAPEL

COLORPLATE 32
American Institute, New York City, ca.
1834–35 (project). Town? & Davis. Front
elevation. Watercolor, ink, and graphite on
paper, 31 x 25 ⅛ in. The Metropolitan Museum
of Art, Harris Brisbane Dick Fund, 1924
(24.66.438).

COLORPLATE 33
Study for the Astor Library, 1843. Front
elevation. Watercolor and ink on paper, 20¾ x
14½ in. The Metropolitan Museum of Art,
Harris Brisbane Dick Fund, 1924 (24.66.419).

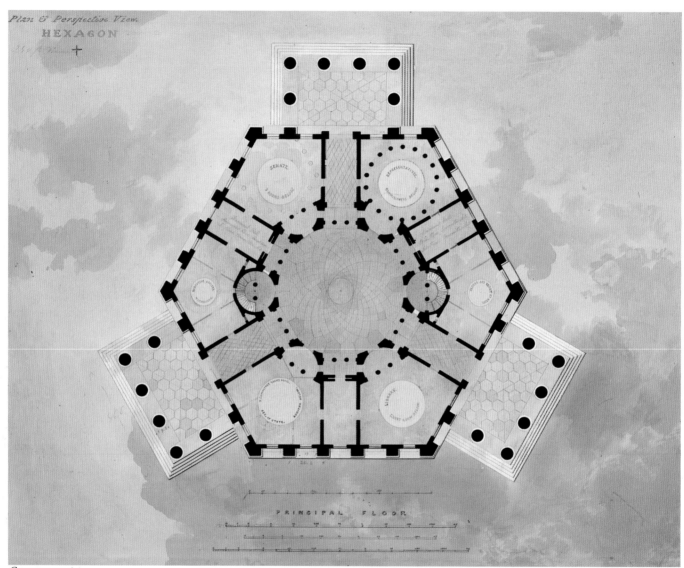

COLORPLATE 34
Competition drawing for the Brooklyn City
Hall, 1835. Plan. Watercolor, ink, and graphite
on paper, 25 ½ x 31 ½ in. The Metropolitan
Museum of Art, Harris Brisbane Dick Fund,
1924 (24.66.471).

COLORPLATE 35
Church of the Holy Apostles, New York City,
1845 (project). Front elevation. Watercolor,
ink, and graphite on paper, 19 ⅞ x 14 ⁵⁄₁₆ in.
The Metropolitan Museum of Art, Harris
Brisbane Dick Fund, 1924 (24.66.88).

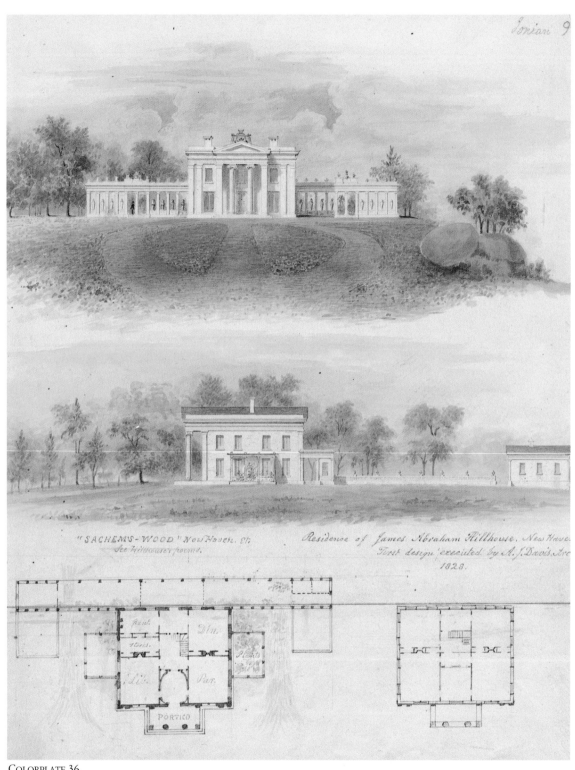

COLORPLATE 36
Study for Highwood for James A. Hillhouse, New
Haven, Connecticut, ca. 1830. Front and side
elevations and two plans. Watercolor, ink, and
graphite on paper, 15 ½ x 12 ⅛ in. The Metropolitan
Museum of Art, Harris Brisbane Dick Fund, 1924
(24.66.1416 [22], vol. XVII, leaf 23).

Highwood for James A. Hillhouse, New
Haven, Connecticut, 1829. Perspective.
Watercolor, ink, and graphite on paper, 14 5/16 x
19 15/16 in. A. J. Davis Collection, The New-
York Historical Society (289).

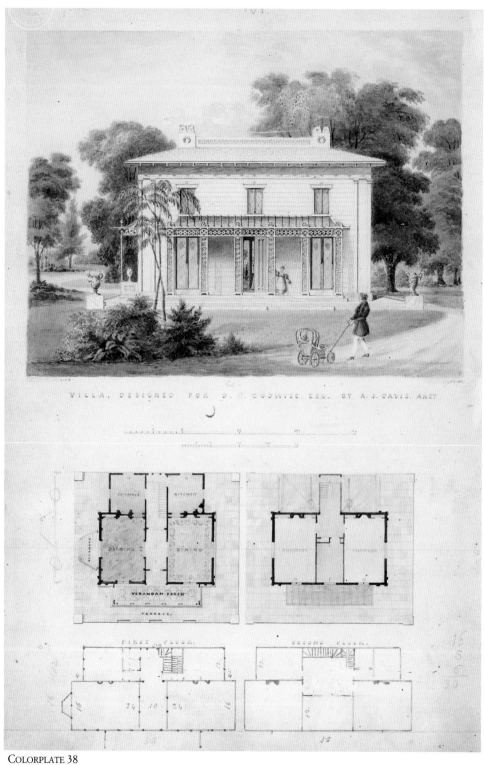

VILLA, DESIGNED FOR D. C. CODWISE ESQ. BY A. J. DAVIS, ARC.T

COLORPLATE 38
House for David Codwise, near New Rochelle, New
York, 1835 (project). Front elevation and four plans.
Watercolor, ink, and graphite on paper, 14⅜ x 9 in.
The Metropolitan Museum of Art, Harris Brisbane
Dick Fund, 1924 (24.66.790).

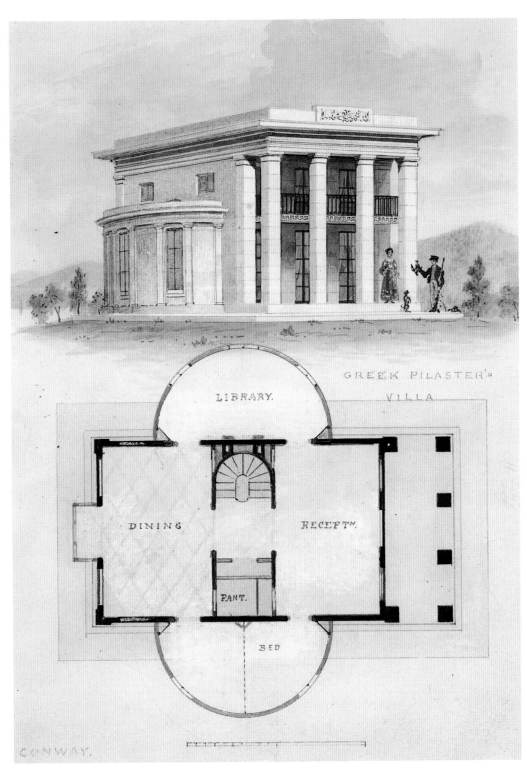

COLORPLATE 40
Hawkwood for Richard O. Morris, Green
Springs, Virginia, 1851–54. Front elevation.
Watercolor and ink on paper, 14 5/16 x 19 15/16 in.
The Metropolitan Museum of Art, Harris
Brisbane Dick Fund, 1924 (24.66.60).

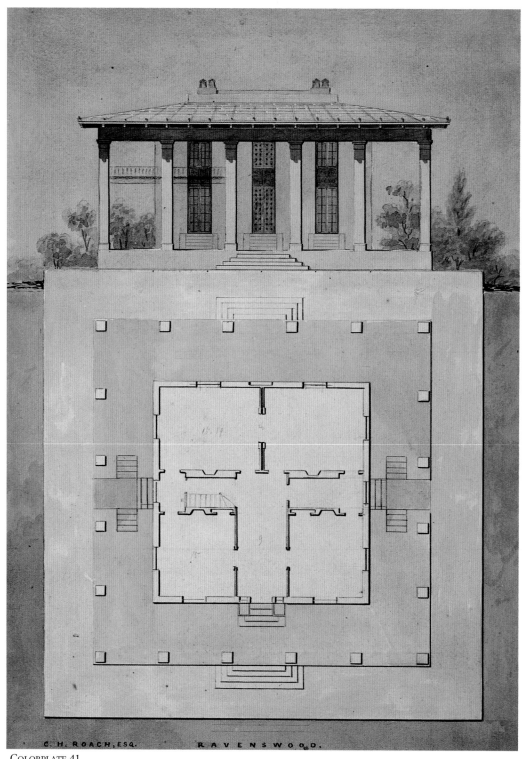

COLORPLATE 41
Ravenswood for Charles H. Roach, Long
Island, New York, 1836. Front elevation and
plan. Watercolor, ink, and graphite on paper,
16 ½ x 12 ⅝ in. Drawings & Archives, Avery
Architectural and Fine Arts Library, Columbia
University (1940.001.00027R).

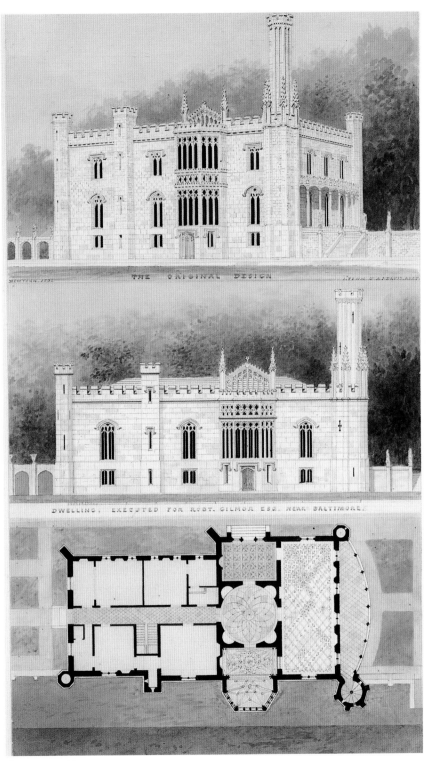

COLORPLATE 42
Glen Ellen for Robert Gilmor, Towson,
Maryland, 1832–33. Perspective, elevation, and
plan. Watercolor, ink, and graphite on paper,
21¾ x 15⅝ in. The Metropolitan Museum of
Art, Harris Brisbane Dick Fund, 1924
(24.66.17).

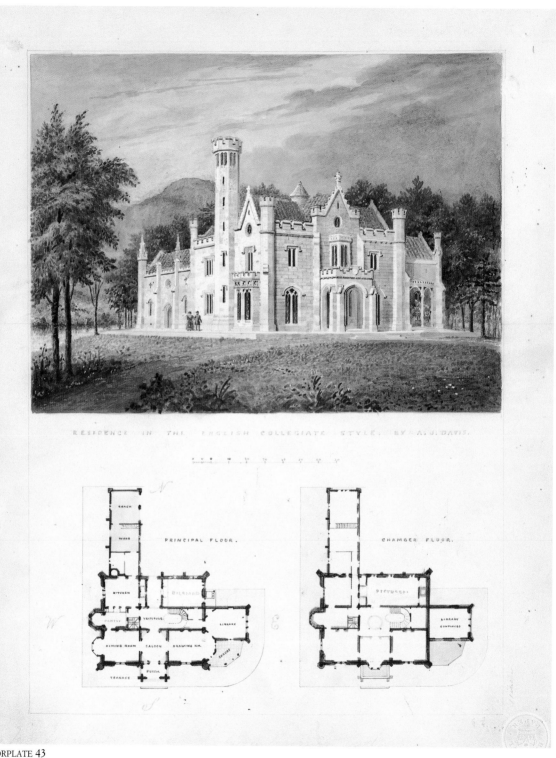

RESIDENCE IN THE ENGLISH COLLEGIATE STYLE. BY A.J. DAVIS.

PRINCIPAL FLOOR.

CHAMBER FLOOR.

COLORPLATE 43
Villa for Robert Donaldson, Fishkill Landing,
New York, 1834 (project). Perspective and two
plans. Watercolor, ink, and graphite on paper,
12 15/16 x 10 in. The Metropolitan Museum of
Art, Harris Brisbane Dick Fund, 1924
(24.66.865).

COLORPLATE 44
Knoll for William and Philip R. Paulding,
Tarrytown, New York, 1838. South and east
(front) elevations. Watercolor and ink on
paper, 14 ¼ x 10 ³⁄₁₆ in. The Metropolitan
Museum of Art, Harris Brisbane Dick Fund,
1924 (24.66.70).

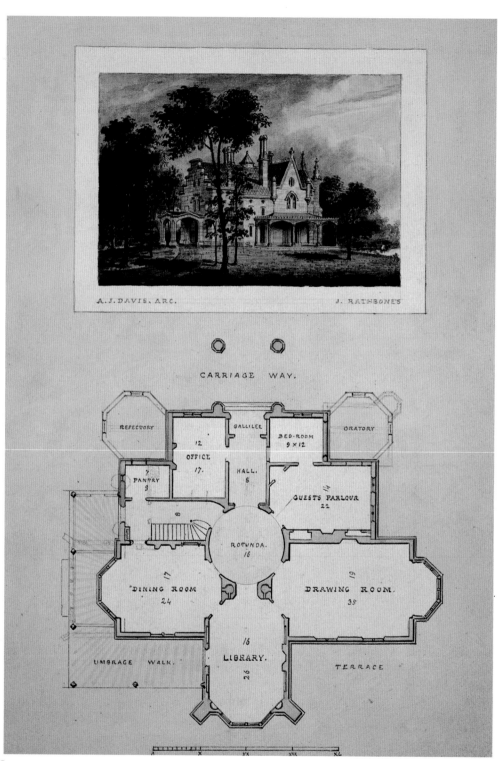

COLORPLATE 45
Kenwood for Joel Rathbone, south of Albany,
New York, 1842. Perspective and plan.
Watercolor, ink, and graphite on paper, 10 3/16 x
7 1/4 in. Drawings & Archives, Avery
Architectural and Fine Arts Library, Columbia
University (1955.001.00133).

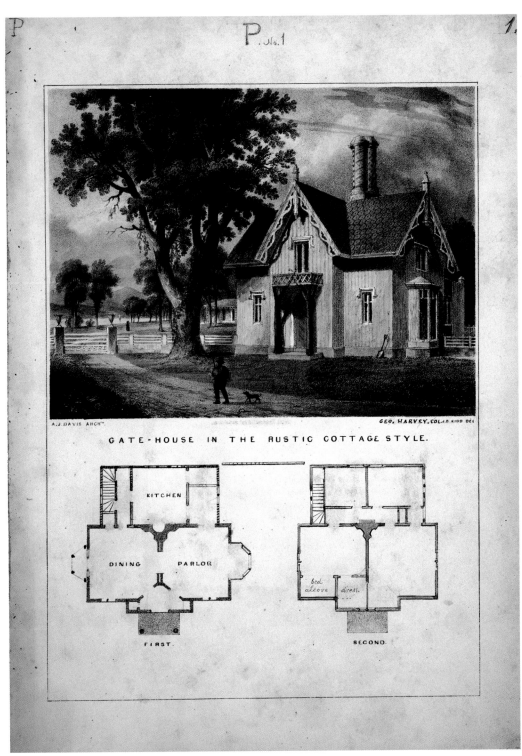

A.J. DAVIS ARCH.T.   GEO. HARVEY. COL. J.B. KIDD DEL.

GATE-HOUSE IN THE RUSTIC COTTAGE STYLE.

KITCHEN

DINING   PARLOR

bed
alcove   dress.

FIRST.   SECOND.

COLORPLATE 46
Gatehouse at Blithewood for Robert Donaldson,
Annandale-on-Hudson, New York, 1836. Perspective
and first and second floor plans. Lithograph,
watercolored by George Harvey, 13 ½ x 9 ⅜ in.
Drawings & Archives, Avery Architectural and Fine
Arts Library, Columbia University (1940.001.00093R).

COLORPLATE 47
House for William J. Rotch, New Bedford,
Massachusetts, 1845. Front elevation.
Watercolor, ink, and graphite on paper, 16 9/16 x
25 3/4 in. The Metropolitan Museum of Art,
Harris Brisbane Dick Fund, 1924 (24.66.20).

Album 2

CASTLEWOOD. SOUTH EAST. ELEVATION

DAVIS.

COLORPLATE 49
Ericstan for John J. Herrick, Tarrytown, New
York, 1855–59. Rear elevation. Watercolor,
ink, and graphite on paper, 25 5/16 x 30 in. The
Metropolitan Museum of Art, Harris Brisbane
Dick Fund, 1924 (24.66.10).

COLORPLATE 50
Wildmont for Alexander J. Davis,
West Orange, New Jersey, ca.
1878. Southeast elevation.
Watercolor, ink, and graphite on
paper, 15 7/16 x 19 3/4 in. Drawings
& Archives, Avery Architectural
and Fine Arts Library, Columbia
University (1940.001.00019).

COLORPLATE 51
Wildmont for Alexander J. Davis,
West Orange, New Jersey, ca.
1878. Perspective. Watercolor
and ink on paper, 4 3/16 in.
diameter. Drawings & Archives,
Avery Architectural and Fine Arts
Library, Columbia University
(1940.001.00018).

COLORPLATE 52
House for William C. H. Waddell, New York City,
1844. Perspective and plan. Watercolor and ink on
paper, 13 ¼ x 9 ⅞ in. I. N. Phelps Stokes Collection,
Miriam and Ira D. Wallach Division of Art, Prints and
Photographs, The New York Public Library, Astor,
Lenox and Tilden Foundations.

COLORPLATE 53
Dining room at Knoll, ca. 1840. Perspective.
Watercolor, ink, and graphite on paper, 13 ½ x
20 ⅛ in. The Metropolitan Museum of Art,
Harris Brisbane Dick Fund, 1924 (24.66.867).

COLORPLATE 54
Study for double parlors in the classical style,
ca. 1830. Perspective. Watercolor and ink on
paper, 13 ¼ x 18 ¼ in. Drawings Collection,
The New-York Historical Society, Gift of
Daniel Parish, Jr., 1908 (1908.28).

COLORPLATE 55
Grace Hill for Edwin C. Litchfield, Brooklyn,
New York, 1854. Front elevation. Watercolor,
ink, and graphite on paper, 20 ¹⁵⁄₁₆ x 27 ⅞ in.
The Metropolitan Museum of Art, Harris
Brisbane Dick Fund, 1924 (24.66.67).

CARRIAGE WAY.

VESTIBULE

STORE
OFFICE. HALL.

DINING. POSTERN

BUTLER

CABINET. 46 LIBRARY. RECEPTION.
10

VERANDA OR

COLORPLATE 56
Lyndhurst for George Merritt, Tarrytown, New York, 1865. West (rear) elevation and plan. Watercolor, ink, and graphite on paper, 18⅞ x 26⅝ in. The Metropolitan Museum of Art, Harris Brisbane Dick Fund, 1924 (24.66.14).

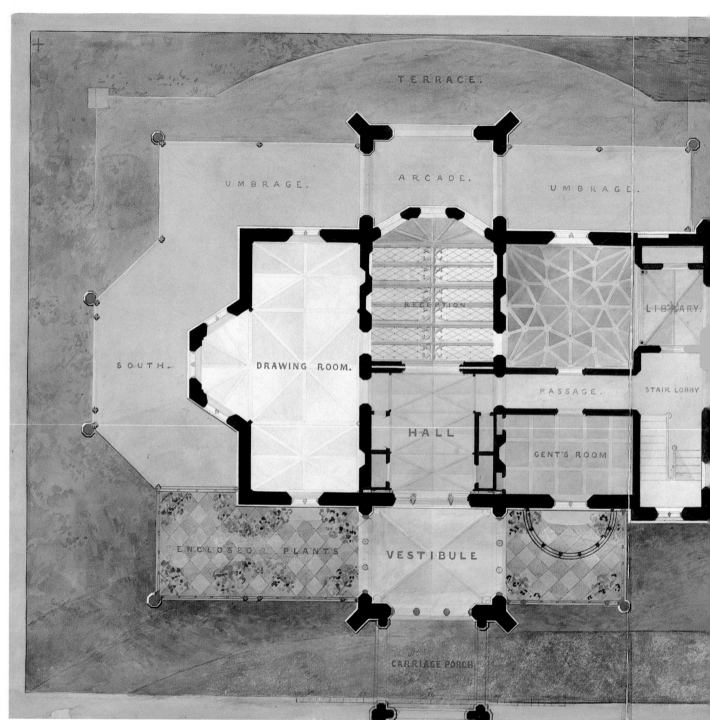

COLORPLATE 57
Lyndhurst for George Merritt, Tarrytown, New
York, 1865. First floor plan. Watercolor, ink,
and graphite on paper, 25 ¼ x 54 ⅛ in. The
Metropolitan Museum of Art, Harris Brisbane
Dick Fund, 1924 (24.66.42).

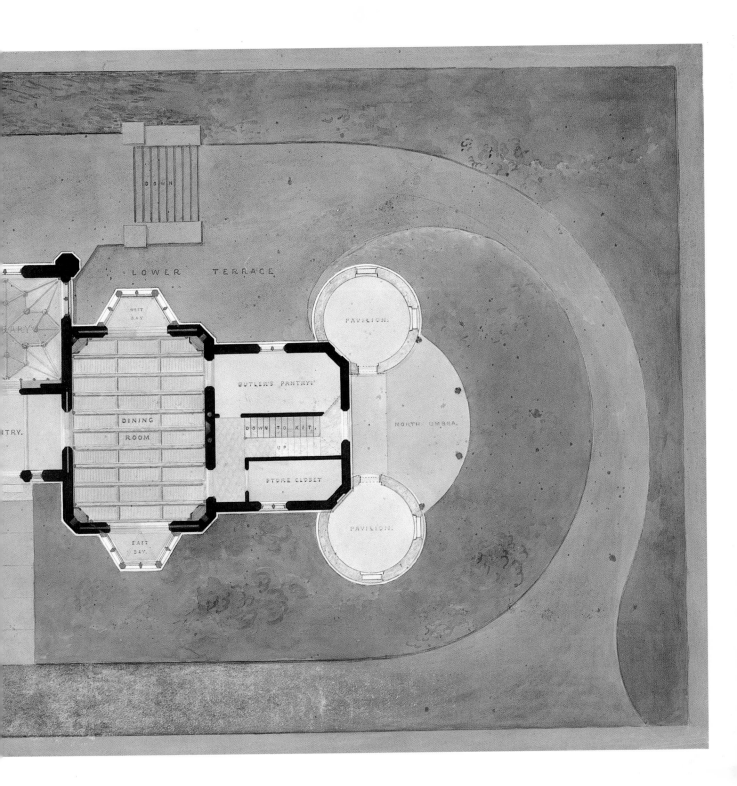

Index